COLLECTIVE FARMS WHICH WORK?

SOVIET AND EAST EUROPEAN STUDIES

COLLECTIVE FARMS
WHICH WORK?

NIGEL SWAIN

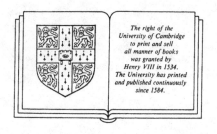

The right of the
University of Cambridge
to print and sell
all manner of books
was granted by
Henry VIII in 1534.
The University has printed
and published continuously
since 1584.

CAMBRIDGE UNIVERSITY PRESS

CAMBRIDGE

LONDON   NEW YORK   NEW ROCHELLE

MELBOURNE   SYDNEY

CAMBRIDGE UNIVERSITY PRESS
Cambridge, New York, Melbourne, Madrid, Cape Town, Singapore, São Paulo

Cambridge University Press
The Edinburgh Building, Cambridge CB2 8RU, UK

Published in the United States of America by Cambridge University Press, New York

www.cambridge.org
Information on this title: www.cambridge.org/9780521268530

© Cambridge University Press 1985

First published 1985
This digitally printed version 2008

A catalogue record for this publication is available from the British Library

Library of Congress Catalogue Card Number: 84–23838

ISBN 978-0-521-26853-0 hardback
ISBN 978-0-521-05759-2 paperback

This book is dedicated to the memory of
KEVIN FRAYNE PARDOE (1950–83),
who shared the more hilarious moments in its research.

Contents

Preface

This book is based on an exhaustive study of primary and secondary, official and unofficial publications, and on first hand evidence gained from interviews and observations made in a number of co-operative farms. There is no shortage of research materials on either Hungarian economy and society in general, or Hungarian agriculture in particular. In addition to the numerous specialist journals which publish articles to a high academic standard, a number of research institutes concern themselves with agriculture and agricultural co-operatives, and publish internal documents which, although of limited circulation, are freely available to the visiting scholar. Hungarian statistical materials are copious and of a generally high standard and, together with major academic journals and legal materials, are mostly available in the British Library in London. Unprocessed survey data are not usually available to the researcher in Hungary, however.

I visited ten agricultural producer co-operative farms in all during a six month research visit to Hungary in 1976–7. In most farms it was possible to interview upper management only. In the pseudonymous 'Red Flag', 'May 1st' and 'Great October' farms, however, permission was given to interview working and retired members in addition to management, and in the 'Red Flag' farm access was granted to official documents, including the minutes of Leadership meetings, and to the year end General Meeting. These three farms were not show-piece farms; but they were economically dynamic and their organisational structure conformed to government recommendation. Other farms visited were less secure, and one had been officially declared 'bankrupt' and was having its finances compulsorily reorganised. Statistical generalisation on the basis of so few farms is impossible. On the other hand, the points that evidence from

ix

Preface

these sources is adduced to support in the book are ones concerned
with the organisation of co-operative management and democracy,
and it is perhaps not entirely unjustified to expect some similarities
between these farms, conforming as they do to government norms,
and other farms which so conform.

This book would not have been possible without the assistance of
the following institutions: the British Council and the Hungarian
Institute for Cultural Relations which granted me two scholarships to
visit Hungary; the Sociological Research Institute of the Hungarian
Academy of Sciences (and especially Attila Gergely) which helped
arrange my research visits and interviews; the British Library,
especially its staff at Woolwich who patiently located Hungarian
statistical and legal materials; and, of course, the members of all the
co-operative farms visited during the course of my research. I grate-
fully acknowledge their role in the production of this work. I naturally
take full responsibility for any of its errors of fact or omission, but
projects of this size are never solely the result of individual effort and I
owe a considerable debt to the following individuals: Mihály Andor
and Pál Juhász, who discussed Hungarian society with me and helped
my ideas to crystallise; István F. Szabó, who taught me Hungarian;
David Lane (my PhD supervisor), Teodor Shanin and Caroline
Humphrey (my PhD examiners) and John Barnes who commented
on various versions of the manuscript; and Geoffrey Hawthorn who
taught me to think critically about sociology. I thank them for their
various contributions.

Finally, I should like to express my thanks to all those friends in
Hungary, England and elsewhere who have supported and encouraged me in this project. Thanks are especially due to Margo and Laci,
Éva and István, Miki and Ági, Zsuzsa, and Kati who made research
in Hungary such an enjoyable experience, and to Eve Rosenhaft who
continues to do the same for research and life in England.

Introduction

In recent years it has become part of the received wisdom of students of Eastern Europe that Hungarian agriculture has been a 'success'. The question mark of the title does not seek to question this view as it is normally understood. Hungarian agricultural policy has been a 'success' in economic terms. While it is accepted that Hungarian agricultural production itself is not especially efficient, overall agricultural policy has led to a situation in which the Hungarian population is well fed; there is extensive consumer choice in agricultural products; and, most important, scarce foreign currency is not squandered importing grain and animal feed which can be home-grown. And collectivisation has been a 'success' in terms of social policy. This agricultural self-sufficiency was achieved without the need to resort to mass starvation or deportation and, although living standards generally are stagnating in the early 1980s, the rural population really has 'never had it so good'. One central concern of this book is to consider aspects of how this 'success' was achieved, to analyse the Hungarian experience suggesting ways in which collectivisation can be made to work and so rescue it as a serious option for nations developing under the banner of socialism. To countries faced with rural underdevelopment, underemployment and poverty, collectivisation can seem an attractive ideal: the Hungarian experience shows that there is no historical imperative to follow Soviet precedent. Collectivisation has suffered too long under the shadow of the Soviet experience. Collective farms can work, and the Hungarian experience shows one way how.

A second aim of the book is to consider some sociological concomitants of this 'success', and this is where the question mark of the title must be introduced. Although Hungarian producer co-operative (collective) farms function as successful production units, questions can be raised about the manner in which they operate and the production relations which obtain within them. Collectivisation has created large-scale socialist enterprises out of peasant agriculture, but were those of all social backgrounds treated equally in the process, and are these socialist enterprises democratically run? Answers to these questions can give us further insights into the political economy of 'actually existing socialism'.

My approach to both questions requires some clarification. Collectivisation is a process of radical, large-scale, socio-economic transformation. The words are chosen carefully. It is difficult to find an analytical approach which is both simple and yet provides sufficient purchase to encapsulate in a single study such a multi-faceted development. The standard approach of Western sociologists to Eastern Europe, that of reprocessing the findings of social stratification and social mobility surveys carried out in these countries, has intrinsic limitations. First, it ignores changes in production relations and the restructuring of the economic context for workplace social relations, areas of considerable importance for the social actors involved. Second, social mobility surveys in particular are of little use in analysing radical social change of this nature because the social and occupational structure itself is changed so fundamentally that almost everyone is socially mobile. Third, this problem is compounded by the social categorisation used in Eastern European social stratification studies. All those involved in agriculture in both the old world of peasant agriculture and the new collective farm tend to be termed 'peasant'. The radical transformation that in reality has taken place is defined away. Those 'peasants' who have not become industrial workers remain 'peasants' on collective farms: but their lives have been totally changed.

The approach adopted here has been to consider the transformations engendered by collectivisation from the point of view of 'labour', a category which spans both the economic and the sociological spheres. We shall examine what has happened to labour as an economic category under collectivisation as well as the changes in the social composition of agricultural labourers and relations between them. More specifically, we shall analyse the consequences for what will be termed 'family labour' and 'socialist wage labour' of socialist economic relations, that is, relations in which, whatever else might be true, individuals' 'labour power' – their ability to labour – is itself no longer a commodity. This will permit us to examine the development of co-operative farms as both distinctly socialist production enterprises and as enterprises into which the 'petty commodity production' of individual farm members is linked.

Collectivisation in Hungary was preceded by a land reform in 1945–6 which, based around the more or less spontaneous demands of the 'land claimants' committees', created predominantly small peasant agriculture in Hungary for the first time. Previously there had been a roughly fifty-fifty split between large hacienda-type estates and an independent peasantry. A first attempt at collectivisation began in 1949 and lasted until 1953. It adopted the traditional techniques of 'stalinist' collectivisation – physical force to collectivise combined with crippling compulsory deliveries once collectivised – and formed part of a traditionally over-ambitious five year plan. It ended in the disbanding of many farms as Hungary shared in the general Eastern European political crisis occasioned by Stalin's death. Imre Nagy's 'New Course' which followed this defeat for the hard-liners promised a much more gradual transformation of agrarian relations but, by the summer of 1955, with Rákosi back in control and Nagy forced to resign, the pace and tactics of collectivisation reverted to the stalinist norm; with the same result. By the next summer, in the wake of publication of Khrushchev's secret speech and Rákosi's resignation, collective farms began to disband once again, a prelude for the revolution in October.

The spirit of reconciliation which ultimately characterised the entire Kádár regime made an early appearance in agrarian policy. The government never rescinded the abolition of compulsory deliveries passed by the Nagy government and almost immediately passed a decree sanctioning the further disbanding of farms. The following July, the new government published its 'Agrarian Theses', setting out its proposed agrarian strategy. These were non-committal on when further collectivisation should take place; adopted a more accommodating attitude towards 'kulaks' and other non-co-operative peasants; and stressed the need to transform existing co-operatives into models of mechanised farming as a precondition for mass collectivisation. However, after renewed pressure from its allies, Hungary's final, and successful, attempt at collectivisation took place sooner than the Theses implied, in the winter periods of 1959, 1959–60 and 1960–1. This time it was achieved with the minimum of actual physical force, especially after 1960 when Kádár replaced Dögei by Losonczi as Minister of Agriculture, and on 17 February 1961 the Central Committee of the Hungarian Socialist Workers' Party declared that collectivisation had been completed. Subsequently, the history of Hungary's collectivisation is the story of changes in policy towards an established, and ultimately well-established, collectivised agriculture, and an analysis of these forms the substance of the first two chapters of this book.

The book ends its detailed analysis in 1977, and there are good reasons for regarding this date as the end of an epoch in the development of collectivised agriculture. First, by 1977 the fundamental change of introducing 100% wages (fully fledged 'socialist wage labour') into co-operative farms had been accomplished. Subsequent developments only confirm this. The same government regulations now apply to both state and co-operative farms, indicating a *de facto* recognition of the unimportance of nominal ownership forms for economic regulation. Second, after vacillation in 1975–6, the framework for support of small-scale private production by farm members has been accepted irrevocably. No significant changes in the pattern of aid have taken place subsequently, although in the early 1980s state farms have involved themselves in the integration of small-scale agriculture to an unprecedented extent. The only developments of any consequence in this area have been attempts to harvest the capital reserves created by 'family labour' by promoting the sale of co-operative farm shares and bonds. Third, social movement as measured by rates of social mobility has died down after the rapid transformations of the 1950s and 1960s (Andorka, 1982). Both socially and organisationally, then, by the late 1970s collective farms had reached relative stasis.

But before we can proceed with an analysis of collectivisation in the key twenty years between 1957 and 1977 we must first clarify the terms 'family labour' and 'socialist wage labour' and examine how both have been affected by thirty years of 'actually existing socialism' in the Hungarian economy. The remaining sections of this introduction address the analytical questions that provide the framework for the rest of the study.

'Family labour' is taken to mean labour performed according to the laws which govern the 'family economy'. The focus will be on the rationality that underpins the use of labour within the family, a joint production–consumption unit, rather than on any specific type of family-based enterprise. The defining characteristic of such 'family labour', as Chayanov argues (1966), is that, because it operates within a more or less closed universe where the producers also constitute the consumption unit, no separately identifiable concept of wage costs need evolve. Time might always be money, but when time spent labouring is one's own, or one's family's, it need not necessarily lead directly to expenditure. Individuals who labour within a 'family economy' do not enter a category of wage-costs into their calculations in the way that profit maximising, labour-hiring enterprises must; and this has a direct effect on their economic behaviour. Since there is no category of wage-costs within the family unit, neither can there be such categories as net profit, rent and interest on capital (Chayanov, 1966, pp. 5–6, 88–9, 228–33). Profit maximisation is replaced by a concern with balancing the utility of output, irrespective of any notional labour costs, and the disutility of having to labour at all.

It might seem unwise to accept without comment Chayanov's views in light of the extended debate which his work has provoked. Fortunately a thorough critique of the pro and anti Chayanov cases is unnecessary for our concerns. This book focuses on a type of labour rather than the internal coherence or explanatory ability of Chayanov's theory of 'peasant economy', and all observers of the economic rationale of family-based economic units agree that labour costs are treated very differently in the family unit (Chayanov, 1966; Galeski, 1975; Harrison, 1975; Marx, 1971, pp. 804–7; Shanin, 1973; Tepicht, 1973). It should be noted that this definition does not preclude the hiring of some occasional day labour. The logic of a 'family economy' can cope with seasonal labour as an occasional cost without having to generate a specific concept of wages. Marxists have traditionally seen the hiring of non-family labour as indicative of capitalist relations within a rural community, but this would seem to be misguided. There can certainly be exploitation of a kind in employer–employee relations within the 'family economy', but it is not the exploitation of capitalist production relations. Day labourers may or may not be fairly treated by their employers, but neither are they paid wages as such and, in many cases, they have a small plot to counterbalance their potential status as 'wage slaves'. It is only confusing to term 'capitalist' a relationship which, however unjust and exploitative, is something rather different.

Two further terminological points should be made in this regard.

First, 'family labour' and 'family economy' are used in preference to 'domestic labour' and 'domestic economy', but for reasons of connotation only. The latter terms are linked too directly with housework and the debates which surround it, debates which have surprisingly ignored the theoretical relevance of Chayanov's work (Coulson *et al.*, 1975; Gardiner, 1975; Molyneux, 1979; Seccombe, 1974; Wajcman, 1981). The focus in this book is on market-oriented work performed within the household rather than its internal services and it is useful to have a distinct term to describe it. Second, the book concerns itself with petty commodity production within the 'family economy' as a process and not on the petty bourgeoisie as a class. It does not search for a new breed of 'kulak', but rather it focuses on how individual labourers following the logic of the socialist and family economies behave.

The term 'socialist wage labour' presents fewer problems. It is understood simply as the sort of labour which is performed for a wage in a socialist economy, with the implicit assumption that there is something fundamentally socialist about Eastern European economies. This doctrinal point cannot be debated fully in this introduction. The assumption rests on the fact that all Eastern European governments have implemented policies which consistently figure at the top of the list of economic demands of any radical socialist party. Major manufacturing industry, banks and insurance are all nationally owned, with co-operative ownership of smaller units in these sectors: there is permanent full employment; and institutional structures have been established for both strategic national economic planning and worker representation in enterprise decision-making. Whether social and political dimensions of these societies are socialist, or whether social, economic and political dimensions can be separated meaningfully in this way are separate issues which, again, cannot be resolved here. There seem to be no *prima facie* reasons why the spheres cannot be treated as distinct; and if this is accepted, there are good nominalist reasons for terming the economic sector 'socialist'.

'Socialist wage labour' differs from 'wage labour' in the capitalist sense in that the ability to perform it is not a commodity in the marxist sense. 'Labour power' has to be purchased since all able members of society are expected to work; and it cannot be relinquished simply because of inadequate demand or low profitability. If planners require an enterprise to shed labour or close down, alternative employment must be found, although this is very often not employment of a similar quality, nor at a convenient location (Berkovits, 1972). Enterprise employees can only be sacked on the grounds of misconduct. The consequence of this *a priori* exclusion of unemployment from economic life is necessarily an increase in 'irrational' employment practices and 'underemployment'. It could not have been otherwise. But this in itself places labour among a sufficiently distinct set of economic parameters to qualify for the appellation 'socialist wage labour' rather than simply 'wage labour'. There is an additional point. The essence of 'socialist wage labour' is not only that it is in receipt of a wage in an economic system which has ruled out the possibility of unemployment and consequently operates according to a different economic logic from capitalist, free market economies. The cost of 'socialist wage labour' must still be entered into enterprise budget calculations. Even if the rationale which underpins a socialist economy does not require labour to be treated as a cost which must be minimised in the pursuit of profit maximisation, it remains a factor which is susceptible to manipulation as to price paid and amount purchased by any group within enterprises which might control such decisions. The essence of 'socialist wage labour' is that it is susceptible to such manipulation should a group with the power to manipulate it exist. The empirical question of whether such groups do exist will be tackled below.

What have been the effects of thirty and more years of 'actually existing socialism' on these two labour types? The effects on 'family labour' have been threefold. First, within the elaboration of an overall economic strategy for socialism, the adoption of certain understandable priorities in industrialisation – investment rather than consumption, heavy industry rather than light – has left space for a private sector to develop. Significant economic development in the sectors which did not figure high on the list of socialist priorities has not taken place. Prioritisation of investment and heavy industry has left Hungary and other Eastern European countries 'underurbanised' in that the percentage of the population dwelling in an urban setting is smaller than would be predicted by statistical extrapolations from its level of industrial development (M. Hegedűs, 1974; Konrád and Szelényi, 1974). Large numbers of Hungarian workers live in villages and commute to work, often over very large distances (Andorka, 1979; Andorka and Harcsa, 1973). In fact, as many workers lived in villages in 1970 as lived in towns, more predominantly unskilled and semi-skilled workers (Andorka, 1979, pp. 78 and 83); and the villages, even those surrounding Budapest, remain villages in terms of their infrastructural development rather than garden cities of the Western Home Counties variety (Berkovits, 1976; Fodor, 1973). While the contribution of the private sector nationally is minimal (1.6% of national income and 1.8% of active earners in 1970), in areas such as services and construction, precisely the areas which were given a low priority in national planning, its contribution is considerable: 48.6% of services, 56.2% of construction generally, and 92% of village construction in 1970 (MKA, 1971, p. 1). Yet this private economic activity has been confined to the family. It has been limited financially by taxation on wages paid, in addition to the general income tax applicable to the sector, and administratively in the form of ceilings, which have changed over the years, placed on the number of workers that can be employed by private entrepreneurs. The private sector which the adoption of socialist priorities in industrialisation allowed to develop is thus predominantly one of petty commodity production making use of 'family labour'.

Second, significant incentives have arisen for individuals to participate in the petty commodity production private sector. These have come from two quarters and again, in both cases, they have been the consequences of avowedly socialist priorities for economic development. Labour was cheap in the immediate post war years when socialist industrialisation relied on the only resource available, a plentiful and underemployed labour force. However, thanks to successful wage regulation and the absence of any form of levy acting as a poll tax on jobs, wages have been kept low and labour has remained a cheap resource for enterprises. A first consequence of this is that wages are felt to be inadequate by workers in relation to their changing needs. Roughly one third of the Hungarian population fell under the official poverty line in 1968 (Kemény, 1979, pp. 248–9), and a family comprising two parents with average industrial male and female earnings and one child in 1967 brought in only 137% of the minimum monthly subsistence level (KSH 214, p. 25). Real incomes have increased since then, but so have demands and expectations, and there continue to be 'large pockets of poverty' (Flakierski, 1979, p. 29).

But enterprises themselves behave in ways that actually encourage private sector activity. Since 1957 wage regulation, which was considered essential to avoid inflation, to ensure a relatively egalitarian distribution of wages and, after 1968, to avoid the danger of unemployment if 'irrationally' employed labour were suddenly exposed to profit-oriented enterprises competing for scarce labour in a market influenced by world market prices (Buda, 1972; Portes, 1977, 1978), has been via a tax on increases in the average wage paid within enterprises. It has been a successful tool in all these respects (Portes, 1972; 1977; 1978; Székffy, 1978; Wiles, 1974a) but, with average wages so near the poverty line, control of the average necessarily places restrictions on differentials and the scope for wage incentives both between grades and, for those who perform better than the average, within grades (Héthy and Makó, 1972a, pp. 50–1; 1975). Workers who expend only an average amount of effort receive not very much less than workers who apply themselves more fully. So, while wages from the socialist economy might be low, in many cases they can be gained without great exertion. Socialist economic relations encourage enterprises to exacerbate this trend. Enterprises manifest an unquenchable thirst for cheap labour, but no incentive to make efficient use of it once obtained. Because, as is argued by Bauer, Laki and others,[1] socialist economies are growth-oriented and experience only physical, not financial, barriers to growth, and because labour is relatively cheap for enterprises, it is quite rational for them to hoard labour, however wastefully it is used. It allows them both to maximise growth with a labour force experiencing weak incentives to exert itself fully and ensure a useful reserve of labour which can cope with the vagaries of supply and pressing deadlines still endemic in Hungary (Laki, 1980) as in traditional centrally planned economies.

The conjunction of these two aspects of socialist economic development – the creation of both space for and incentives for 'family labour' in the private sector – had a further consequence: the growth of a unique form of labour market. On this market, two parallel, non-capitalist economic systems coexist, and individual workers are economically active both as 'socialist wage labour' in the one and, in their 'marginal labour time', as 'family labour' in the other.[2] Rather than extend themselves fully in the socialist economy, workers retain some of their 'labour power' for use after work in the 'second economy'. They lose very little in wages by saving energy in this way because of the weak labour incentives in the socialist economy, and the energy saved can be devoted to much greater rewards obtainable in the private sector. So, although 'certain objects which are considered part of the conditions of life (a flat or some other consumer durables) cannot be procured from today's average basic wage' (Hegedűs and Márkus, 1976, p. 109), almost a half of the average worker's monthly salary can be earned in a week-end by an electrician working in the private sector:

'It's only worth while doing new stuff – electrical heating or an electric cooker where you need a separate circuit. It's done in a day and you can ask 1000–2000 forints for it. Wiring a family house, which needs two men for a Saturday and a Sunday, comes to 4000–5000 forints if I supply the materials ... If you really have a go at the private sector, you can earn 50 000–100 000. From spring till autumn they pass you on from person to person.' (Héthy, 1978, pp. 83–4)

Héthy and Makó estimate that at the time the above quotation was collected work in the private sector could bring in between 25 and 50 forints an hour compared with an overtime rate of 20 forints an hour. Not all are lucky enough to be able to earn the high incomes available in the construction sector, but most Hungarians are in on the act. In 1972 over half of the Hungarian population, 5.2 million people, lived in a household which operated some sort of small-scale agricultural plot (Andorka and Harcsa, 1973, p. 97) and in 1980 István Hétényi, then secretary of the National Planning Office, revealed that according to official estimates some 70–75% of Hungarian families had some sort of secondary income (*Figyelő*, 1980, No. 12, pp. 1 and 4).

In 1982, drawing on the success achieved in agriculture which will be considered in subsequent chapters, the government sought to extend its integration of 'family labour' to the industrial and service sectors of the economy. Measures introduced at the beginning of that year allowed for the creation of a number of new types of smaller, less closely regulated production units, and the most interesting of these are the 'economic work partnerships'. These consist of 2–30 individuals working either full-time in the group or having full-time employment elsewhere and working only part-time for the partnership. They are allowed to undertake production or service activities on condition that at least one member possesses the necessary trade qualification and can lease space and machinery from the state enterprises and subcontract to them. A particular case of such 'economic work partnerships' is the 'enterprise economic work partnership' where all members are employees or pensioners of the same parent enterprise, which also takes on additional financial responsibility for the partnership. The industrial and service 'co-operative

groups' of the co-operative sector function in an analogous manner
and are exact equivalents of the 'agricultural specialist groups' which
will be discussed in chapter 2.

The focus for all the units introduced in 1982, from 'economic work
partnership' to 'small co-operative' and 'small enterprise', is on
subcontracting for a lump sum to the larger state enterprises.
Furthermore, although full-time employment in the work partnerships is possible, the emphasis has been on encouraging those who are
already employed full-time in some other area to join them in their
spare time, on integrating into the socialist economy, and in the case
of the 'enterprise economic work partnership' the enterprise itself, the
'marginal labour time' of industrial and service workers which had
previously been spent performing these same tasks in the 'second' or
'black' economy (*Figyelő*, 1984, No. 18, p. 4). By the end of 1983 some
5399 'enterprise economic work partnerships' had been set up in
industrial enterprises with a further 2166 in the construction sector.
By the same date the number of independent 'economic work partnerships' in industry was 1684, with 1194 in construction. These 'enterprise economic work partnerships' concentrated mainly on tasks
related to ensuring the continuity of intra-enterprise activity rather
than contracting with other enterprises or producing directly for the
market (*Figyelő*, 1984, No. 10, p. 5). And these new contractual
systems not only integrate 'family labour', they also mirror the
symbiosis between 'family labour' and 'socialist wage labour' which
was created in agriculture and which will be discussed in chapter 2.
Private artisans, or 'enterprise economic work partnerships' which
subcontract to their full-time employer, enjoy pension rights and
rights to other social benefits, entitlement being based on the average
income of a wage labourer doing the same job (TRHGY, 30/1981
(IX.14) MT 10§).

The consequences of more than thirty years of 'actually existing
socialism' for 'socialist wage labour' require slightly lengthier analysis.
We need to look at labour, and the control of labour, within the network of overlapping management relations in a socialist economy; and
we should focus on those who control production at the point of production – enterprise managers. Can managers make independent
decisions at all? If so, over which areas, how independent can they be
from central government and party apparatuses, and how do they behave towards labour? These questions will be considered in turn: first,
the degree of operational autonomy enjoyed by top level enterprise

management under Hungary's New Economic Mechanism and the role of ministries and central planners.

In principle, the system of economic planning in Hungary operates as follows. The National Planning Office directs and organises the elaboration of plans and establishes the main ratios for balanced economic growth. In this process it relies on information provided by the Central Statistical Office, the banks, the ministries, the federations of co-operatives, large national enterprises, county and town councils, research institutes and individuals commissioned to investigate specific problems. There are three tiers to planning: long term plans of about fifteen years which outline general factors such as growth rate, general trends in social policy and international economic relations; one year plans, which are limited to short term adjustments, adapting credit policy, labour policy and so on to immediate budget constraints; and five year plans. These remain the most important level of planning and establish major economic regulators for enterprise income and fund formation, prices and wages policies, and major investment programmes. At none of these levels does planning take the traditional form of targets expressed in physical units; rather they modify at the appropriate level of generality the economic regulators which mediate market forces in the national interest.

Beneath this planning apparatus enterprise managers enjoy some freedom in determining how to meet the plan objective of profit maximisation within a mediated market context. Freedom as to the manner of plan fulfilment is an area in which management has always enjoyed some autonomy, even under the most centralised of socialist economic systems. But the point that needs to be made here is that, even under Hungary's New Economic Mechanism, managerial autonomy in this respect remains restricted. Investment funds and capital flows are strictly controlled. Investment decisions, except those relating to major national projects, were decentralised initially under the New Economic Mechanism, and finances for them were awarded on the basis of the projected return on investment alone (B. Balassa, 1973, p. 362). But this era of decentralised investment lasted only until Hungary suffered another of its endemic crises of over-investment (Bauer, 1981; Portes, 1972; Wiles, 1974a). Politically perceived needs rather than the projected return on investment then regained predominance (Bauer, 1975, pp. 728–9), and profit turned into a falsifiable plan indicator rather than the centre of interest in a controlled market economy (Bauer, 1970; Laki, 1980, pp. 95–7). Large enterprises reverted to direct bargaining with ministries – investment funds granted in return for increasing the output of unprofitable goods required by the state (Laki, 1980, pp. 78–9) – and smaller ones concentrated on accommodating themselves to existing ministerial projects as a means of gaining access to funds (A. Balassa, 1975; Laky, 1976; 1979).

In other areas operational autonomy is less restricted. Management has effective control of the product mix within the enterprise's permitted 'profile', although it cannot produce goods or supply services which lie outside it (B. Balassa, 1973, p. 360), and it has some freedom with regard to prices if the goods are in the free or 'competitive' pricing categories (*Figyelő*, 1979, No. 45, pp. 3–4; Hare, 1976a, pp. 202–6). But, most important, it has control over labour, over enterprise labour inputs, however constrained by the ever-present scarcity of labour referred to above. Labour policy is subject to some restriction. Wage levels are regulated, there are certain restrictions on labour mobility,[3] and wage increases are controlled by taxation; but these regulations still permit management considerable flexibility with regard to the quantity of labour employed and the size of rewards paid to it.

The apparatus of central government is not the only channel for influencing management behaviour from above, however, and we should also consider the impact of the party apparatus before turning to consider pressures from the shop floor below. It is important when considering the role of the Party in economic decision-making to distinguish between strategic and operational decisions. Clearly the Party, or rather its ruling group, has a profound effect on national economic strategy, as it does over all major governmental decisions. For all the Hungarian leadership's emphasis on the role of parliament in official and semi-official publications (Erdei, 1968, pp. 344–5), few would seriously argue that it is not the Political Committee of the Hungarian Socialist Workers' Party that is the ultimate arbiter of strategic policy decisions. But this in itself indicates little about the role of the Party when less far-reaching decisions are being made at either the local area level or at the workplace. The Party is omnipresent, but is it everywhere and at every level the decider of policy?

The role of the national and county Party organisation in day-to-day economic decision-making is one of 'control' in the sense of supervision, and it achieves this in three ways: by monitoring and influencing enterprise plans; by monitoring, vetoing and in some cases actually making appointments; and by requiring economic leaders, even if they are not themselves Party members, to report back regularly on their performance. But it does not decide day-to-day economic policy. As Lantos states, 'It should be emphasised that the preparation and implementation of economic plans are the task of economic leaders' (Lantos, 1976, p. 20). The county Party organisation is the most important area organ. Although enterprise directors and other senior managers are appointed by the appropriate 'supervisory organ', usually the ministry, it is the county Party organisation which approves their appointment. This informal control is likely to be only marginally diminished by the increased use of competitive applications for managerial posts in the early 1980s, for it is unlikely that such candidates will be appointed without Party approval. The county Party organ's jurisdiction also extends to the appointment of Party secretaries within enterprises in its area.

The Party organisation within the enterprise plays a similar role. It supervises the appointment of middle and lower management and, in practice if not in theory, has the right to, for example, 'freeze' the appointment of non-Party managers in cases where a large number of non-Party managers had already been appointed within an enterprise (Héthy and Makó, 1979, p. 100). It is under an obligation to take a position on general policy goals in the light of government and Party decrees and on questions which have a fundamental effect on workers' living and working conditions; and it uses its right to receive reports from economic leaders to ensure that the spirit of the plan is being adhered to in both its social and economic aspects (Gy. Juhász, 1974, p. 48). But it is under the same obligation as the county Party organ not to interfere in economic decisions itself (Merényi and Simon, 1979, pp. 71–5). Finally, at the very bottom of the Party hierarchy, the workplace Party groups concentrate more on busying themselves with propaganda work and with 'socialist brigade' activity (Merényi and Simon, 1979, p. 87), although they too perform a supervisory function in that Party members are enjoined to inform the relevant Party organs of the atmosphere amongst, and opinions of, non-Party members in the workplace (Gy. Juhász, 1974, p. 50).

The Party's role in economic planning in Hungary's socialism, then, can be summarised as follows. Although it determines overall policy goals and decides general economic strategy, its control over tactics is much weaker. It supervises generally, uses 'moral suasion' on enterprise leaders to undertake politically desired but unprofitable production, and controls the appointment of key personnel in order to ensure that executive decisions are not wholly out of line with the prescribed economic policy. But it does not pretend to determine what those executive decisions should be. Party omnipresence restricts management to an approved type of person and to an approved range of policies; it does not decide which policy should be implemented within that range, nor who, at every level, management should be.

The constraints on managerial autonomy from the shop floor, from the trade unions, from the institutions of workplace democracy, and from the unofficial activity of workers are considerably less severe. Although trade unions do take up cases of injustice in relation to individual workers (Gál, 1975), are powerful political institutions in their own right, and enjoy formal rights of suggestion and veto with regard to certain managerial decisions,[4] structural limitations prevent them from acting as an independent institutional body whose primary purpose is to defend the interests of labour within the workplace. The central problem with trade unions in this respect is that union and management are insufficiently distinct. Full-time union officials receive their bonuses and profit shares, some 10% of their salary, from the enterprise (Andor, 1979, p. 45) and, as Andor also reports, management, trade union and indeed Party posts within the enterprise can be seen to form a single career structure. Shop floor trade union committees, on the other hand, are dominated not by workers but by foremen and administrators and cannot be expected to act unambiguously in the workers' interests. In both the Győr engineering works and the Budapest construction company studies by Héthy and Makó the shop floor trade union committee typified this trend (1972a, p. 177; 1978, p. 252). Not surprisingly, workers place little reliance on their trade unions when they have a problem and, in the same Győr factory, members of the Trade Union Theoretical Institute found that only 1% of workers consulted their trade union on matters concerning norms and wages, and that only 1.5% consulted it in connection with the improvement of conditions of work (Héthy, 1979b, pp. 46–7). On the other hand, 75% turned to their immediate superiors on issues of norms and wages, 87% on other matters (Héthy, 1980, p. 88).

If trade unions are ineffective in defending the interests of labour, the institutions which exist to promote industrial democracy within

Hungarian enterprises fare no better. The Party group at the workplace level tends to be staffed by the lower echelons of management (Héthy and Makó, 1972a, p. 177), while at the enterprise committee level it is part of the same general managerial career structure mentioned above. Enterprise Party secretaries go on to become heads of personnel departments and so on (Héthy and Makó, 1979, pp. 30–1). Nor are 'production meetings' conducive to worker participation. Management considers them to be simply forums for informing workers of decisions already taken, rather than opportunities for considering worker suggestions and entering into reasoned debate; and, consequently, very little serious discussion takes place at them (Andor, 1979; Halmos, 1978, pp. 50–1; Kozák and Mód, 1974; Kunszabó, 1980). At Győr, Héthy and Makó found that, despite 90% of workers wanting to have a say in general enterprise affairs, no matters of serious concern to labour were discussed at production meetings (1972b, p. 146). 'Easy questions' were answered by management on the spot; 'difficult questions', such as the need to clean factory windows in order to illuminate the workshop better, were replied to in writing within seven days; 'awkward questions', such as norms and wages, were not even recorded in the minutes of the meetings (1970, pp. 115–16). Not surprisingly, attendance at such meetings is low, considerably lower than the official attendance figures (Andor, 1979, p. 6; Kunszabó, 1980, pp. 97–9), and workers' opinions, as gauged by the surveys of Andor, Kunszabó, Héthy and Makó, and others, reflect the inevitable disillusionment with 'production meetings' which this engenders. 'There's no point going to a meeting and saying this, that or the other need doing. Nothing changes' (Andor, 1979, p. 20). 'At our place industrial democracy follows the director's orders' (Lunczer, 1974, p. 77).

Of course, the fact that workers have no effective influence on enterprise decision-making via institutional channels does not mean that they are entirely impotent. Indirect and negative forms of control are possible and have been studied at length by Héthy and Makó and some other industrial sociologists. The best documented informal shop floor tactic is the systematic 'go-slow', used to blackmail management into increasing wage rates, not cutting overtime, or not increasing norms (1972a, pp. 89–106; 1972b; Héthy, 1978). They also cite workers who mention 'working to rule' in order to put pressure on management (1978, pp. 188–90). Such threats to management bonuses for successful plan fulfilment can only be used successfully by groups of workers who occupy a position of strength in relation to the production process, who have a monopoly control over a key stage in production and who have evolved enough of a collective spirit to be willing to endure relatively low wages in the short term for considerably higher wages later. This in effect means that such tactics can be applied successfully only by elder skilled workers who have their skill to sell, considerable experience of the rules of the game, and fewer financial pressures on them to maximise immediate income (Héthy and Makó, 1972b, pp. 140–5; Kemény, 1978b, pp. 68–74).[5]

Other workers are more impotent. Strikes, or the threat of them, can yield results. Héthy and Makó describe how workers at Győr extracted both a pay rise and the opportunity for considerable overtime by walking out and threatening a strike (1972a, pp. 258–61), and the first issue of Hungary's *samizdat* magazine, *Beszélő*, describes how 34 building workers secured an improvement in changing room conditions after downing tools in November 1980 (*Beszélő*, No. 1, pp. 31–3). In both cases, significantly, the trade union organisation gave no support. But strikes are relatively unusual events and, where matters do not reach such a head, the absence of a strong informal group, or the inability to control a stage in production, obliges workers to accept work on management's terms, fight against sometimes impossible norms and complain, or bribe foremen, in order to obtain overtime or a well-paying job (Andor, 1974, p. 170; Földvári and Zsille, 1978; Haraszti, 1977, p. 23; Héthy and Makó, 1978, p. 188).

It is clear, then, that under the production relations of Hungary's version of a socialist economy, management does enjoy considerable autonomy in the method of plan fulfilment and this is manifest mainly in respect of labour. We must now consider what it does with this power. We have defined 'socialist wage labour' as being susceptible to manipulation by those who might have control over labour, and have located management as such a group. How does it use its power? There are three strands to this question. Does management have any particular group interest in favour of which it might be expected to exercise its control over the method of plan fulfilment? Is that interest threatened from any quarter over which it is capable of exercising control – for example labour and its associated costs? Does management take self-interested, evasive action to promote its interests? Is it, that is, part of the nature of 'socialist wage labour' to be manipulated by management in the pursuit of managerial, group self-interest?

In order to answer the first of these questions, we must consider the bonuses which lubricate relations within economic planning and which encourage individuals to behave in the manner required by the plan. Interest in bonuses is not uniform. Management receives large bonuses in respect of successful performance: 30% to 50%, and in some cases even more, of basic salary (Andor, 1979, p. 39; *Figyelő*, 1979, No. 47, p. 5; 1982, No. 48, p. 4). Workers can look forward to only relatively small end of year profit shares, rarely as much as 10% of basic salary and dependent on factors over which they have no control (Andor, 1979, p. 39; Hegedűs and Márkus, 1966, p. 108; Héthy, 1979a, p. 28; Tardos, 1972, p. 925). What is more, while workers have the fallback of working overtime, it is only by winning bonuses that management can hope to receive more than its basic salary.

But managerial bonuses are under a tax threat from a source which requires some familiarisation with the forms of wage regulation which have operated since 1968. The details of these regulations are complex,[6] and we should note the continued element of 'average wage level' regulation in the form of the 'average wage brake' even within the 'wage bill' regulation which was predominant in the late 1970s but which has been abandoned again in favour of 'wage-level' regulation. The crux of the matter, however, is that under all the systems, as soon as any annual tax-free increase in the level of the average wage for an enterprise has been exceeded, an exceptionally progressive levy – termed (until modifications in the 1980s) the 'wage development payment' – is imposed which very quickly reaches a highest marginal rate of some 300–600%, depending on the precise system in operation. Furthermore, this levy is paid from the 'sharing fund' element of enterprise profits and hence, if incurred, adversely affects management's chances of getting its bonuses. Managerial bonuses have come either from the same source as the 'wage development payment' or, since 1976, from a different one, but one whose size is adversely affected by payment of the levy. From 1976 to the end of the period under detailed consideration (and only the details have changed since) bonuses could only be awarded once all the funds to be created out of profit had been established and once the 'sharing fund' (out of which the 'wage development payments' were made) had itself been subjected to progressive taxation. In addition, until 1976, the economic indicator on which managerial bonuses were themselves based (overall profit between 1968 and 1970, and 'sharing fund' divided by wage-costs between 1971 and 1976) was adversely affected by making 'wage development payments'. After 1976, enterprises did have the theoretical option of not forming a 'sharing fund' at all, but failure to do so would prevent the payment of end of year profit shares to either other levels of management or workers, and enterprises have been reluctant to follow this course (Laky, 1979).

Whatever the precise method of wage regulation, a situation has developed in which bonuses have been considerably at risk should a 'wage development payment' be made. It would not be surprising therefore if management adopted strategies to avoid incurring the payment, and there is considerable evidence to show that it does. Or rather, there is copious evidence that enterprises behave in a way which has the consequence of avoiding 'wage development payments', but it is less easy to show that the adoption of these strategies is the result of management self-consciously perceiving its separate group interest and acting in order to maximise it. Sufficient secondary evidence exists even for this latter claim, however, for it to be forwarded as a plausible causal hypothesis which could at least be refuted if there were easier access to the minds and budgets of enterprise managers.

The most common strategy adopted by enterprise management to avoid the payment of taxation on excessively high increases in wages is usually termed 'labour force dilution'. This is the practice of employing reserves of cheap labour in order to keep the average wage low and thus allow some flexibility in paying higher wages to skilled workers since skilled labour is constantly in short supply. This tendency was noticed immediately after the introduction of average wage control in 1957 (A. Hegedűs, 1960); it came under particularly close scrutiny during the first few years of the New Economic Mechanism as enterprises experienced labour problems when labour mobility increased (MTA–KISZ, 1971); and it continues to be the subject of comment in economic journals.[7] But is this the result of self-conscious, self-interested management policy? Héthy and Makó reproduce some management comments which provide the best evidence in support of the case. In their study of a Budapest construction enterprise, they reproduce verbatim a discussion which reveals both the importance attached by managers to keeping within the wage level regulations and their ability to juggle with labour inputs over the course of the year.

'There is another worker . . . who has been with us for a long time and we only keep him on because he is a cheap duffer, he improves the average wage.' Mattheisz [the site manager] explains that a bonus of 20 000 forints is at risk if the average wage is exceeded by half a percent. 'If we exceed the average wage then we cannot pick up a bonus during the year however many flats we finish. We only get a bonus at the end of the year if I've got the average wage to balance by then.' (1978, p. 231)

Management decision-making is clearly structured around avoiding 'wage development payments'. There are, as Héthy and Makó recount, many ways of getting round actually making these payments, by employing cheap labour, by using students and soldiers, and by falsifying the books (1979, p. 45). But to acknowledge this is to reinforce the determining influence that these payments have on behaviour, and the threat that they represent to bonuses. It might well be possible to manipulate labour inputs at the enterprise level so that the levy is avoided, but the middle manager is faced with the danger that 'If he doesn't succeed [in keeping increases in average wages within the tax-free limits], he is considered the sort of person who cannot manage' (Héthy and Makó, 1979, p. 159). Management would appear, then, to be quite aware of where its interests lie and how it can manipulate labour inputs so as to maximise them.

If effects on labour are to be our key to unlocking the experience of collectivisation in Hungary, the two central points made in this introduction should be restated. First, socialist priorities in industrial development and socialist concerns in economic organisation have created a situation in which there is both space for 'family labour' to operate and incentive for its operation. As we have seen in the brief résumé above, Hungary's 'actually existing' socialist economy has gone further than most Eastern European countries in institutionalising the integration of the family and state sectors. Second, socialist relations of production in Hungary have developed in such a way that part of what it means to be 'socialist wage labour' is to be an economic category which is capable of manipulation by those who control the method of plan fulfilment, and which is so manipulated by management in pursuit of its group self-interest.

The remainder of this book will consider the interplay of these factors for labour, both as an economic category and as an amalgam of social factors, as socio-economic relations in agriculture were revolutionised; as the peasant family farm was first universalised under the land reform, then squeezed out of, and finally integrated into, the socialist economy; as male and female poor peasants, middle peasants and agrarian proletarians were transformed into managers and operatives within a highly structured, complex division of labour on agricultural producer co-operatives. Comparisons will be made from time to time with Soviet collective farms and Chinese communes so as to highlight the contrasts, but also to establish the many similarities in all these experiences of collectivisation.

PART I

'FAMILY LABOUR' AND 'SOCIALIST WAGE LABOUR' IN HUNGARY'S CO-OPERATIVE AGRICULTURE: THE INCORPORATION OF PETTY COMMODITY PRODUCTION

I

'Family labour' in the achievement and consolidation of collectivised agriculture, 1946–68

In the years between 1946 and 1968 Hungary not only established collectivised agriculture throughout the country, it also provided it with a sound financial basis on which to build successfully in the 1970s. These two processes – establishment and consolidation – were not straightforward, nor were they unidirectional, and the approach adopted towards labour, and primarily 'family labour', was central to the final realisation of both. Concessions in favour of private peasant production played a central role in Hungary's successful third collectivisation in 1959–61; whilst a crucial factor in the consolidation process from the early 1960s to 1968 was the recognition that, for collective agriculture to be successful, it could not be based on farm-wide, communal 'family labour' alone. That is, Hungarian agricultural co-operatives very soon realised that the logic of the 'family economy' in relation to individuals' income and wage-costs could not be extended from the family farm to a large, complex organisation. Thus, while incorporating and indirectly relying on private sector 'family labour' on members' household plots, the communal sector of the farm replaced 'family labour' writ large with a form of wage labour. These two concerns – the need for concessions to private 'family labour' in the achievement of collectivised agriculture and the retreat from communal 'family labour' in its consolidation – constitute the primary focus of this chapter. A subsidiary interest is collectivised agriculture's readiness to incorporate certain forms of individual 'family labour' into the communal sector as well. Although it is not argued that the approach adopted towards labour was the single most important determinant of successful collectivisation – the government's readiness to provide sufficient funds to cover the costs of collectivisation being equally significant – its centrality to the process will be clear.

25

There is no need to repeat here the history of land reform and collectivisation given in the introduction. Suffice it to recall that the land reform of the immediate post war years universalised for the first time small-scale proprietorship and that, from the late 1940s until the debacle of 1956, there were two unsuccessful attempts at collectivisation using traditional 'stalinist' tactics before the Kádár government finally succeeded in 1959–61 using policies more or less in keeping with its Agrarian Theses of 1957. Why was it that the respective attempts at collectivisation of the Rákosi and Kádár governments produced such different results? What were the crucial differences in policy?

The key differences would appear to have been in three areas. First, there was a substantial change in the overall economic policy towards agriculture. It was actually given finance and capital in order to transform its productive base, and was no longer treated as a branch of the economy out of which surplus had to be extracted for industrial development. Second, social concessions were made to middle peasants and even 'kulaks'; and, third, economic concessions were made to middle peasants and, indeed, to all co-operative farm members, in the form of revised household plot regulations. Although the pace of collectivisation was rather more rapid than was implied by the Agrarian Theses, in the manner of collectivisation their spirit was more or less obeyed. Before turning to the second issue of how and why co-operatives subsequently succeeded in consolidating themselves we must analyse the reasons for this successful realisation at the third attempt more closely. Our focus will be on differences in social and economic policy, although it should be noted that psychological factors may also have played an important role. Hungary was a demoralised country in the years immediately following 1956 and in many cases the peasantry, having already endured two attempts at collectivisation, was resigned to its inevitability.

The Kádár regime's Agrarian Theses had introduced a new attitude to agriculture generally. Collectivisation was no longer seen as an end in itself, but as a method whereby large-scale agriculture would bring about an ever-increasing standard of living (AT, p. 69). Existing co-operatives were rationalised and enlarged to make them suitable for large-scale agriculture (Appendix I), and there was a concerted policy of aid directed towards them, both direct and indirect, totalling 18 000 million forints. However, although aid was successful in raising both production levels on the co-operative farms and the standard of living of the members (Orbán, 1972, pp. 199–203), private peasants were not enticed away from their plots in large numbers, and the new members who did join between 1957 and 1959 were predominantly from the former landless poor (MAR, Vol. 2, p. 13). Compulsory deliveries, abolished by the Nagy government (Vali, 1961, p. 293), were not reintroduced, despite their retention in the Soviet Union (Nove, 1980, p. 151); and the state provided positive aid to agriculture to cover this period of fundamental reorganisation. As part of its general economic reform, in 1957, the government raised agriculture's portion of national investment (Berend, 1974a, pp. 94 and 102).[1] This aid was continued during the years of collectivisation itself and, as a consequence, collectivised agriculture was established with no substantial fall in overall agricultural production, and with no dramatic fall in members' living standards. Figures for gross production value between 1958 and 1962 do not fluctuate enormously and the gross production index (taking 1950 as 100) oscillated around 122 (see Appendix I). The figures for net production reflect the costs involved in collectivisation, however. The net production index (again taking 1950 as 100) rose to 114 in 1959, but plummeted to 96 in 1961 before rising slightly to 101 in 1962 (see Appendix I). Although not profitable, collectivisation did not lead to a fall in production.

This successful provision of economic aid compares very markedly with the earlier attempts at collectivisation, when co-operatives were heavily burdened with compulsory deliveries, low agricultural producer prices (M. Hegedűs, 1971) and inadequate government aid. For example, only half of the 22 000 tractors projected in the first five year plan saw the light of day (Orbán, 1972, p. 120), and use of fertiliser remained below planned levels, with the ratio of fertiliser per hectare falling continually as the co-operative land holdings increased (Orbán, 1972, p. 121). At the same time, the original 11 milliard forints of credit planned for the co-operative farms for the years up to 1953 were reduced to 8 milliard forints during the course of the first five year plan; by 1953, only 5 milliard had materialised (Orbán, 1972, p. 116). The New Course, introduced in 1954, provided temporary relief for the co-operatives thus starved of resources. In that year, for example, agriculture received an unprecedented 23% of national investment, and more tractors were put into service than during the entire 1950–3 period (Orbán, 1972, pp. 141–3). However, by March 1956, official bodies noted that farms could neither meet their compulsory deliveries nor pay their members, and were citing the inadequate economic base of the co-operatives as the reason for their break-up (Orbán, 1972, p. 154).

Such a policy of collectivisation on the cheap was, of course, similar to the pattern of collectivisation undertaken by Stalin in the 1930s and maintained by Soviet policy makers until the mid 1960s (Nove, 1980, pp. 135–6), a policy which might be taken as the 'socialist norm'. The theory that this 'socialist norm' actually extracted funds from agriculture and the peasantry which were then used to fuel industrialisation has been criticised as being incomplete on two counts. First, it takes insufficient account of the fact that, because of general food shortages, the local market price for agricultural products remained high and that, by exploiting this shortage, peasant incomes did not suffer. Second, the price disparities between agricultural and industrial products did not lead to an extraction of surplus from agriculture at all between 1928 and 1932; if anything, the reverse was the case (Ellman, 1975; Millar, 1970). Neither criticism alters the fact, however, that stalinist development strategy put its emphasis on industry rather than agriculture and, relative to the demands made on them, starved the state and co-operative sectors in agriculture of funds. Even if no levy was extracted from agriculture, the consequence of the 'socialist norm' in collectivisation was that farms could not reap the potential fruits of large-scale, mechanised production, and kolkhoz peasants retreated into production for autoconsumption and for the local, private market. Agricultural produce for the state sector had to be extracted by force. The peasantry as a group might not have suffered any more greatly than the urban proletariat under such policies (Ellman, 1975), but the squeeze on agriculture certainly prevented kolkhozy from developing as effective large-scale production units. A decade after collectivisation in Hungary, most farms had fully mechanised cereal production, were undertaking large-scale investments in animal sheds and were diversifying into non-agricultural production. A decade after collectivisation in the Soviet Union, only 4.2% of collective farms had electricity (Nove, 1980, p. 243).

Although the organisation of Chinese collectivised agriculture differs in many respects from that in Eastern Europe and the Soviet Union, the same 'socialist norm' appears to have been followed in its creation. Collectivisation was accompanied by the same low priority for agriculture within the national budget (Gurley, 1976, p. 125);

Chinese collectivisation was carried out at similarly break-neck speed from the spring of 1956 to the spring of 1959 (Grays, 1982, p. 151; Gurley, 1976, pp. 159–60); the decision for rapid full-scale collectivisation rather than a steady progression to mechanised agriculture was the result of the sudden re-emergence of Mao in 1956 (Selden, 1979, pp. 56–7), just as Soviet collectivisation followed on from Stalin's victory in political struggle; and collectivisation was accompanied by starvation in China just as it was in the Soviet Union (Gittings, 1982; Nove, 1969, p. 108). In fact, real differences of organisational form are not so very great despite the use of different terminology in China. This will become apparent below when we compare Hungarian, Soviet and Chinese attitudes to such factors as the household plot, but here it is worth noting that after the Lushan Declaration of August 1959, only a matter of months after the completion of 100% communalisation, the main units of account in agriculture became production brigades, that is villages, and later work teams, and that the communes were reduced to the status of administrative units (Wheelwright and McFarlane, 1970, p. 50). In general, the small work teams were responsible for field cultivation, while the village-sized production brigade had responsibility for such things as the piggery, the duck farm and the dairy (Wheelwright and McFarlane, 1970, p. 131). Although there was reference during the Cultural Revolution to re-activating the communes as production units, it was not followed up (Leys, 1977, p. 197), and recent developments indicate further decentralisation (Grays, 1982), as we shall see below.

Clearly, then, the Kádár government's readiness to pay the price of providing a sound productive base for collectivisation was of fundamental importance to its ultimate success. However, collectivisation entails social as well as economic reorganisation, and the third attempt at collectivisation was characterised by social and political initiatives on top of the more narrowly economic incentives offered to those who participated in co-operative agriculture. Since those who were already committed to co-operative farming tended to be the former landless proletarians or estate workers, this translated itself, in effect, into making co-operative agriculture attractive to, or at least not prohibitively unattractive to, those who had been successful peasant farmers, the middle peasants and the 'kulaks'. Similar policies may also have accounted for China's relative success in initially establishing collective farms (Nolan, 1976).

Hungary's third collectivisation was altogether less coercive and punitive than the previous attempts had been. No quotas were set for the number of co-operatives to be formed in a given district (PHI, 1972, p. 338), and a more positive approach was adopted towards the 'kulaks' and middle peasants. The 1959 law on co-operative farms not only allowed for the 'kulaks' to join co-operatives, from which they had previously been excluded,[2] it also provided for their election, after two years' exemplary work, into the co-operative leadership (TRHGY, 1959 évi 7 tvr). In addition since the presidents of the newly formed farms were no longer appointees from the central or local administration (Kunszabó, 1974a; PHI, 1972, p. 339), farms were able to elect well-respected successful middle peasants as their heads in the hope that their experience would make a viable economic concern of the co-operative (Erdei, 1969, p. 83; Orbán, 1972, p. 221). Furthermore, former middle peasants were allowed to establish their own separate co-operative rather than join in with the poor peasants who formed the core of the existing farms. This was beneficial because middle peasants were reluctant to join forces on equal terms with those who had formerly been their day labourers, while the former poor peasantry feared that, in an integrated farm, they would once again be relegated to the role of day labourers for middle peasant masters (Kunszabó, 1970a, p. 10; Orbán, 1972, p. 241).

During the first two collectivisation campaigns, by contrast, the most successful elements in government policy had been those directed against the 'kulak', and since the definition of the term in terms of size of land holding bore little relationship to a single social group, many peasants were included within its compass for whom the term 'middle peasant' would have been more accurate.[3] The aim was to abolish the 'kulaks' completely as a class. Socially they were excluded from all forms of political life and the co-operative movement, whilst economically the attack came from two quarters: restrictions were placed on the scope of their economic activity, and there was an increase in their economic obligations to the state. *De facto* restrictions were placed on the employment of outside labour by limiting the working day to 8–10 hours, and wage increases of 50–100% were enforced (Orbán, 1972, p. 109); limitations were placed on the amount of land that could be sold privately (Orbán, 1972, pp. 78–9); and both taxes and compulsory deliveries to the state were increased.

The anti-'kulak' elements in collectivisation are again part of the 'socialist norm', but their origins are more purely ideological than in the case of 'collectivisation on the cheap'. They stem ultimately from Lenin's emphasis on class formation in the Russian countryside in the early part of the twentieth century. Lenin saw embryonic capitalism in any relationship where material reward passed from one person to another in return for services rendered. But peasant society is complex, and there are many relationships of dependence and reward, and even of exploitation, which are in no way analogous to the relationship of labour to capital in a capitalist economy; however unjust they are, they should not be confused as such. In both Hungary in the immediate post war years and the Soviet Union in the 1920s, there was much hiring of seasonal labour, much loaning of carts or draught animals in return for labour services, much 'exploitation'; but there were very few farmers who could accurately be termed 'kulak' if this is to mean an embryonic market-oriented, profit maximising, wage labour employing capitalist farmer (Lewin, 1968; Orbán, 1972, p. 78). At the third attempt, and in the wake of 1956, Hungary had the political courage to break the leninist mould.

Equally significant for the final achievement of collectivised agriculture, the cost to the member of joining the co-operative farm was reduced, and this benefited poor and middle peasant alike. Costs were reduced both in terms of the immediate loss of property to the co-operative on joining and of lost potential earnings. All livestock, equipment and fodder had to be handed over to the co-operative as before, but instead of being obliged to forfeit 15% of its value, the member could now receive, as reimbursement, a sum fixed by the General Meeting of the co-operative, at which every member had a vote.[4] Furthermore, no land tax was to be subtracted from the 'rental' which members received from the co-operative in respect of the land they had contributed, as had been the case previously. The value of this rental was not altered substantially, but it was now to be paid in cash rather than kind.[5] Finally, and most significantly, while there was no change in the restrictions on the size or scope of the household plot, there were relaxations in regulations which, in effect, supported the members in their private 'family economy'.

A brief excursus on household plot regulation is necessary here to make this point clearly. The 1948 legislation on producer co-operatives set the size of the household plot at 0.86 ha on the most developed type III co-operative groups and independent producer co-operatives. In addition to this land, the member could keep as many animals as he needed to meet his personal needs (MK, 14.000/1948). At this stage, the simpler forms of co-operative did not require a specific household plot since members gave only a certain portion of their land over to collective cultivation (MK, 14.000/1948), a fact which itself led to considerable conflict because peasants gave only inferior land to the co-operatives and kept the best land for themselves (Donáth, 1949, pp. 118–20; A. Hegedűs, 1949, p. 468).

Decrees on co-operative agriculture passed in 1949 and 1950 established a lower limit of 0.28 ha for the household plot with an upper limit of 0.43 ha (TRHGY, 1949 (163) Korm sz r; 133/1950 (V.7) MT), and those joining without land were allowed a plot of the lower limit only. The permitted area included both arable land outside the village and any garden area immediately surrounding the house.[6] Later in 1950, the number of animals permitted on the household plot of the type III co-operative group and independent producer co-operative was set at one calf, one sow and its young, five sheep, one or two fattening pigs and unlimited poultry and rabbits. In 1951 acreage limitations were extended to the looser type I and type II farms as members of such co-operatives were obliged to give over all their land to communal production (TRHGY, 18.010/1951 (I.20) FM). In 1953, however, as co-operatives were spontaneously breaking up, restrictions on the household plot were relaxed. The upper limit was increased to 0.57 ha; it was stressed that the plot was given to a household rather than a family, so ensuring that newly married children of existing members would get their own plot; members were specifically allowed to retain simple tools; and the limits on animal holding were increased, the permitted number of calves, sows and fattening pigs being doubled (TRHGY, 1038/1953 (VIII.2) MT; 1070/1953 (XI.12) MT).

During the Rákosi era of collectivisation, then, the houshold plot was seen as a threat, a bastion of private agriculture which had to be severely restricted. It was subjected to compulsory deliveries (J.Juhász, 1973, p. 103) and the upper limit was apparently strictly enforced, the average size quoted by Juhász being considerably below the permitted upper limit (J.Juhász, 1973, pp. 103–4). In 1954–5, under the 'New Course', although there was no change in the view that the household plot ought to be strictly controlled, and there was no idea of its serving more than the family's basic needs, it was acknowledged that the plot would remain within co-operative agriculture for a long time (J.Juhász, 1973, p. 109).[7]

In 1959, the limitations on the area of household plots and on the number of animals to be kept on them were not modified. However, a number of other measures certainly benefited household plot agriculture. New members who joined without land were no longer restricted to 0.29 ha, indicating perhaps that all members now received the upper limit where possible (TRHGY, 1959 évi 7 tvr 28). Again, it was stressed that if family members set up an independent household, they too qualified for a separate plot (TRHGY, 19/1959 (VII.12) FM 64§ (4)). In addition, the new regulations not only allowed for co-operatives to be created where there existed no adequate facilities for animal husbandry, they further endorsed the practice adopted since the Agrarian Theses of allowing communal animals to be kept on members' household plots in such circumstances (TRHGY, 1959 évi 7 tvr; 3004/2/1959). This was a pragmatic move to prevent the slaughter of animals and was informed by a recognition that co-operatives could not build the facilities for communal animal husbandry at once. In the interim, co-operative farm members were allowed to profit from the compromise. Milk, calves and piglets deriving from these animals could be retained by the member until their number exceeded the maximum permitted by the household plot regulations, in which case, once communal stabling was available, the co-operative was obliged to purchase them at the official state purchase price. In addition, the co-operative was placed under an obligation to supply the necessary fodder for such animals (TRHGY, 19/1959 (VII.12) FM 63§(5) (6)). It should also be noted that Márkus claims that statistics for the numbers of animals kept on private plots were not held and that, on outlying farmsteads ('tanya'), the limits were never seriously enforced (1979, p. 160).

Social, political and economic concessions to those who had been successful practitioners of 'family labour' on their peasant farms were, then, an imporant factor in the successful establishment of collectivised agriculture in Hungary. So too was the readiness to retain a private sector, based on family labour, within the bosom of collectivised agriculture. At this stage, such a move was a calculated risk in the light of the experience of the 1950s. Not only were co-operatives scarcely better endowed with capital equipment and machinery than their peasant members, the financial and organisational regulations circumscribing their operation remained imbued with the same logic of a 'family economy'. While certain measures were taken by the Agrarian Theses to alter this capital situation, it was the failure in practice of co-operative farms, operating as communal family units, to attract labour (that is to induce membership participation) that convinced agrarian planners that a radical reorganisation of financial principles within the co-operative farm was necessary. As we shall see below, while the Agrarian Theses stimulated policies that increased the economic strength of the co-operatives and went some way to giving the co-operative farm member the functional equivalents of what his private land had given him – a regular income and life-long security – further financial reorganisation was necessary to complete the task, and such reorganisation initiated the movement towards the use of 'socialist wage labour' within co-operative agriculture.

But, before we go on to analyse this new development in Hungarian agriculture, we should briefly review Soviet and Chinese attitudes to private agriculture. Regulations concerning the size of household plots for kolkhoz members in the Soviet Union have varied somewhat since the first model statute was presented in March 1931 (Davies, 1980b, p. 107), but, by and large, they have been similar to Hungarian ones. In 1935, the land area limit was between a quarter and a half of a hectare, with a livestock limit of one cow and its calves, a sow and its piglets, four sheep and any number of rabbits and poultry (Nove, 1969, p. 241). The current regulations allow the same land area, although this now includes the immediate farmyard which had previously been excluded (Wädekin, 1973, p. 349) and allows the ownership of one cow, two calves, ten goats or sheep and unlimited poultry and rabbits. There are also special regulations allowing larger animal holdings in primarily livestock areas (Hill, 1974, p. 493). These limits on animal holdings are considerably larger than the average numbers owned by kolkhoz members (Wädekin, 1973, p. 349). Arutyunyan, for example, found that the average acreage of plot in the area he studied was 0.4 ha, whilst only one household in three kept a cow (1969, p. 240).

In China, the regulations are rather different and the plot's size is much smaller, although it should be borne in mind that the land holdings in China and throughout Asia have always been much smaller than those in Europe. The average landlord land holding in China before the 'Land Revolution' of 8.13 ha (Selden, 1979, p. 37) would scarcely have counted as a middle peasant holding in Hungary. Private plots in China are allocated by the 5% principle, that is, the per capita area of private land in a given village should not exceed 5% of the arable land per capita in the village (Gurley, 1976, p. 159). This was increased to 10% for a time in the 1950s (Gurley, 1976, p. 159), but observers in the 1970s refer to a 5% norm (Aubert, 1975); in the 1980s, it was increased again to 15% (Mandel, 1982, p. 202). In the Hua Dong commune visited by Aubert, this amounted to 165 square metres per family (Aubert, 1975, p. 91). Regulations concerning livestock holding are unclear, but on this same commune, 60% of the 67 208 pigs on farms encompassed by it were privately owned. The whole commune only worked 400 meat and 10 milk buffalo, none of which were privately owned (Aubert, 1975, p. 89). As in Soviet and Hungarian practice, official figures for the commune livestock holdings include the private holdings of the commune members. Household plots elsewhere in socialist Asia are also small. In Korea they are only 50 square metres (Brun and Hersh, 1976, p. 342), and in Vietnam they are 200 square metres (Gough, 1978, p. 70). (The Hungarian limit is 6000 square metres.)

The organisational model of the very first Hungarian co-operative farms in the 1940s had been rudimentary. There was no concept of a wage, nor was there a developed division of labour. Members received a share in kind from the total surplus production in relation to the amount of work they had performed on the farm. The president was a genuine *primus inter pares* taking part in communal work and doing the necessary paperwork in moments of free time (Gyenes, 1968). The means of production consisted of whatever simple machinery the members had brought into the co-operative with them. In the first two attempts at collectivisation, three types of producer co-operative group were forwarded (types I, II and III), together with an independent producer co-operative which was organised on the same lines as the type III co-operative group, but which was entirely independent of any other co-operative organisation. The difference between the three types of co-operative group related to the amount of communal production and manner in which the harvest was shared. On the type I farm the members sowed jointly, but harvested individually, and kept their harvested produce for themselves. On type II farms, the members cut the harvest on an individual basis but then pooled it. Type III groups and independent farms operated on an entirely co-operative basis, distributing the surplus in relation to the amount of work performed. The conception underlying all the groups was the same. Producer co-operatives were groups of peasants operating jointly on land they had formerly owned, and with machinery they themselves had brought into the farm. The state might award them additional land, and type III groups and independent farms might receive some animals, but modern equipment had to be hired from the state-owned machine stations and tractor drivers were employees of these stations and not the farm (TRHGY, 104/1952 (XI.28) MT). Thus, horse power was the most usual form of traction, and even horses were in short supply initially since landless labourers made up the majority of the membership of the earlier co-operatives.

The organisation of work was decided on a daily basis at the early morning meeting of all the members who were prepared to work. The smallness of the farm, the antipathy felt towards them by other peasants in the village, and the level of sacrifice necessary for the co-operative to survive all helped to develop a collective spirit, though sometimes even this was not enough to overcome the problems they faced.[8] Remuneration was based on sharing the surplus in proportion to the amount of work performed, but only after all compulsory deliveries had been made. The co-operative was an amalgam of peasant farmers producing jointly in a manner similar to the traditional 'family economy' in that there was no specific notion of fixed wage-costs.

The Agrarian Theses of 1957 initiated a change in the whole conception of co-operative farming. The scale of the farms was increased; only one form of co-operative, corresponding to the former type III variety, was permitted except in poorer areas;[9] farms gained permission to own capital equipment; and government funds were made available to facilitate these changes. More important, however, the government realised that some inducement had to be offered to the members to stay in agriculture once their land had entered collective cultivation. The co-operative had to provide the member with the equivalent of those functions which land had previously offered: the provision of income in the present and security for the future.

Government policy towards collectivised agriculture after its establishment consisted of lessening the burden on agriculture within the national plan, continuing aid, and encouraging experimentation with novel forms of work organisation and remuneration, even if this entailed turning a blind eye to local initiatives which questioned certain socialist shibboleths. We have already seen how a transfer of economic resources to agriculture helped to establish co-operative farms. This policy was continued during its consolidation and, in addition, a special programme of decrees was introduced to direct aid and investment to the farms.[10] Despite this, however, the price of agricultural products remained comparatively low for the major part of the period until 1968. This seriously affected the co-operatives' profitability, although it did mean that central organs could retain some *de facto* control over co-operatives and co-operative economic policy via their control of investment credit and loans.

The aim of this combination of aid, low prices and directed investment was to transform co-operatives into large-scale production enterprises, relatively autonomous from government control. As an initial step towards the realisation of these goals, the government encouraged the amalgamation of farms, and from 1956, and especially between 1960 and 1968, there was a phenomenal increase in both the average acreage and average membership of the co-operative farms (see Appendix I). Amalgamations took place predominantly in 1961 (the final year in the period of collectivisation) and in 1965 at the end of the second five year plan (Szerdahelyi *et al.*, 1976, p. 10). This reflected Soviet developments towards larger farms. The number of kolkhozy in the Soviet Union was almost halved between 1950 and 1958 and almost halved again between 1958 and the mid 1960s (Nove, 1969, p. 336).

More important, consonant with the policy of greater autonomy for the co-operatives, collective farms were allowed to become owners of machinery in their own right. This right was first conceded in 1957 (TRHGY, 1.091/1956 (IX.11) MT 9§). Co-operatives were encouraged to buy for themselves all forms of machinery other than combine harvesters and heavy tractors (AT, p. 70) and in that year alone over 1000 light tractors were purchased by the 2557 producer co-operatives. A further 800 had been purchased by the end of 1959 when the number of co-operative farms was 4185 (Pelva, 1960, p. 842). After 1959, further measures were taken in this direction, when a government decree of 1959 provided for the easy purchase by the co-operative farm of tractors and agricultural machinery. This decree and subsequent amendments allowed 75% credit for the purchase of such equipment repayable over six to eight years.[11]

A further move in this process was the decision announced as a government decree in January 1963 to turn the agricultural machine stations into machine repair stations and transfer their machinery to the co-operatives themselves. This followed, rather more belatedly than was sometimes the case, the Soviet decision to abolish the Machine Tractor Stations (MTSs) in 1958 (Nove, 1969, p. 363). Soviet repair stations apparently never got off the ground (Nove, 1969, p. 363), while the Hungarian ones did for a time (*Figyelő*, 1969, No. 22), although they were ultimately transformed into the basis of Hungary's agricultural equipment producing industry.[12] In China, it was during the Cultural Revolution that tractor power ceased to be a gift from the state and communes and brigades began to buy their own equipment (Selden, 1979, p. 125). The Hua Dong commune visited by Aubert operated a sort of compromise system in which the commune owned the eleven tractors, while each work team owned its own power cultivators (1975, p. 89). North Korea opposed suggestions to abolish its MTSs in 1958, but changed its mind in the 1960s (Brun and Hersh, 1976, p. 333; Noumoff, 1979, p. 40). Romania continued to ignore hints and still retains its MTSs.

As a result of these measures, by 1967 the mechanical base for large-scale independent agriculture in Hungary was well on the way to being laid. In 1960, there had been only one tractor for every 112 ha of arable land. By 1968, this ratio had been reduced to one tractor per 50 ha; similarly, the number of combine harvesters increased from 4200 to 9800 between 1960 and 1967 (Berend, 1974a, pp. 146–7). Nor were tractors emphasised at the expense of fertilisers. Fertilisers per hectare increased from 25 kg in 1960 to 50 kg in 1965, 122 kg in 1970 and 224 kg in 1975, after which they stabilised and fell slightly to 211 kg in 1980 (MGSZS, 1981, pp. 104–5). In fact, Hungary's position in international comparisons of kilos per hectare use of fertilisers is rather higher than when hectares per tractor are concerned (MGSZS, 1981, p. 291). Hungary would thus appear to have avoided the fetishisation of tractor power which was committed in the Soviet Union and other socialist countries (Magdoff, 1982).

In consequence, 92% of wheat harvesting was mechanised by the late 1960s compared with 43% in 1960 (Berend, 1974a, pp. 146–7), as was 99% of heavy and 95% of light ploughing (Fazekas, 1976, p. 187). On the other hand, green fodder and hay harvesting was only 50% mechanised, as was only 66% of sugar beet production (Fazekas, 1976, p. 187), while as little as 23% of potato production was performed with the aid of machinery (Berend, 1974a, p. 147). Vegetable production generally was hardly mechanised and, while the basic work of tending and spraying crops was mechanised, hoeing and weeding were not, and these comprised 90% of the necessary work between sowing and harvest (Fazekas, 1976, p. 187). Manual labour was still a fundamental requirement for these stages in the production process.

Such an increase was, of course, more related to the provision of credits and the will of government to develop agriculture than simply to the organisational changes associated with the abolition of the machine stations. In the Soviet Union, Nove reports the reverse process. After the abolition of the MTSs, the kolkhozy were still not provided with agricultural machinery, presumably because of their status as second-class, non-state bodies. As a result, the output of many kinds of agricultural machinery fell (1969, p. 363).

Agricultural policy after 1957 not only changed the scale of the production unit in Hungary and its degree of mechanisation. With the introduction of systematic pension provision for co-operative farm members, it attempted to introduce, in a modified form, one of the functions that their privately owned land had performed previously: the provision of life-long security (TRHGY, 1957 évi 65 tvr). The significance of this source of income which did not depend on labour cannot be overestimated.

Before 1958, the size of pensions and eligibility for them had not been set down in government regulation. In 1951, the type III co-operatives were obliged to form a cultural fund to help look after members who were too old to work (TRHGY, 18.010/1951 (I.20) FM), and the subsequent legislation in 1953 went further, specifying that the fund should provide for old and ill members if they had been members of the co-operative for two years. The fund was also to pay the social insurance contributions of such members and purchase any necessary medicines (TRHGY, 1.070/1953 (XI.12) MT). In 1958, precise regulations for a state-administered pension scheme were introduced. The old age pension was to begin at 65 for men and 60 for women, five years higher in each case than that of workers and employees. The regulation also provided disablement pensions, widows' pensions and additional supplements to pensions if there was a family to support. All these benefits were dependent on joining co-operatives by the end of 1960 (TRHGY, 1957 évi 65 tvr). In 1960 itself, an additional category of old age and disablement supplements was introduced for members of newly formed co-operatives who did not otherwise qualify for normal pension benefits,[13] while in 1961, the deadline for joining a co-operative and qualifying for a pension was extended to the end of that year (TRHGY, 1967 évi 17 tvr). In 1967, there was a wholesale reorganisation of the system, increasing the level and extending the scope of benefit, relating it more closely in principle to the quality of work performed on the co-operative (TRHGY, 1966 évi 30 tvr). The qualifying age for the old age pension for both men and women remained five years higher than that in state industry, however, although a minimum of 33% of the member's previous average income was awarded on the completion of ten pension years, and an absolute minimum of 400 forints per month was established (TRHGY, 1966 évi 30 tvr; 30/1966 (XII.24) Korm).

A similar pattern is visible in the case of other social benefits. Certain provision was made in 1953, but more systematic benefits were only begun with the Agrarian Theses and subsequently expanded considerably during the consolidation years of the 1960s. Thus, in 1953 a family allowance, considerably inferior to that provided in industry, was offered to type III co-operative members with three or more children of up to ten years if the member had completed 120 work days.[14] By 1959 the regulations stated that the social-cultural fund should further provide the members with social insurance benefits, and women members with maternity allowances for twelve weeks at a level of three quarters of the previous year's average work unit, provided the woman had worked regularly on the farm (TRHGY, 19/1959 (VII.12) FM 14§ and 15§). But it was only in 1966 that sickness and maternity benefits were further improved in a systematic way. Sickness benefit was set at between 50% and 75% of the member's yearly income (excluding rent on land) and at between 65% and 75% of the same sum if he had completed 200 work days in the previous year. Benefit was also received for share-cropping missed through illness, if the members had no family member who could perform it for them. At the same time, maternity benefits were increased to 20 weeks on full pay, provided the member had completed 120 work days during the preceding year.[15]

Social benefits also exist in Chinese and Soviet collectivised agri-culture, their degree of sophistication reflecting their overall level of development. The social insurance provision for commune members in China is not subject to national regulation. There are apparently no pensions as such, and handicapped or other members who cannot work are looked after out of the brigade's welfare fund (Selden, 1979, p. 122). This fund may not be large, however. In the Hua Dong commune, the welfare funds of the various work teams making up the commune consisted of 1% of income (Aubert, 1975, p. 91), although

Wheelwright and McFarlane imply that 5–10% of income should be put into this fund (1970, p. 193). A state-administered insurance programme for the Soviet kolkhoz sector was introduced in 1965, one year previous to the reorganisation of the Hungarian system. Prior to this, pensions for kolkhoz members were organised on a local basis out of the farm's 'social composition funds'. Henceforth, they were to be administered at a uniform level from a fund created by a 4% levy on kolkhoz incomes (Bronson and Krueger, 1971, pp. 220–4). Between 1965 and 1967 the size of the pensions and the age of eligibility were less advantageous than those in the state sector. In 1967, they were brought into line, although all those resident in rural areas received only 85% of the sum received by city dwellers. In 1968 maternity benefits for a total of 112 days were introduced (Brown *et al.*, 1982) for kolkhoz members. Soviet social insurance benefits, then, are similar to, and may well have been the inspiration for, Hungarian ones.

However, the increased capital strength of Hungarian agricultural co-operatives and this attempt to provide a substitute for the life-long security function of privately owned land were not in themselves sufficient to make co-operative agriculture attractive to many other than the ideologically committed. The size of this problem was enormous. Between 1961 and 1964, 20–25% of nominal co-operative members took no part in communal work (Donáth, 1977a, p. 200). At this period, it was common throughout the country, at peak periods such as harvest, for the co-operative leadership to go from door to door every morning at dawn in an attempt to persuade the members to work, and every year the harvest was brought in by soldiers, students and office workers from the towns, while the members, or large numbers of them, stayed away (Donáth, 1977a, pp. 200–2). Since, for a third of the co-operative membership, income from communal work did not exceed a third of the average yearly wage of the state farm worker, and for a further 30% it did not exceed 50% of state farm worker incomes, this reticence to perform communal work was understandable (Donáth, 1977a, p. 201). On top of these low participation rates for existing members, large numbers of peasants were giving up agriculture altogether. Active earners in agriculture dropped steadily both during collectivisation, from 37.7% of the economically active population in 1960 to 31.7% in 1962, and during the period of the farms' consolidation, so that by 1965 workers in agriculture formed only 27.4% of the economically active population (see Appendix I). The only way to attract labour into the co-operatives, or prevent it leaving and persuade it to participate, was to make work in communal agriculture materially attractive to the co-operative farm member. This the government did in the following ways. It encouraged the ending of the work unit and 'remainder system' and replaced it by a system of guaranteed wages. More important in the short term, it closed its eyes to two ploys: that of taking on 'employees' to perform essential skilled labour in the mechanised sectors of production; and that of using share-cropping as a system of reward for the still considerable areas where production remained predominantly labour-intensive. And, in addition to these policies aimed at making participation in communal agriculture more attractive, it adopted a lenient policy towards the household plot, so increasing the overall attractiveness of co-operative farm membership.

Remuneration on the co-operatives had previously been based on the 'work unit' and 'remainder principle',[16] a system analogous to the labour day system in the Soviet Union and the work point system in China. This system had been institutionalised in the Soviet Union by a series of decisions between April and June 1930 (Davies, 1980b, p. 141), was legalised in a decree of 5 July 1932, and was more fully defined in January 1933 (Nove, 1969, p. 181). Payment was made predominantly in kind and in proportion to the number of work days performed. The absolute value of the payment (rather than its relative size) depended on the amount of surplus the co-operative had left after meeting its financial obligations to the state. To use Nove's terminology, the kolkhoz peasant and his Chinese and Hungarian counterparts had 'residual legatee' status (1969, p. 241). Like the peasant's income, theirs was directly dependent on the state of the market and the quality of the harvest. Unlike the peasant's income, however, there was only a very indirect link between the amount of work put in and the size of the reward that came out. Traditional peasant farmers might not have a concept of wages, but they could link a specific level of 'drudgery' directly to a specific reward. In communal agriculture, where there was the mediation of so many hands between ploughing and harvest, no such direct link between 'drudgery' and reward could be established for any single member. As Soviet commentators have also noted, the labour day system acted as an inadequate incentive (Aitov, 1969, p. 131). The problem was compounded in Hungary, as in the Soviet Union, by the steady growth in the average size of farms; and was further aggravated by the low level of agricultural prices which precluded the possibility of farms earning a large surplus to share out on the basis of work units performed. Where there was no clear link between effort and reward, and where the size of the reward was inevitably low, it is understandable that members were not motivated to participate.

The period of co-operative consolidation between 1961 and 1968 witnessed two important changes in the area of rewards for labour: a dramatic increase in the value of the incomes of co-operative farm members and, more important, an increase in the payment of advances on income throughout the year, culminating in the payment of guaranteed wage incomes. The average income of co-operative farm members grew steadily as a result of the aid given to agriculture, especially the aid to weaker farms, so that by 1967 it was 50% higher than it had been in 1962 (Vági, 1969, p. 29). Payment of guaranteed wages grew out of the custom of paying an advance on the members' ultimate share (which was in money and kind) of the year's surplus. Payment of some sort of advance of this kind began as early as 1953 (Donáth, 1977a, p. 119), and the majority of farms were paying one by 1963, although the size of the advance was not great and in a number of farms no actual money was paid, the co-operative contenting itself with paying the members' social insurance contributions (E.-né Csizmadia, 1963, pp. 1398 and 1400). But, in the early 1960s, guaranteed wages as such were not generally paid. Only 4% of co-operatives were paying them in 1962 (E.-né Csizmadia, 1963, p. 1401) and this figure had only risen to 10% by 1966 (Fehér, 1970, p. 83). By this date, however, it had been recognised that a radical change in the status of members' incomes would be necessary if labour of sufficient quality were to remain in agriculture. The logic of a communal 'family economy', implicit in the 'remainder system', no longer squared with the size and capital base of co-operative farms. It would have to be transcended if members were to receive the regular monetary payments at a more or less guaranteed level which were necessary to keep labour in agriculture. Wage labour, or an approximation towards it, would have to replace 'family labour' and co-operatives would have to budget with regular labour costs. The attraction to the membership of a regular monetary payment throughout the year had become clear from research carried out in the early 1960s. In the 32 co-operatives which, in 1961, started experimenting with the regular payment of a percentage of the estimated monthly wage, 300 people aged under 30 requested to join the farm

(E.-né Csizmadia, 1963, p. 1402), and this at a time when the general trend, especially among the young, was to leave agriculture (see chapter 3). In 1966 the Central Committee of the Hungarian Socialist Workers' Party therefore proposed that the guaranteed wages should be introduced throughout co-operative agriculture, although not at state farm levels (E.-né Csizmadia, 1966). The system was accepted with alacrity, and by 1967 the work unit system was only used in weaker co-operatives (Fazekas, 1976, pp. 178–9) or as an additional form of payment specific for certain types of job (Kalocsay, 1970). Under the system proposed, members did not receive full wages throughout the year. Instead, they received a percentage of the projected wage (usually 80%) at the end of each month – the so-called 'work payment' – and then at the end of the year, provided the co-operative farm was sufficiently successful, the remaining 20% was awarded, with perhaps a further few percentage points (occasionally as high as 10%) as a profit share. Not all farms were sufficiently secure financially to pay even 80% work payments, but the fundamental change that was represented by even a 30% or 50% guaranteed monthly work payment is clear enough.

A similar system of guaranteed payment schemes had also been adopted in the Soviet Union in 1966, after a resolution to that effect was passed by the 23rd Party Congress (Arutyunyan, 1969, p. 234). The precise workings of the system are not entirely clear from secondary sources, but its essence is that a certain minimum payment is guaranteed to members (Wädekin, 1973, p. 207) according to a system of wage rates identical to state farm wage rates (Bronson and Krueger, 1971, p. 220). In order to finance these payments, short term loans are available from the State Bank (Millar, 1971, p. 278) and it seems that most farms which do pay guaranteed wages are obliged to avail themselves of this facility (Aitov, 1969, p. 128). Payment of some sort of advance to kolkhoz members, but not a guaranteed money income to ease them through the year, was begun in 1952, again, just before the adoption of the same practice in Hungary. The practice was widespread by 1957 (Nove, 1969, p. 337), but in itself proved inadequate as a solution to the disincentives associated with the work unit and remainder system. It is interesting to note, in passing, that the payment of advances on future wage income to co-operative members was not new to Soviet agriculture in the 1960s. Before mass collectivisation, some kolkhozy were making advance payments to members according to a provisional payment scale and then making final adjustments after the harvest. Such arrangements were partly financed out of advances from the state agencies on contracts for the sale of kolkhoz products (Davies, 1980b, p. 134). Payment of advances of this type was explicitly prohibited in an 'explanatory note' of 13 April 1930 (Davies, 1980b, p. 140) and it is quite possible that Soviet planners were not conscious of this historical precedent when they reinvented it in the 1950s.

In China, the work point system is still in use, although there has been criticism of the scales used within it and the criteria on which they have been based. Recent criticism has claimed that differentials within the system are narrow (Gittings, 1982), and that it does not distinguish adequately between diligent and lazy workers. During the Cultural Revolution the criticism came from the opposite direction. The allocation of incomes was to be based on discussion and not on a rigid application of work points (Wheelwright and McFarlane, 1970, p. 131). Thus, the Tachai Brigade, which was set up as a model for others to follow, used a modified version of the work point system where an individual's political attitudes were taken into account as well as skill required and difficulty of job (Selden, 1979, p. 121). The work unit multiplied by the number of days worked determined the share of distributed income. The Tachai system also paid an advance in the form of the grain needs of each household, provided from the brigade's own resources. The advance was then deducted from the member's year end income (Selden, 1979, p. 122). It is not clear from secondary sources how much of this represented a departure from the previous practice and, if so, whether what was new was the payment of advances or the fact that the brigade and not the state financed them. The Grays report that in the prosperous Liaoning province weekly wages have been introduced, although they stress that this is wholly exceptional (1982, pp. 155–6).

But Hungary's official solution to the problem of guaranteed incomes was made universal only at the end of the period of co-operative consolidation. In the intervening years, co-operatives had to fend for themselves and adopt whatever semi-official solutions they could. The two most common of these were the hiring of employees and a reliance on share-cropping or kindred systems of reward. The former solution, utilising wage labour, was applicable in areas where skilled labour was required, the latter, utilising 'family labour', was best suited to traditional labour-intensive tasks. Employees were first taken on in about 1962 as labour was being freed from the machine stations (Gyenes, 1973, p. 39), and they were mainly tractor drivers or skilled workers. As employees, they received a regular wage irrespective of the co-operative's surplus, their wages counted as a production cost, and it was hoped that their extra production would cover the additional costs of their employment. If not, the farm could turn to forms of government aid that were provided specifically to cover such costs, although the expectation was that such employees would be experts and administrators rather than manual workers.

The hiring of employees was the only way that co-operatives could attract (from its former employment in machine stations) the skilled labour necessary to run the new agricultural technology they were acquiring as the machine stations themselves were being run down. Fazekas shows the growth of employees during this period. In 1961 there were 10 000 employees in agricultural co-operatives; by 1967 there were 200 000 of whom 80 000 were permanent (1976, p. 186). The increase within a single co-operative could be even more startling. The Baska co-operative in Baranya county had 3 employees in 1961, but 236 by 1966, and they completed the majority of the working days on the farm (A. Hegedűs, 1977, pp. 131–2).[17]

The same phenomenon accompanied the break-up of the MTSs in the Soviet Union. Their employees were given a privileged status on the farms with incomes higher than those of the average member (Nove, 1980, p. 141) while the state authorised long term loans to finance the pay of both administrators and machine operators at state farm rates (Bronson and Krueger, 1971, p. 220). Despite this, many mechanics and tractor drivers left villages rather than become kolkhoz peasants (Nove, 1969, p. 363), unlike Hungary where, as we shall see later, there was a movement of skilled workers into agriculture.

The hiring of employees was clearly only possible in certain sectors of the co-operative. Government sources could not finance all agricultural labour, and each farm possessed in any case large reserves of albeit 'unskilled'[18] labour which remained untapped. For sectors of the farm where traditional labour was required, the traditional method of share-cropping, or related systems such as the 'Nádudvar system' (where a minimum monetary payment was guaranteed in addition to the member's share of the crop or its cash value), were introduced (Jacobs, 1970, p. 346; Lázár, 1976). Share-cropping had already appeared within co-operative agriculture in 1954–5 and from 1957 onwards when, with the break-up of many farms, the remaining co-operatives found themselves with a very high ratio of land to members (Orbán, 1972, pp. 138 and 174; Donáth, 1977a, p. 163). With the successful establishment of collectivised agriculture, some share-cropping was retained for certain crops in poorer areas (Erdei, 1973, pp. 263–4). Initially, it was stressed that such solutions were temporary, but share-cropping and 'family cropping' later gained semi-official acceptance as a socialist form of remuneration. First used by the 'more courageous' co-operative leaders (Kemény, 1978a, p. 32),[19] it was finally claimed as a 'socialist' form of remuneration because it conformed to the principle of 'to each according to his work' (Fehér, 1970, p. 84). Significantly, it avoided all the difficulties associated with the 'work unit' system since income was directly related to the individual's effort. In addition, since the reward was related to the final product only, rather than measured labour inputs, it was well suited to labour-intensive tasks. With reward related to the end result, the individuals budgeted labour inputs for themselves in a way analogous to the individual peasant within the 'family economy'. By utilising the peasant's capacity for 'self-exploitation', the co-operative could offer relatively attractive and predictable rewards, without incurring the prohibitive costs which would have been associated with a wage form directly linked to the quantity of labour. With official acceptance, share-cropping, either for a percentage of the crop or for a percentage of its market value, became a recognised form of payment for non-mechanised sectors of co-operative pro-duction and by 1977 even figured in official government ordinances on wage regulation (TRHGY, 19/1977 (V.25) MEM–MUM).

Share-cropping as such was never a major component of Soviet agriculture, although Wädekin does point to its use in the 1960s on poor kolkhoz land as a means whereby members could acquire fodder for their household plot animals (1973, p. 323). However, arrange-ments of a similar type have a long pedigree in Soviet agriculture. The term 'link system' has meant different things at different periods in the history of Soviet collectivisation (Pospielovsky, 1970, p. 411), and the reality behind the first coining of the term was not dissimilar to Hungarian share-cropping. Under this original link system, groups of four to six people, often linked by kinship ties, took responsibility for a certain area of the farm (Pospielovsky, 1970, p. 413), and sold the produce to the collective at a pre-arranged price. It was a method used mainly for manual work in monoculture (Pospielovsky, 1970, p. 413). Such an organisation is very different from the 'self-administered, mechanised, multi-purpose work teams' (of which more later) to which the term 'link system' has also been applied, and is a clear cousin of Hungary's share-cropping. The crucial difference is that, under the Hungarian system, it was acknowledged that the members were working for two masters, for themselves and for the collective farm, and private use of, and even sale of, the member's share was accepted, if not actively encouraged. Regulations concerning the use of link group produce not sold to the collective are unclear. This link system was widely used between 1939 and 1950 when many farms were merged and it was announced that brigades should be the basic unit in field work (Pospielovsky, 1970, pp. 412–14).

The Soviet Union is not the only socialist country whose leaders have felt the need to introduce into agricultural production a system akin to Hungary's share-cropping of the 1960s. A further cousin has recently been born in China, this time called the 'responsibility system' (Grays, 1982, esp. pp. 182–3). Under this system, started in Anhui in 1979, the brigade's land is divided up between households, although the brigade still holds title to the land and can re-assign it. Each peasant household farms the land, pays state taxes, fulfils state quotas, contributes to the collective welfare fund and then keeps the balance for itself. The details vary (Grays, 1982), but in all the systems, the essence is clear: peasants, or their families, can experience a direct relationship between the effort put in and the rewards taken out. The important point is not that the members and their families work for themselves, but that differing degrees of labour produce tangible results. Work and varying degrees of work can be directly experienced as meaningful in a way that is impossible when workers are expected to maximise work points for a share in a final sum whose overall size they have only the most indirect means of influencing. The new system was given great encouragement at the 12th Congress of the Chinese Communist Party (SWB, 10 Sept. 1982, FE/7127/C/3; FE/7L25/C/6), but has existed in some form in North Korea since the 1960s (Brun and Hersh, 1976, p. 340).

Finally, as co-operative agriculture developed in Hungary, the official silence about the role of the household plot which had characterised the period after 1957 was ended. The 1959 regulations on co-operative agriculture made no mention of whether the plot should involve itself in commodity production or not. However, official statements in 1960 recognised that it had a role as a commodity producer, as well as constituting the temporary locus for a large amount of the nation's animal husbandry, and as provider of income supplements for co-operative members (Fazekas, 1976, p. 157). The government had evidently decided that, since there were good reasons for retaining household plots, members might as well be encouraged to farm them efficiently. Household plots remained in the interests of both the national economy and individual co-operatives. In 1962, 25% of all animal produce still came from the household plot, figures which included 55% of pigs for slaughter, 53% of eggs and 45% of chickens for slaughter (K. Kovács, 1964, p. 926); clearly the nation could not afford to lose this supply of food.

Within the co-operative, household plots were necessary for two reasons. For the members, they were an essential source of extra income at a time when incomes from the communal farm were low and the work offered by it often seasonal in nature. In 1960, 1961 and 1962 the proportion of income from the household plot within total family income was 51%, 54% and 53% respectively (F. Szabó, 1964, p. 21), and it played an especially significant role for those with an overall low income from the co-operative (F. Szabó, 1964, p. 23). For the co-operative as a whole, the household plot was essential to the farm in order to retain reserves of labour which, even though they could only be employed on a seasonal basis, were nevertheless essential if the farm were to produce at all. There were, as yet, few alternative solutions to the problem of providing off-season employment for members, and mechanisation had not yet begun to iron out seasonal fluctuations in the demand for labour. The household plot had to be retained, even if it entailed the risk that, at peak periods, members might be reluctant to take part in communal work. Fazekas estimates, however, that on balance in the years between 1961 and 1967 the household plot was more likely to be fulfilling one of its positive roles as petty commodity producer, temporary locus of animal husbandry, or provider of supplementary incomes than taking essential labour away from collective work (1976, p. 189), a view shared by Wädekin in his assessment of the Soviet household plot (1973, p. 200).

By the mid 1960s, then, it was beginning to be acknowledged that the household plot, based on the private 'family labour' of the co-operative farm member, might have a role as an integral part of socialist agriculture (F. Szabó, 1964, p. 23). Concessions to the private 'family economy' had been essential to the establishment of collectivised agriculture, while, in the process of consolidating it, it had been realised that within large-scale agriculture the logic of the 'family economy' would have to be transcended and wage labour introduced in its place. Once these steps had been taken, and it had been seen that no adverse effects stemmed from commodity production on the household plot, the stage was set for integrating communal agriculture (with predominantly 'socialist wage labour', but some 'family labour' in the form of share-cropping) and the household plot (based on private 'family labour') more fully. Whilst Soviet precedent and Hungary's tradition of 'feudal', hacienda-type pre-war agricultural estates (Illyés, 1967, p. 151) lay behind the decision to retain household plots in co-operative agriculture (P.Juhász, 1977, pp. 414–17), it was now recognised that there might also be sound economic reasons for their retention.

2

'Family labour' and 'socialist wage labour': from integration to symbiosis, 1968–77

In chapter 1 we saw how the co-operative farm developed from an amalgam of peasant farmers producing jointly to an intricate mixture of 'family' and wage labour using both industrial and traditional technology. Between 1968 and 1977, after the introduction of the New Economic Mechanism, agricultural producer co-operatives developed further, becoming economically more autonomous, large-scale production units, subject to more or less the same financial constraints as industrial enterprises. This was accompanied by two changes in the nature of agricultural labour. First, the form of income from the communal farm changed gradually so that it finally became equivalent to the monetary wage paid to 'socialist wage labour' in industry, an economic category counted as a production cost, paid fully throughout the year, and located within a complex structure of enterprise funds and taxes. Second, there was a self-conscious attempt to integrate 'family labour' performed in the 'marginal labour time' of members into the socialist sector and into the co-operative farm. 'Family labour' and the socialist sector became related in a system of mutual benefit or symbiosis. This chapter considers these two developments in the nature of agricultural labour in turn.

The major stages in the further development of 'socialist wage labour' within agricultural co-operatives are summarised in Table 2.1, which includes some of the developments referred to in the previous chapter. The crucial dates are 1968, when the new statutes on agricultural co-operatives established the system of 'work payments' in law and insisted that such 80% wages should be treated as production costs, and 1977, when it was recommended that co-operatives move beyond the 'work payment' system, and pay

Table 2.1 *Stages in the growth of the institutional and financial context for 'socialist wage labour' on agricultural producer co-operatives*

Publication of Agrarian Theses	1957
Co-operative ownership of capital equipment	1957
Introduction of pensions	1958
Introduction of depreciation funds	1966
Establishment of National Producer Co-operative Council	1967
Co-operative ownership of land	1968
Reorganisation of co-operative funds	1968
'Work payments' to be treated as production costs	1968
Introduction of maternity allowances	1968
Introduction of production tax	1971
Introduction of new income tax regulations with differential rates	1971
Introduction of 'increase in income' tax	1971
Obligation to form reserve fund	1972
Virtual parity of wages within co-operative agriculture and state industry	Early 1970s
Recommendations for length of working day	1974
Recommendation for national table of wage rates	1975
Ministerial decree on national table of wage rates	1977
100% wages recommended rather than the system of 'wage payments' followed by 'wage supplements'	1977
Introduction of official overtime rates for night work	1977
Introduction of mandatory qualifications for some manual jobs on co-operatives	1977

100% wages throughout the year. This was, in fact, an *ex post* recognition of a practice that had already become common among the stronger co-operatives by this date. In order to understand 'socialist wage labour' as an economic category within co-operative agriculture and appreciate the implications of the distinction between 'family labour' and 'socialist wage labour', for both those who perform them and those who might manipulate them, it is necessary to look first in some detail at changes in the status of agricultural producer co-operatives and the financial context within which they operate.

In 1968, the economic status of the co-operative farm was changed, bringing with it modifications in the financial context of 'socialist wage labour' within the co-operative budget. As part of the preparation for the New Economic Mechanism, the preconditions for relatively autonomous economic activity, the hallmark of the reform, were created within co-operative agriculture. The aim was to strengthen the 'enterprise-like' activities of the co-operative farm (TRHGY, 1028/1967 (IX.8) Korm). The November–December 1966 Congress of the Hungarian Socialist Workers' Party decided on these measures in principle (Fazekas, 1976, p. 166), and legislation and ministerial decrees in 1967 put them into effect. As a preliminary, indicating the mood of the reform, the Ministry of Agriculture and the Ministry of Food Supply were merged into a single Ministry of Agriculture and Food Supply on 4 April 1967 (Fazekas, 1976, p. 227). Next, the legal status of the agricultural co-operative was modified and it gained the right to own land in its own name.

New co-operative legislation in 1967 both confirmed in law the right of agricultural co-operatives to exist and gave them legal autonomy of action, made meaningful by separate decrees establishing their rights to make contracts with other bodies and to market goods (TRHGY, 1020/1967 (VII.11) Korm). This was of considerable symbolic significance since it removed from co-operative farms the stigma of being a 'second class' socialist form, a factor which has contributed to the relative disregard of agriculture in the Soviet Union. Legislation also made it clear that the co-operative farm itself had the right to draw up co-operative plans with maximum autonomy, although within the context of certain ministerial suggestions (TRHGY, 1967 III Tv 46§). Independence was further bolstered by the creation of the National Producer Co-operative Council on 20 April 1967 whose sole aim was to defend the interests of co-operative farms (Fazekas, 1976, p. 226). This time it was the Soviet Union that followed suit with the creation of a Kolkhoz Council in 1968 which, it appears, has little influence on kolkhoz affairs (Nove, 1978, p. 11).

Equally novel was the provision that the co-operatives could, as legal entities, themselves own land rather than rent it from their members. This concept of co-operative property was a natural extension of the right co-operatives already possessed to own their own capital equipment. There was a further justification, however. With the mass exodus from agriculture that had accompanied collectivisation (see chapter 3), and the gradual inheritance in name of co-operatively farmed land by a generation no longer employed in agriculture, by 1966 a fifth of the land farmed by agricultural co-operatives was owned by individuals who were not members. In addition, a further 30% of co-operatively farmed land belonged to the state, or to certain disbanded organisations, and approximately 200 000 hectares of land had no living owner (G. Soós, 1969, p. 76). Not only was this anomalous, it was also costing co-operatives 230 million forints a year in land rent (Fehér, 1970, p. 142), and so the law on land ownership initiated the change to co-operative land owner-ship (TRHGY, IV Tv).

More important than changes in legal status, the conception of agricultural co-operatives as independently operating large-scale economic agents further required modification of the financial regu-lations to which they were subject. The key changes of this nature concerned the reorganisation of co-operative funds. Under the pre-vious price system, income from agriculture had been so small that regulations concerning the funds to be formed from surpluses were minimal. As a prelude to restructuring co-operative farm budgets, therefore, there was, first in 1966 and again in 1968, a substantial increase in agricultural producer prices, by 10% and then 9%; and in 1966 there was also a cancellation of 60% of co-operative farm debts (W. Robinson, 1973, p. 67). The underlying theory was to transform 'price-centred' regulation into 'tax-centred' regulation. For 'tax-centred' regulation to be possible, farms had to be able to generate a sufficiently large surplus to be taxed, and producer price increases were aimed at making this possible.

Steady increases in procurement prices have also been a feature of Soviet agriculture from 1958 when the dual system of pricing for over-quota and quota deliveries was abolished. Livestock prices were increased in 1962 and there were across the board increases in 1965 and 1970. In 1965, a bonus for over-quota deliveries was reintro-duced; however, certain products, especially livestock, remained unprofitable even after the increase (Nove, 1980, pp. 196–8). Chinese procurement prices have also been increased recently and the price of farm inputs reduced (Grays, 1982, p. 171).

Under the initial system of fund formation on Hungarian co-operatives, the greater part of co-operative income was divided among the members as personal income; in addition to this, a 'co-operative fund' was established which had to be increased annually by 10% of the sum paid out to the members as income; a seed and fodder fund also had to be formed, together with a social-cultural fund of 4% of the income distributed to members (TRHGY, 1959, évi 7 tvr). In 1966, co-operatives were additionally obliged to form a depreciation fund (TRHGY, 12/1965(XII.11) FM; 2/1966

(I.11) FM).[1] The 1967/8 reorganisation created a system of fund formation more like that in industry. In addition to the new obligation to count 'work payments' as production costs, depreciation had to be so counted, and all such costs had to be met before co-operative funds could be formed. The social-cultural fund was retained, but the co-operative fund was replaced by a development fund (F-fund), a sharing fund (R-fund), and an income guaranteeing fund. The co-operative itself was given the right to decide on the size of funds, although the law required that the sharing fund and the development fund be increased at the same rate (TRHGY, 1967 III Tv). With growing surpluses and the increased scale of co-operative agriculture, a further compulsory 'reserve fund' was introduced in 1972 (see chapter 6), and depreciation rates were re-assessed in 1976 and again in 1980 (TRHGY, 10/1976 (III.7) MT; 41/1979 (XI.1) PM–MEM).

Co-operative taxation was also modified during this period. Farms continued to pay land tax after 1968 but, despite attempts to make it reflect land values more realistically, it remained, until further changes in 1980, essentially a levy on all farms with little discriminatory power (TRHGY, 32/1970 (XI.15) PM; 30/1972 (XI.13) PM; 38/1974 (XII.24) PM; 39/1975 (XI.15) PM; 39/1979 (XI.1) MT; Gadó, 1976, p. 140). The other major tax paid by co-operative farms before 1968 was an income tax. In 1952, this stood at 10% of net income after fund formation and meeting external obligations (TRHGY, 1952 (I.27) MT); in 1955 the base for the tax was changed to shared income in both money and kind (TRHGY, 16/1955 (III.4) MT); and in 1958 these two components were taxed separately, income in kind at 10% and cash incomes at 5% (TRHGY, 11/1958 (II.9) Korm). A uniform rate at 7% was reintroduced in 1964 as money incomes became more common (TRHGY, 42/1963 (XII.30) Korm), and in 1967, when additional financial burdens on co-operatives were introduced, income tax was reduced to 6% (TRHGY, 30/1967 (IX.13) Korm).

This structure of taxation and fund formation is more or less in line with the regulations affecting collectivised agriculture in the Soviet Union and China. In the former, a 12% tax was levied on gross income prior to 1965 and, after that date, this same percentage was levied on net income (Millar, 1971, p. 278). An accumulation fund, cultural fund and fund to cover the payment of bonuses also has to be formed, and the farm has to cover the members' social security payments (Nove, 1980, p. 148). In China, 5–6% of commune income is paid in tax (Aubert, 1975, p. 91; Wheelwright and McFarlane, 1970, p. 193), an additional 5–10% of income is placed in an accumulation fund (Wheelwright and McFarlane, 1970, p. 193) and a further 5–10% is supposed to go to the welfare fund (Wheelwright and McFarlane, 1970, p. 193) although, as has already been noted, on the Hua Dong commune, only 1% of income was devoted to this fund (Aubert, 1975, p. 91).

In Hungary, however, a new tax was introduced in 1968 in conjunction with the changes in the income tax: a tax to control increases in members' incomes. Under this 'regulating tax', for every percentage rise in per capita income over a permitted limit of 2%, a progressive tax was brought to bear on the co-operative. In 1971, the basis of co-operative taxation was reorganised again because of the increased economic strength of the farms. The rate of income tax was made variable upon the average daily income of members taking part in communal work (TRHGY, 36/1970 (XI.24) PM), and a much more progressive 'increase in income' tax was introduced in order to control the level of average incomes within the farm. As with the 'wage-development payments' in industry, marginal tax rates of as high as 300% were charged to the co-operative if increases in per capita income exceeded permitted levels.[2] In 1980, this 'increase in income tax' was replaced by an essentially similar 'work payments tax' (TRHGY, 39/1979 (XI.1) MT). Meanwhile, in 1976, there had been a major revision of income (not 'increase in income') taxation.[3] The basis of the tax was changed from shared personal income per active member to per capita value-added (gross income) (TRHGY, 40/1975 (VI.30) PM). The reason for this change can be located in the differential strength of co-operatives. By basing the tax on per capita value-added rather than shared income, weaker farms effectively paid less tax (Kostyál and Enyedi, 1977, p. 905; Vendégh and Enyedi, 1976), a bias which was retained when further changes were introduced in 1980 (TRHGY, 39/1979 (XI.1) MT).

Of the remaining taxes levied on agricultural co-operatives, the production tax is the most significant. Introduced in 1971 in response to the co-operatives' increased diversification out of agriculture, it imposed taxation at similar rates to those in industry for farms which had a significant income from non-agricultural sources. Agricultural co-operatives also paid a town/village contribution (a form of local government tax) fixed at 1% of value-added (TRHGY, 31/1970 (XI.15) PM), and a social insurance levy of 13% of members' incomes and 17% of employees' wages (Kis, 1976, p. 110) which has been greatly increased in the 1980s. Finally, we might also note that new regulations in 1980 imposed an additional and extremely progressive 'sharing fund' tax on the profit which remained after wages and all other taxes had been met, a tax which was analogous to the one introduced for industrial enterprises in the same year (TRHGY, 36/1979 (XI.1) MT; 39/1979 (XI.1) MT).

This, then, was the financial context of 'socialist wage labour' on the Hungarian co-operative farm by 1977. Before turning to the question of its integration with 'family labour', however, we should examine some secondary characteristics of 'socialist wage labour' in agriculture so as to heighten the contrast between the two labour forms. A preliminary point to be made is that, by the early 1970s, the value of 'socialist wage labour' in agriculture was more or less on a par with that in industry. The incomes of co-operative farm members increased most quickly between 1960 and 1965, and the rate of their increase slackened as they approached industrial levels. Overall peasant monetary incomes had already surpassed those of workers by 1966, registering 108.8% of worker levels; and by 1971–2 they had reached 110.7%. However, if the components of this figure and the value of social benefits are taken into account, the relative situation changes. Members of agricultural co-operatives received only 66.1% of the value of industrial workers' social benefits. What is more, if nominal monthly incomes, rather than actual earnings, are considered, then between 1971 and 1973 the income of members of agricultural co-operatives was only 91.1% that of industrial workers. And if this is further calculated on the basis of an hourly wage, the monthly income of co-operative farm members falls to 77.2% of industrial workers' because of the normal 60 hour week on the farm compared with a 44 hour week in industry (L. Nagy, 1976).[4]

In the Soviet Union, the average kolkhoz worker was considerably worse off in the mid 1960s and, on the basis of both national statistics and a local survey, Arutyunyan states that the income of the kolkhoz farmer is between 30% and 39% lower than that of state farm workers (1969, p. 239). Perendentsev claims that the value of the 'labour day' at 0.3 rubles plus 1.5 kg of grain was little more than 50% of the pay in the state farm sector in 1963–4. At the same time, the average state farm wage was only 58% of the average wage in industry (Nove, 1980, p. 217). The introduction of pensions in the 1960s has improved the lot of the kolkhoznik somewhat, but it is unlikely to have bridged the gap between industrial and agricultural incomes.

Not only does the value of 'socialist wage labour' on Hungarian agricultural producer co-operatives approximate that in industry, so too does the wage form. Payment of wages in co-operative agriculture, whether at 80% or 100%, is based on a system of piece-rates wherever possible, unless there is an overriding concern for the quality of labour performed (TRHGY, 1977, évi 9 tvr 67§). Thus, on the Red Flag co-operative farm, for example, while piece-rates were the general rule, hourly rates were paid in the repair shop. In pig rearing, the piece-rate is related to the number of piglets born; in dairy farming it depends on the volume of milk produced; in cereal production, the rate is fixed in accordance with the type of machinery used, the type of crop involved, the nature of the job and the acreage covered. Thus, drivers of the MTZ 45 and 50 tractors received 12 forints per hectare for sowing soya beans, but only 8 forints per hectare for lucerne, while drivers of the JD 4620, with an eight row sowing drill, received only 4.2 forints per hectare. With these new wage forms, there developed a new area of potential conflict between members. The establishment of a wage form provided a clear basis for comparing individuals' effort and drudgery between piece-rates, and between piece-rate workers and those paid on an hourly basis. Unfortunately such conflicts, real and potential, have not yet been studied in co-operative agriculture.[5]

In addition to developments in the wage form, the latter years of the period 1968–77 saw the beginnings of a concept of 'overtime' for co-operative agricultural labour and, as we saw in the introduction, overtime is a central area for management–labour conflicts in socialist industry. In 1974, the national Co-operative Council established guidelines for the length of the normal working day (Donáth, 1976b, p. 25) as a necessary preliminary for the introduction of overtime. Overtime, as such, for members has not yet been regulated centrally, but in 1977 an income supplement for night work (TRHGY, 19/1977 (V.25) MEM–MUM 17§) was introduced, as were suggested overtime rates of between 25% and 100% of the basic wage, or a system of days in lieu, for work performed over and above the normal working day[6] (TRHGY, 7/1977 (III.2) MT. 77§; 12/1977 (III.12) MEM 29§). This same period saw the beginnings of regulation of the quality or type of labour allowed to perform certain jobs. In 1968 women were excluded from certain jobs that were considered too dangerous or arduous for them (TRHGY, 20/1968 (VI.4) MEM).

These included a number of better paying jobs such as driving the new heavy tractors, but did not cover traditional 'back-breaking' peasant labour. In 1977, the requirement of certain minimal educational qualifications, which had existed in upper management for some time, was extended throughout the organisational structure down to the level of brigade leader.

Finally, the period after 1968 witnessed an improvement in co-operative farm members' social benefits. A new maternity allowance, introduced nationally in 1968, was immediately extended to co-operative farm members. Although it was worth 100 forints less a month than the sum paid to industrial workers, this was perhaps symptomatic of the new status of agricultural co-operative labour. In 1976, receipt of this benefit was facilitated[7] and in 1977 it was extended to the members of the looser 'specialised' co-operatives. Family allowances were improved, as were pensions. The size of pensions increased steadily; they were extended to 'specialised' co-operatives in 1970; and the limit on the size of additional income earned before the right to a pension was forfeited was raised. As a consequence, the value of pensions of agricultural producer co-operative members reached 63% that of industrial worker and employee pensions by 1975 (Fazekas, 1976, p. 279).[8]

By 1977, then, labour within the communal farm was (predominantly) a form of 'socialist wage labour' more or less equivalent to that in socialist industry. It was an economic category which counted as a production cost and figured within a similar constellation of enterprise funds and taxes. Its value was equivalent to that in industry, as were its form and other secondary characteristics. What is more, it participated in what were by this time both physically large, and economically large-scale, production enterprises. As Appendix I shows, throughout the period farms continued to amalgamate so that by 1977, for example, the average agricultural producer co-operative farmed 3224 ha with an average membership of 644, of whom 388 were fully employed members or employees and the remainder retired. The average gross value of these farms' stock of fixed capital was 110.7 million forints, and the average farm owned 32 tractors (with a pulling capacity of 32 horsepower per 100 ha), 12 lorries and 49 trailers. Average value-added in 1976 (when there were rather more farms) was 21.6 million forints[9] and bigger farms were naturally the locus of even larger-scale operations. The Red Flag co-operative generated value-added of 87 million forints from a farm of just over 8000 ha with fixed capital valued at 552 million forints.

The average Soviet kolkhoz was equally large by the 1970s. It comprised 443 households, 6200 ha of agricultural land, of which 3200 ha were arable, 32 tractors, 1388 cattle, 964 pigs, and 1680 sheep (Nove, 1978, p. 12). These huge Soviet and Hungarian farms contrast starkly with the organisation of collective production in China. Although communes themselves are enormous, numbering 20 000–25 000 members, the basic production unit since the 1960s, the work team, which operates and has title to the land and distributes income from it, consists of only 20–35 families. The village sized production brigades of 5–15 work teams help the commune in co-ordinating the use of tractors, local industrial, health and educational activities, while the commune, consisting of 10–30 brigades, co-ordinates regional planning, rural industry, electrification and plan co-ordination (Colliers, 1973, p. 170; Selden, 1979, p. 77). These are the functions which in Eastern Europe and the Soviet Union are performed by the district council and the district Party machine. The actual producing unit in China has dimensions more in line with the very earliest co-operatives in Hungary and the Soviet Union when farms of under 20 families were the norm (Appendix I; Davies, 1980a, pp. 10–11). This is not surprising given their low level of mechanisation, and is consistent with their more rudimentary forms of remuneration and social welfare.

Before analysing the process by which the policies initiated between 1968 and 1977 in Hungary created a symbiotic relationship between communal 'socialist wage labour' and private 'family labour', we should first confirm that 'family labour' is involved on the household plot and, indeed, in small-scale agriculture generally, and consider which family members it concerns. The small size of the household plot is, of course, the most important factor limiting its scope to the confines of the family. The regulations restricting the size of household plots have already been considered. A survey in 1972 of all small-scale agriculture, including household plots, confirmed their success. The average size of all small-scale plots was between 0.5 and 1 ha. Within this total, household plots were more likely to fall into this size category, while the plots of 'specialised co-operative' members were likely to be between 1 and 2 ha, and those of 'others' tended to be between 0.2 and 0.4 ha, with a significant proportion even smaller than 0.2 ha. Similarly, the number of animals kept on household plots is not large (AMO, Vol. 14, pp. 225 and 261).

However, in addition to physical limitations of size, the state imposes financial limitations on the scope of household plots in the form of the General Tax on Agricultural Incomes. This tax comprises three elements: a tax on the size, type and quality of the land; an additional tax on 'excessive' incomes from that land; and a separate tax on horses. Before 1976, the tax rate on household plot land was different from that levied on other small plots, in that it was not related to the quality of the land;[10] subsequently, differential tax according to the quality of land was applied throughout. The tax on 'excessive' incomes applies to both; and built into this tax is a restriction on the regular employment of outside labour. If such labour is employed, the tax threshold is lowered and the tax rate increased.[11] The different rates of taxation are such that they provide a strong disincentive to the employment of outside labour. In addition to this indirect restriction on the hiring of labour, and despite measures taken to encourage the purchase of small-scale machinery by household plot farmers, administrative restrictions are placed on the use of larger machinery on household plots (TRHGY, 26/1972 (XII.29) MEM); and the co-operatives are prevented from selling off old scrapped machinery to members for their private use (Zám, 1977, p. 57).[12]

Household plots in the Soviet Union are also subject to tax, although the tax rate has recently been reduced to 'insignificant' levels (Hill, 1975a, p. 94); and until 1958 they were obliged to make compulsory deliveries to the state (Nove, 1969, p. 337). In 1953, the basis of the household plot tax was changed from the oppressive estimate of the potential income of the plot to one based simply on the area of the plot (Nove, 1969, p. 329). Livestock was not taxed unless it exceeded Republican norms (Nove, 1980, p. 240) and peasants were freed from the obligation of making compulsory deliveries of meat even if they kept no livestock (Nove, 1969, p. 329). Despite articles in the press encouraging the provision of small-scale machinery for kolkhoz private plots, there is no evidence that such machinery has been provided in sizeable numbers (Nove, 1980, p. 128).

In order to show how successful Hungarian attempts at keeping the household plot within the confines of the family were, it would be convenient at this point to be able to refer to figures for the proportion of the working population employed as full-time agricultural labour outside state or co-operative farms. Unfortunately such a category does not even figure in recent statistics (presumably because it is so small). In 1964, however, the Central Statistical Office found that less than 0.1% of the village population earned its living entirely from day labouring (TT, p. 285). On the other hand, Hann in his study of a 'specialised co-operative' village (where there are more likely to be full-time day labourers) does refer to a number of people eking out an existence of extreme poverty on the basis of day labour for other peasants (1980, pp. 151–2).

Generally, household plot agriculture does not appear to rely on hired labour. In fact, as File remarked, 'The basis of small-scale agricultural production is essentially the residual labour time of family members' (File, 1977). This is especially true of the co-operative farm member, though not surprisingly, in the light of their proximity to their work and the seasonal nature of some of their employment, they also spend longer hours on their plots than other part-time farmers. Andorka and Harcsa report that manual workers on co-operative farms spent a daily average of 3.3 hours working on their plots, compared with 2.4 hours for state farm workers and 2.8 hours for those with 'other' small-scale plots (1973, pp. 107–8). Small-scale farming is clearly a time-consuming and yet not full-time occupation.

One perhaps surprising consequence of this is the insignificant role played by children in this 'family economy'. Survey evidence on this point is not extensive, and no study looks specifically at the co-operative peasant's household plot within small-scale agriculture as a whole. Individual village studies indicate that in very backward areas constantly (Végh, 1972, p. 111), in fruit growing areas at peak periods (Hann, 1980, p. 60), and during the school holidays in villages which specialise in market gardening for Budapest (Márkus, 1973, p. 58), considerable use is made of children's contribution to the 'family economy'. On the other hand, representative data from a county-wide survey reveal a different picture. Analysing data from 1756 families in Békés county, Sas found that 78.8% of families had a plot of some sort (1972, p. 249), 27% kept pigs for commercial purposes and 26% had a plough-pulling animal (1976, p. 98). Nevertheless, she concluded that children were being deliberately detached from the traditional (peasant) culture of hard work. In only 5.7% of families did children living at home help in the garden or feed the animals (1972, p. 251), whilst even the easy work of shopping and cleaning was performed by children in only 18–22% of households (1972, p. 249). More important, in a situation where private land cultivation itself was of diminishing importance and a source of supplementary income only (but where plots other than co-operative household plots could be inherited), 'peasants' manifested no desire for their children to take over the family farm. In Sas' survey, only 1.5% of respondents wanted their children to become manual workers in agriculture (1972, p. 258).

In order to get a fully rounded picture of 'family labour' on the household plot and its significance to the economy, a number of further points should be made. First, unlike the 'second economy' in construction, the return on these inputs of labour is not large. Calculations by the Central Statistical Office estimate that the hourly wage rate which corresponds to the 16 forints' worth of produce created hourly on average in small-scale agriculture is only 9 forints (E.-né. Csizmadia, 1978, p. 84). This is an exceptionally low hourly rate for the late 1970s, lower even than the hourly rates in industry ten years previously which led to the unrest at the Győr based company studied by Héthy and Makó and referred to in the introduction, and well below the average wage for the early 1970s (SPB, p. 262). However, it is a convenient form of supplementary income to add to co-operative wages or 'work payments' which, although equivalent to those in industry are, as we also saw in the introduction, by that same token barely adequate for growing demands.

Thus, second, despite this low return, household plot agriculture remains very popular. Figures reflecting the general popularity of small-scale agriculture were given in the introduction. Within the co-operative farm every member has the right to a plot, and over 80% maintain one (Simó, 1977, p. 487). Significant commodity production is undertaken by 19.8% of co-operative farm members in their plots, and 52% use it 'mainly' for their personal consumption (Simó, 1977, p. 487).[13] Estimates for the proportion of the members' total income supplied by the household plot vary from 30% to 50%. Csizmadia puts the figure at 32% in 1975 (E.-né. Csizmadia, 1978, p. 83), a decrease on the 38.9% in 1970 (Andorka, 1979, p. 133). Égető estimates it at around 40% (1976, p. 150), while unofficial sources would estimate it at nearer 50%.[14]

Third, small-scale agriculture remains of central importance both to the national economy and to co-operative agriculture. In 1977 it was estimated that production on small-scale agricultural plots, including both the product marketed nationally and that consumed by the producing family, accounted for more than 40% of the nation's food supply (File, 1977). In addition, 90% of the nation's land under market gardening was in the small-scale sector in 1977, as was 60% of the land under wine cultivation (File, 1977); while, in the previous year, 57% of the nation's pigs were kept on small-scale farms (*Figyelő*, 1976, No. 7). A considerable proportion of Hungary's agricultural foodstuff exports, which provide a quarter of all exports and a third of all hard currency exports (Gy. Varga, 1982, p. 689), comes from the private sector. Pork, fruit, vegetables and products made from them constitute important elements in these exports, while wheat and cereals, where the communal sector is so successful, are rather less important. Virtually no wheat is exported to the West, although some maize is (KSE, pp. 129, 72–5 and 125). Within the co-operative itself 'family labour' in household plot animal husbandry, although declining at an alarming rate in the case of dairy farming,[15] has kept Hungarian agriculture buoyant in the late 1970s and early 1980s despite increasing economic difficulties and drought.

Similar points about the centrality of household plot agriculture can be made in relation to the Soviet Union and, to a more limited extent, China. In the Soviet Union some 25–30% by value of total agricultural output comes from the private sector – a ratio that has remained remarkably constant since the 1930s (Davies, 1980b, p. 161) – and some 80% of vegetables consumed in the Soviet Union are produced on private plots (Hill, 1974, p. 495). Since the fall of Khrushchev, these plots have provided the kolkhoz members with about a third of their total income; previously, the private plot revenue rather than the kolkhoz wage was the peasant's major source of income (Wädekin, 1973, p. 190). Of course, the size of the income varies by region, and Hill reports that in the mid 1960s, private plots continued to provide over 50% of kolkhoz members' income in the Baltic states, in Georgia and in Belorussia (1974, p. 495). There has been a steady decline in the numbers of animals held on these plots over the 1960s and 1970s (Nove, 1978, p. 7); some 15–20% of plot produce is marketed, within which 8% via state procurement agencies; 60% is consumed and 20% is for productive use on the plot (Hill, 1974, p. 495). As in Hungary, the plot demands essentially part-time work (Hill, 1974, p. 495), although there are indications that the contribution of children is more significant than in Hungary (Selivanov, 1969, p. 149).

Secondary sources on China do not give an indication of the importance to the national economy of private agricultural production. Some figures are available estimating the contribution of private plots to household incomes – Wheelwright and McFarlane give a figure of 12% (1970, p. 189), while Mandel, more recently, gives a figure of 30% (1982, p. 189) – but it is only possible to get a feel for the importance of the plots by reference to passages describing peasant behaviour towards them. The Chinese government, until the very latest policy changes, has been more or less consistently hostile to private agriculture, and peasants have reacted by killing livestock, the traditional peasant response. In 1956, there was a squeeze on private plots (Gurley, 1976, pp. 159–60; Selden, 1979, p. 54) which led to the slaughter of animals and exacerbated the decline in livestock which had begun with collectivisation itself in 1954; and in 1958 there was a further squeeze on the plots, leading to their abolition. However, because this drastic move resulted in food shortages, serious malnutrition and indeed starvation in some areas (Selden, 1979, p. 54), private plots were reintroduced in 1960 and have coexisted with collective production ever since. During the Cultural Revolution, peasant families were allowed to eat their pigs themselves or give them to urban friends or relatives. They were not allowed to sell them privately (Colliers, 1973, p. 163). Over the middle 1970s the policy became more tolerant of private agriculture, a policy begun with the fall of Ch'en Po-ta in 1970 and Lin Piao the following year (Leys, 1978, pp. 121–2), and this new line has been encouraged more strongly since the death of Mao with an increase in the permitted size of the private sector to 7% and then 15% of cultivated land and an encouragement of private markets (Mandel, 1982, p. 202).

The importance of private economic activity to the Chinese peasant is reflected in an account reproduced by Selden of peasant harvesting of grass at a brickworks:

'On the mountain sides, there's grass that can be sold to the village brickworks for 1.4 yuan per 100 catties; in a good year you'd only earn one yuan for a whole day's collective work, while some folks can cut up to 200 catties of grass in the same day. As soon as collective work stopped for lunch, folks would immediately clamber up the mountain sides, running along cutting grass . . . When collective labour resumes they are pooped and so relax in the fields for a bit.' (Jonathan Unger, 'Collective incentives in a peasant community: lessons from a Chinese village', *Social Scientist* (May/June 1977), p. 48, quoted in Selden, 1979, pp. 123–4)

Some sort of supplementary private sector income is clearly very important to the Chinese peasant. More important than this, however, the low level of technical development in Chinese agriculture means that there remains a more real conflict of interest between private and collective labour. All agricultural work is labour-intensive. The distinction between mechanisation of extensive production on the collective and labour-intensive production of vegetables and livestock on the members' household plots, which is commonplace in both the Soviet Union and Hungary, appears to be only rudimentary. It exists to the extent that the collective sector concentrates on grain and staples production, as in other socialist economies; but the labour inputs in both sectors are of the same type.

The general attitude towards the private sector in both Chinese and Soviet agriculture appears to have been one of attack first and then make concessions when the crises provoked by the attack ensue. All pro-peasant measures have been forced on their governments by obdurate reality and they are retracted almost as soon as they begin to have positive results. The source of this type of policy lies in an inability to transcend a restricted version of marxism which sees all private economic activity as a harbinger of capitalism. Repressive policies in the Soviet Union ceased once Brezhnev and Kosygin had ousted Khrushchev. Policy has progressed from conflict to uneasy coexistence, as Wädekin has expressed it (1973, p. 365); but positive, active encouragement has not materialised. China now appears to be vacillating between coexistence and encouragement.

In Hungary positive aid did materialise. The peasant family economy has been actively encouraged and integrated into the co-operative farm because it was no longer perceived as a threat. There is now a relationship of symbiosis between private 'family labour' and the communal part of the co-operative, which relies overwhelmingly on 'socialist wage labour'. The most important elements to this symbiosis, which is discussed below, are summarised in Table 2.2 (including a number of developments that took place before 1968). There are two aspects to the symbiosis. First, there is the way in which household plot agriculture, as a variety of small-scale agriculture, has been integrated into the national economy. Second, there are changes internal to the agricultural co-operative farm itself which made symbiosis complete.[16]

Once the ideological barrier against small-scale commodity farming had been crossed, the government was faced with the

Table 2.2. *Stages in the integration of 'family labour' on the co-operative farm*

Publication of the Agrarian Theses	1957
Concessions in regulations concerning size of household plot and number of animals to be kept on it	1959
Role of household plot in commodity production acknowledged	1960
Extensive use of share-cropping	1960s
Household plots awarded to individuals rather than families	1968
New emphasis on General Consumer and Marketing Co-operatives	1968
Beginnings of purchasing arrangements between small-scale agriculture and state enterprises	1968
Ending of restrictions on number of animals held on household plots	1970
Recommendation that co-operatives hire a household plot agronomist	1970
Work on household plot with animals marketed via co-operative counts towards member's social benefits	1970
Establishing of Agricultural Specialised Groups	1971
Co-operatives recommended to form a household plot committee	1971
State aid in purchase of machinery for small-scale production	1971
Co-operatives receive state aid to encourage integration of household plot animal husbandry	1972
State aid in purchase of polythene sheeting for small-scale vegetable production	1974
Work on household plot with vegetables marketed via co-operative counts towards member's social benefits	1974
Regulations apparently conceding the transformation of the household plot into a money relationship	1974
Small-scale producers can rent additional unused state land	1977
End of prohibition of horse ownership on household plot	1977
Obligation on co-operatives to form household plot committee	1977
Prohibition on household plot becoming a money relationship	1977
Improvement of household plot production becomes a criterion on which part of managerial bonuses can be based	1977

problem of ensuring that as much small-scale production as possible would be channelled into state hands. This problem was solved in two ways. An institutional framework was created by which small-scale farms of all kinds could be integrated into the national economy, and financial incentives were offered to producers if they made use of this form of marketing. The new institutional framework comprised the General Consumer and Marketing Co-operatives (GCMCs), re-vamped versions of the land cultivating co-operatives, and the 'agricultural specialised groups'. Although the GCMCs do a great deal in addition to purchasing from small-scale agricultural producers, their relative weakness when compared with state buying enterprises means that such buying as they do direct from producers is predominantly from the small-scale producer (M.-né Hegedűs, 1975, pp. 212–13).[17]

Both the Soviet Union and China have networks of wholesale and retail co-operatives to which above-quota produce is sold and from which the collective farms/communes and their members can purchase supplies (Wheelwright and McFarlane, 1970, p. 131; Wronski, 1971). In the Soviet Union there is also a system of 'commission' sales under which these co-operatives will market produce on behalf of kolkhoz peasants (Nove, 1980, p. 128). However, Nove refers to Soviet literature, complaining that such co-operatives are often inadequately organised and many peasants prefer to make the laborious journey themselves to distant market towns to sell their produce (Nove, 1980, p. 128). Generally, the organisation of such co-operatives leaves ample scope for improvement (Nove, 1980, p. 150), and they share the same reluctance as all Soviet wholesale and retail organs to handle perishable goods. With fixed margins and insufficient resources to cover costs, they resist handling goods which they cannot be sure they can resell (Nove, 1980, pp. 262–3). This problem is compounded by the Soviet Union's well-known lack of adequate roads (Nove, 1980) which increases the chances of goods perishing. Whilst an institutional structure exists to direct the produce of private petty commodity agriculture to the state sector, it does not appear to flourish.

In Hungary, where 'lack of roads' has not been a problem since the 1950s, the GCMCs grew rapidly after 1968. However, since purchase from small-scale producers is only one of their activities, it was soon felt that they might become too remote from their suppliers (Agonács and Mészáros, 1977, pp. 10–11; M.-né Hegedűs, 1975, p. 206). In order to cope with this, a further institution was revamped, the 'Agricultural Specialised Group', and government regulations in 1971 and 1972 gave a new importance to this old form. The 1971 law on consumer co-operatives made provision for self-governing 'specialised groups' to be set up within the framework of the GCMCs (TRHGY, 1971, évi 35 tvr), and a government regulation determined their sphere of operation more completely, making provision for their establishment within producer co-operatives as well (TRHGY,

28/1972 (IX.27) MT). The aim of these co-operative groups was to give the members assistance with the acquisition of tools and equipment, and to help sell the produce of their small-scale farms.

By 1973, there were 1906 specialised groups functioning within the framework of the GCMCs and by 1977 this figure had risen to 2238 with a total of 164000 members (Agonács and Mészáros, 1977, p. 50).[18] 'Specialised groups' qualify for government support in their own right, and are eligible for the same sorts of investment aid as producer co-operatives.[19] Membership is open to all small-scale producers and only 39.6% of members are simultaneously members of producer co-operatives (Győry and Tiszolczy, 1975, p. 17). While the regulations allow for them to be established within producer co-operatives, in the 1970s they were set up mainly in the GCMCs (M.-né Hegedűs, 1975, p. 225). Membership of such a group brings additional tax advantages to members. They receive a reduction in land tax of 15%, pay no income tax on greenhouse production unless income is in excess of 24 000 forints a year, nor on animal husbandry if income from that sector is less than 30 000 forints a year; and wine marketed via 'specialised groups' is exempt from the wine-marketing tax (Győry and Tiszolczy, 1975, pp. 77–80).[20]

With the GCMCs and the 'specialised groups' the government created an extensive institutional framework for the marketing of small-scale agricultural produce. In addition, it offered considerable, and increasing, positive economic incentives to take part in such production in areas where it was felt there was a particular need. On the condition that produce be marketed via a state or co-operative institution of some kind, thus finding its way on to the national market, the small-scale producer could be the recipient of considerable financial aid. This aid was initially for the purchase of milking cattle, because of the recognition in 1967, and again in 1969 and 1972, of the decline of this sector in both small- and large-scale agriculture. Later it was extended to vegetable production for the purchase of equipment and machinery, and finally, in the form of price support, to pig rearing, after the catastrophic drop in the nation's pig stocks in the mid 1970s. In the case of milking cattle the need was so great that the contractual obligation was waived and replaced by a straight grant (see below).

The major forms of contractual relationship in the fields in which they are most extensively used – the purchase and maintenance of milking cattle, the purchase of machinery and specialist equipment

Table 2.3. *Aid to small-scale farming*

Date	Milking cattle	Vegetables/Fruit	Machinery	Conditions
1968	5000 Ft price concession on cow purchase	—	—	Cow must be kept for a year. Purchase from AM & MIT
1970	8000 Ft price concession on cow purchase		—	Cow must be kept for 4 years. Purchase from AM & MIT
1971	8000 Ft price concession on cow purchase[a]	—	Purchase price concession	Purchase at trade prices of garden tractors, spraying and animal husbandry equipment.
1972	8000 Ft price concession on cow purchase	Machinery purchase concession	Purchase price concession	The 1971 concession is extended to machinery for vegetable growing.
1973	1500 Ft grant per cow per year[b]	Machinery purchase concession	Purchase price concession	Cows must be kept for a year to qualify for grant
1974	1500 Ft grant per cow per year	30% price concession for polythene, etc.	Purchase price concession	Concession on polythene sheeting and metal frames for vegetable production if purchased from GCMC and if farmer has 2 year contract to sell via GCMC or other national marketing enterprise.
1976	1500 Ft grant for one cow per year and 3000 Ft for additional cows	20% price concession for polythene, etc.	20–40% purchase price concession	Cows must be kept for a year. Four years' total may be paid in advance. Contract period for eligibility for concession extended to 3 years.

| 1977 | 2500 Ft grant for one cow per year and 5000 Ft for additional cows | 40% price concession for polythene, etc. | 20–40% purchase price concession | No change. |

Notes:

a. In 1971, the AHC mediated in this relationship. Money was to be paid immediately by the AHC rather than being paid in instalments by the AM & MIT, once proof of milking was available.

b. In addition, up to 25 000 Ft worth of credit available from National Savings Bank for cow purchase.

AHC: Animal Husbandry Commission. AM & MIT: Animal Marketing and Meat Industry Trust.

Sources: TRHGY, 2/1967 (XII.22) PM; 5/1969 (II.19) MEM–PM; 18/1969 (XI.29) MEM–PM; 1041/1969 (XII.7) Korm; 1045/1970 (X.17) Korm; 43/1970 (XII.13) MEM–PM; 1050/1971 (XII.29) Korm; 1026/1972 (III.30) MT; 1010/1974 (III.6) MT; 10/1974 (IV.8) PM–MEM; 1030/1975 (XI.15) MT; 42/1975 (XI.15) PM–MEM; 1028/1976 (IX.16) MT; 53/1976 (XII.29) PM–MEM; 28/1976 (VIII.15) MEM–AH; 67 698/1976 Vsz PM leirat (*Magyar Mezőgazdaság*, 1977, No. 5); 29/1977 (XI.5) PM–MEM.

for vegetable production – are summarised in Table 2.3. In addition to this, in 1976 price support was offered to small-producers who contracted to sell 20 fattened pigs a year to the state meat industry, and in 1977 the state decided to pay price support to the GCMCs, agricultural producer co-operatives and other buying enterprises for pigs purchased on a contractual basis of three or more years from all small-scale producers (TRHGY, 53/1976 (XII.29) PM–MEM). Fruit and wine production was also aided in 1977 when sums were made available for re-planting small-scale vineyards and orchards (*Magyar Mezőgazdaság*, 1977, No. 5).

However, the rehabilitation of small-scale farming is perhaps best epitomised by regulations in 1977 permitting small-scale producers to acquire for their own use up to 0.6 ha of state or co-operative land not suited to large-scale cultivation. Farmers of household plots could thus double their acreage, and other small-scale producers could more than double theirs. The cost of leasing such land was fixed at a maximum of 50% of its market value and payment could be spread over ten years (TRHGY, 6/1977 (I.28) MEM–EVM–PM–IM). Quite clearly, by the time that 100% wages were being paid on the technologically advanced communal farm, small-scale agriculture with its 'family labour' was no longer seen as a threat.

Developments in regulations concerning small-scale agriculture within the producer co-operative – the household plots – paralleled, more or less, those taken towards this sector generally. After initial measures supporting milk production, more general aid was introduced, extending to all branches of animal husbandry and to vegetable production. More important than the simple fact of support was the manner in which household plot and communal agriculture were effectively integrated.

In the late 1960s a number of purely administrative changes were made in favour of the household plot. As we have seen, such plots had been allocated on a family basis since 1953, as they have been since the 1930s, and still are, in the Soviet Union (Davies, 1980b, p. 57; Hill, 1974, p. 493). Each family had a right to a single plot no matter how many family members worked on the co-operative. Since 1968, household plots have been awarded on an individual basis in Hungary. All members have the right to a plot, irrespective of their familial status (TRHGY, 1967 III Tv, 69§), provided they perform the required minimum number of days' labour. The restrictions on livestock holding on the household plot had been confirmed in the

1968 legislation at the 1959 level. Two years later, however, they were removed entirely, in line with the general change of policy towards small-scale agriculture, so that between 1970 and 1977, the only restriction on animal holding was the prohibition on horse ownership (TRHGY, 19/1969 (XII.31) MEM), and, in 1977, even this anachronistic limitation was removed, provided the Leadership of the individual co-operatives concurred.[21] In addition to relaxing size restrictions, positive institutional measures were taken to strengthen the status of the household plot within the co-operative. In 1970, it was recommended that every farm appoint an agronomist with special responsibility for members' household plots (W. Robinson, 1973, p. 119), and in 1971 provision was made for co-operatives to set up a household plot committee in addition to the other governing committees that constitute the farm's democratic management. By 1977, the establisnment of such a committee had been made compulsory (TRHGY, 7/1977 (III.12) MT), although the appointment of a household plot agronomist remained a recommendation only.

Elements of mutual aid of this sort exist in both the Soviet Union and China. The kolkhoz is 'recommended' to provide grazing rights for the private cattle of its members, and the kolkhoz usually sells fodder to its members (Hill, 1974, pp. 493–4). Since the fall of Khrushchev, it has also been recommended that the kolkhoz hire out horses to members (Wädekin, 1973, p. 203). The sale of feed grain to private livestock owners in urban settlements has been sanctioned (Wädekin, 1973, p. 229) and the State Bank offers loans to kolkhoz members and sovkhoz workers to buy cows (Wädekin, 1973, p. 321). The Soviet Union also allows a form of subcontracting by kolkhoz members to the collective farm. Members can buy pigs via the kolkhoz which they then rear on their plot and sell to the state at a net gain equivalent to one and a half months' salary. The pigs can, of course, also be sold for more (or less) on the private 'kolkhoz market' (Wädekin, 1973, pp. 217–19). Sales of private livestock generally to the kolkhoz increased after 1958 when compulsory deliveries from household plots were abolished (Wädekin, 1973, p. 232). In 1969, 4.2 million head of cattle were purchased from private owners, comprising 65% of all animals in that year (Wädekin, 1973, p. 243), while in 1963 the collective farms purchased 249.4 million rubles' worth of livestock from private owners for fattening or restocking (Wädekin, 1973, p. 244). Unfortunately, figures which might indicate the proportion of contract sales as described above within this total are not available (Wädekin, 1973, p. 245).

Two additional points about contract sales of this type should be made. First, although it has only been resurrected as a form relatively recently, it has a long pedigree and was suggested in an article in *Pravda* during the first debates on kolkhoz organisation in 1930 (Davies, 1980b, p. 110). Second, the kolkhoz itself benefits from the arrangement, either because the animals are necessary in order to meet the farm's procurement plan, or because they increase the percentage of sales at over-quota prices to the state. In such cases, the additional income the kolkhoz receives can be shared with the peasants (Nove, 1980, p. 128).

In China, similar integration of private and communal exists, and, on some communes, a form of subcontracting has been reported. In the absence of chemical fertilisers, production brigades are reliant on pig manure. Attempts to build lavish pigsties on communes in the 1960s were a failure, and the brigades had to fall back on the private sector as a source of supply and purchase manure from the brigade members (Gurley, 1976, p. 160). On the Changsha commune visited by Collier, this had been taken a step further and, in the absence of a large piggery and with the need to fulfil its state quota, the various teams allowed pigs to be raised privately by the members which were then sold back to the team some ten months later (Colliers, 1973, p. 163).

In Hungary, integration of this type went a degree further and elements of symbiosis in such relationships began as early as 1970. At the beginning of that year, co-operatives were exhorted to ensure that the household plot was supplied with adequate fodder (TRHGY, 1041/1969 (XII.7) MT), and in the spring steps were taken so that the performance of private 'family labour' on the household plot led to social benefits for the member paid out of communal co-operative funds. Work performed on the household plot in connection with any animal husbandry which was subsequently marketed via the co-operative farm henceforth counted towards the member's labour days, and these, in turn, counted towards the necessary labour requirements for sickness benefits, pensions, holiday allowances and maternity benefits (TRHGY, 5/1970 (III.22) Korm; 9/1970 (III.22) MEM). Keeping a milking cow, for example, counted for 3 labour days a month; the rearing of calves for 1 labour day per calf per month; and fattening pigs for 0.25 of a labour day per pig per month

(TRHGY, 9/1970 (III.22) MEM). Although the labour day allowance was not very generous, this was clearly a radical new development.

In 1974, a similar system was introduced for vegetable growing. In this case, the household plot-produced goods could be marketed either via the producer co-operative, the GCMCs or a state enterprise. Provided the vegetables were supplied on a contractual basis to one of these agencies, the work spent producing them on the plot would count towards labour days, and again ultimately towards social benefits (TRHGY, 13/1974 (VI.30) MEM). After government and ministerial regulations further systematising this form of integration for both animal husbandry and vegetable production in 1976, the labour day allowances were set at, for example, 1.3 days per quintal of green beans or peas, 0.6 days per quintal of cabbage, 3 days per quintal of plums and 4 days per quintal of apricots (TRHGY, 19/1976 (V.27) MEM). Again, while the labour day allowance was not very generous, the principle of mutual benefit is quite clear.

Meanwhile, in 1973, the government initiated a programme which gave state aid for such forms of integration. Co-operatives which engaged in a 'raising action' programme with their members, whereby members raised heifers on their household plots and then sold them to the communal farm, were eligible for government investment aid to build sheds to accommodate the animals. The only condition was that the buildings projected conform to state health and technological norms, and the farm sign a five year contract with the local Animal Husbandry Commission (TRHGY, 37/1972 (XII.7) PM–MEM). Thus, the state provided aid to the co-operative, and the co-operative aided the household plot by allowing labour performed in the 'raising action' to count towards the member's social benefits. In 1976 there was a call to develop this system further (TRHGY, 1038/1976 (XI.29) MT) although there was no increase in the amount of state aid towards sheds for heifers (TRHGY, 53/1976 (XII.29) PM–MEM; 37/1972 (XII.7) PM). At the end of 1977, in response to a catastrophic fall in pig production caused by short-lived political threats to small-scale agriculture (Swain, 1981, pp. 244–7), it was decided to provide aid for the improvement of pig sheds built before 1968 for farms which engaged in a 'breeding action' for pigs with members' household plots, or those of other small-scale producers (TRHGY, 29/1977 (VI.5) PM–MEM).

Such arrangements may not be unique to Hungary. Wädekin refers to a somewhat similar case in the Baltic states in the Soviet Union. He reports that until the end of the 1960s, kolkhozniks could commit themselves to raise calves and piglets for the kolkhoz; in exchange they received fodder and plots for growing additional fodder near to their private plots and received wages as if they had raised the animals in public sheds (Wädekin, 1973, p. 245). However, he does not give precise details about how the system works, how the wages are calculated and whether social security benefits are also included; and the impression given is that this was a temporary measure used to ensure some systematic livestock production at a time when large-scale animal husbandry had not been developed. It seems to refer to rewards for what is essentially the full-time activity of farm members rather than an official state recognition of their private part-time 'family labour'.

The benefits from such relationships were not one-sided. Household plot goods marketed via the producer co-operative count towards overall co-operative income (TJ, 1/1972, TOT), as do household plot animals sold via the Soviet collective farms, (Wädekin, 1973, p. 246). What is more, since improved income is one of the factors on which the co-operative management's bonuses are based (see chapter 6), management has a certain interest in developing the symbiosis. In 1974, almost 8 thousand million forints' worth of household plot goods were marketed by the producer co-operatives (MAK, 1976, No. 2, p. 105). In addition, the household plot constituted a market for 3.75 thousand million forints' worth of goods and services for the producer co-operatives in that year.[22] In 1977, the co-operative farm management was made materially interested in household plot production in a more direct fashion. The reorganisation of the regulations concerning management bonuses in that year gave, as one of the criteria on which a 20% bonus could be based, the development and improvement of systems of contractual household plot animal husbandry and vegetable production (TRHGY, 19/1977 (V.25) MEM–MUM 11 § (2) b). Co-operative farm management can increase its own income by attention to the 'family labour' of members on their household plots.

Within a single production unit, then, workers can increase their rewards from the enterprise by 'family labour' in the private sector, while management can increase its bonuses by encouraging such activity. In a symbiotic fashion, activities in one sector can lead to benefits in the other: the economic categories of 'family labour' and 'socialist wage labour' no longer compete. Co-operative farm management, the government and the local administration can be less concerned about 'lax discipline' in the one sector because the same individual's labour, in a different form, can be used to advantage in the other.

An additional change during this period which should be noted in connection with the encouragement of 'family labour' in the 'marginal labour time' of members was the trend, in the arable sector, towards ending the physical separation of co-operative and household plot land. The 'household plot' became a relationship of income in cash or kind rather than a physical expanse of arable land to be farmed. 'Family economy' in animal husbandry was further aided by taking away the drudgery involved in the family cultivation of feedstocks.

With the increased mechanisation of ploughing, sowing and harvesting, and with the increased capacity of the new agricultural machinery, co-operatives experienced growing difficulty meeting the obligation they had accepted since the early 1960s of contract ploughing the small, dispersed plots of co-operative members.[23] The practice therefore developed of the co-operative ploughing of all household plot land jointly, sowing it and harvesting the crop. Members then received a share of the final surplus proportionate to the per hectare yield of their notional 0.6 ha plot, less a fee for the cost of the service performed. If members did not want an income in kind, they could be paid the money value, at state buying prices, of what their notional plot would have produced. This latter procedure, which was clearly in the interests of white-collar and non-agricultural workers on the farm, gained official approval in 1974 (TRHGY, 18/1974 (VII.25) MEM) and an upper limit was set on the size of the income in cash or kind that could be paid in lieu of a plot. However, the Central Committee meeting of 1975 took up a position critical of the trend towards 'household plot' money, since it resembled too greatly a form of unearned income, and new regulations in 1977 prohibited the transformation of the household plot into a purely money relationship, although the practice of retaining the plot as a form of income in kind was reinforced (TRHGY, 7/1977 (III.12) MT).[24]

Finally, on the theme of integration we should note that the integration of 'family labour' and 'socialist wage labour' within the co-operative was not restricted to the creation of symbiosis between communal farm and household plot. We have already seen how the utilisation of 'family labour' in share-cropping contributed to the successful consolidation of collectivised agriculture; it continued to be an important aspect of co-operative agriculture between 1968 and 1977. From the middle to late 1960s the use of share-cropping as a means of payment became more marginal as the production of an increasing number of crops, and an increasing number of the stages within the production of a single crop, became mechanised. As mechanisation spread, share-cropping and kindred methods were used only for a limited number of special crops where mechanisation was not highly developed and there was still a need for a high labour input. The only basic crop where it was retained to any significant extent was sugar beet. More specialist crops where it was commonly used were open field vegetable growing. On the Red Flag co-operative, for example, it was used to great effect in the growing of onions for pickling. By this time, payment tended to be in cash rather than for a share in kind. While share-cropping remained a common form of remuneration for fodder crops such as maize, payment in kind had been demanded by members.[25] In fact, the ending of this source of fodder with the mechanisation of maize harvesting led to some tension between members and management until producer co-operatives found an alternative, commercial source of fodder, the other side of the deal with the GCMCs (P. Juhász, 1976). Once alternative sources of fodder were guaranteed and share-cropping moved into more marginal products, income in money rather than kind proved acceptable to all.

Before turning to consider the more sociological aspects of 'family labour' and 'socialist wage labour' in Hungary's collectivisation – who became what in the new world, and who enjoys which powers over whom – and in view of Hungary's manifest economic success compared with the Soviet Union's continuing failure and reliance on imported cereals from the West, we should conclude this section by reviewing the ways in which the organisation of collective agriculture differs in the two countries. As we have seen at various points in this chapter and the preceding one, the similarities are much greater than their differing economic success might suggest. The size of the household plot is similar, as were the limitations on livestock holding until these were removed altogether in Hungary in 1970. Hungary followed Soviet initiatives in the introduction of guaranteed wages, in the extension of social insurance to co-operative agriculture and in the abolition of the machine and tractor stations. In both countries, the collective helps plough household plot land and offers services to sell its produce. Until Hungary's New Economic Mechanism, the structure of farm taxation was essentially the same, and both countries have made use of a system akin to share-cropping to encourage production in those labour-intensive sectors which had yet to be mechanised.

Significant differences are only apparent in three areas. First, although both countries now offer considerable aid to agriculture, Hungary (at the third attempt) did not try to establish collective farms 'on the cheap'. Second, Hungary has given considerable material encouragement to petty commodity production on the household plot and 'family labour', in the form of share-cropping, within the co-operative farm. It has encouraged the symbiosis within the agricultural producer co-operative described above and has ensured that adequate channels exist to direct the product of this 'family labour' to the socialist market. Finally, because of the relatively effective price reform and, as we shall see in chapter 5, more or less real freedom as to choice of product created first by the abolition of compulsory deliveries and then the New Economic Mechanism, Hungarian farms have been able to offer guaranteed monthly wages which are competitive with those in industry. Soviet kolkhoz incomes might be guaranteed, but they are still much lower than those in industry. The most significant differences, then, are ones of trust: trust in co-operative farms as socialist forms of production unit, and trust in individual peasants to sell via the state if the state price is right and the state's marketing channels exist to be made use of.

Comparisons with China, such as they have been possible, reveal that Chinese agriculture is relatively underdeveloped, but that it conforms to a perhaps surprising extent to the 'socialist norm' of the Soviet Union. Meaningful comparisons can be made between contemporary Chinese agriculture and the pre-mechanisation Soviet and Hungarian collective farms.

PART II

MEMBERS AND MANAGERS

3

The social composition of the agricultural producer co-operative labour force

In this chapter we shall consider the social composition of the agricultural producer co-operative labour force which was created as the two labour types – 'family labour' and 'socialist wage labour' – were integrated within Hungarian co-operative farms. Who became what in the new agricultural world; and how, and by whom, are 'family labour' and 'socialist wage labour' combined? What were the effects of collectivisation and the growth and integration of 'family labour' and 'socialist wage labour' on peasants as social groups? As a prelude for these sociological questions, however, we should focus first on two issues of a more economic nature: the changes which took place in the demand for labour, and types of labour, as collective farms developed, and the transformation of the farms' occupational structure.

Demand for labour within Hungarian agriculture changed considerably throughout the 1960s as mechanisation and the evolution of the wage-labour form not only modified the degree of the intensity of demand, but also created a complex occupational structure with new skills and new occupational categories. The general pattern of the relationship between labour supply and mechanisation was the following. Mechanisation first, belatedly, made up for the shortage of suitably qualified labour that had prevailed as labour moved out of agriculture *en masse* and that which remained was reticent about joining in communal agriculture. It then proceeded to compound the continuing problem of periodic unemployment and underemployment of suitably qualified labour by increasing the seasonality of demand. At the same time, mechanisation increased enormously the number of 'skilled' tasks in agriculture, as well as those which were intrinsically industrial in nature.

In the early 1960s, then, many agricultural co-operatives experienced a shortage of labour (Fazekas, 1976, p. 182). The shortage, however, was not so much one in absolute terms as a shortage of labour of an acceptable quality and willing to work within communal agriculture. Taken as a national average, there was sufficient labour to perform all the necessary work on both communal and household plot land (Fazekas, 1976, p. 182). The shortage reflected the absence of sufficient young males within the membership, many of whom had either taken on industrial employment, while still retaining links with a co-operative farm family, or had given up agriculture altogether; and it was compounded by the general unwillingness of many existing members to take part in communal work at all (Fazekas, 1976, pp. 184–5; Fehér, 1970, p. 58) (see chapter 1). Thus, between 1962 and 1967, co-operative farm membership fell by 95000, only 7% of which could be explained by the retirement and death of members (Fazekas, 1976, p. 184); and the average age of members rose from 51.6 years in 1961 to 54.0 years in 1967 (Fazekas, 1976, p. 186). In 1964, 41.6% of the membership was over 60, with men slightly over-represented in those over 70. Less significantly, but nevertheless steadily, the proportion of women overall in the membership was growing, from 38.1% in 1962 to 38.4% in 1963 and 38.5% in 1964 (MAR, Vol. 2, p. 22).

Until 1965, mechanisation, experimentation with wage forms, and the taking on of 'employees' (chapter 1) did no more than make up for the shortfall (Fazekas, 1976, p. 187; Szilágyi, 1969, p. 1206). From that date on, mechanisation, as it saved labour days (134 million in 1966 and 144 million in 1967) (Szilágyi, 1969, p. 1201), also saved labour. By 1966/7, 75% of the labour days necessary for the wheat harvest had been saved, although the saving for other crops was less radical, 50% for green fodder and 50% for maize, while remaining under 10% for sugar beet and potatoes (Szilágyi, 1969, p. 1204). As a result, the co-operatives' demand for traditional manual labour decreased, and continued to decrease as mechanisation developed further. The situation in which a large proportion of the co-operative membership did not find full-time employment on the co-operative remained constant. Now, however, it was increasingly due to the inability of the co-operatives to provide the work, rather than members' unwillingness to join in. According to a representative sample of 334 agricultural co-operatives in 1966, only 58.7% of male members under pensionable age could be provided with full-time (over 200 work days) employment, as could only 12% of female members. In addition, the seasonality of agricultural labour both increased as a result of mechanisation, and its periodisation changed. An index of seasonality calculated by Szilágyi revealed a disparity of 53.9% against 59.4% between non-mechanised and mechanised branches in 1967; although the summer peak of work intensity disappeared, it was replaced by two lower peaks in May–June and September–October (1969, pp. 1207–8).

From the mid 1960s onwards, agricultural co-operatives had the twin labour problems of a surplus of manual traditional peasant labour, for which employment of some description had to be found, and a potential, and periodically real, shortage of skilled labour for its ever more numerous mechanised branches. The development of relatively high wage payments solved the latter problem, for the richer farms at least. A conciliatory attitude to the household plot and forays into processing and ancillary industrial and service activities were the solutions adopted for the rest (see chapter 5). Precisely because of the increasing level of mechanisation, labour on the relatively non-mechanised household plot was no longer seen as a threat to the co-operative. Unwanted labour could be safely parked there, ignored, and brought out at peak periods to help, as 'family labour' performing share-croppers, with the as yet unmechanised stages of production.

As a consequence, the flood of people out of agriculture was stayed somewhat after 1966. Between 1967 and 1970, there was even a temporary rise (Fazekas, 1976, p. 234), although this could well be attributable to expansion, in these years, of ancillary enterprises. By 1974, co-operative farm membership was only 7% down on 1967 (Fazekas, 1976, p. 234). Although the membership fell, the increased scope of the farms, and their continued amalgamation, resulted in a more rational use of labour. A smaller working population completed the same number of 'labour days' (Fazekas, 1976, p. 234), resulting in more permanent employment for those who did get work. In 1974, male active members worked on average 290 ten hour days, while economically active women worked an average of 193 ten hour days.[1] This represented a 20% improvement on 1967. The average age of the membership also improved as new members joined. The average age of all members fell from 54.0 years in 1967 to 53.3 years in 1974, and the fall in the average age of members actively employed on the farm was more significant, from 46.5 years in 1967 to 41.5 years in 1974.

There was also a considerable rise in the percentage within the active membership of those aged under 27 years, from 9.5% of the total to 17% in 1974 (Fazekas, 1976, pp. 236–40).

From the middle to late 1960s then, the consequence of mechanisation for the co-operative farm labour market was the creation of a relatively stable situation, in which there was no great shortage of labour for full-time employment on the farms, although there was no over-supply of adequately qualified labour either (Donáth, 1976a, p. 673), and where there was a large residue of relatively unqualified labour who could only be provided with seasonal employment. This can be contrasted with the Soviet Union, where the general picture is still one of a shortage of labour in agriculture, except in Estonia, which is the country's most prosperous agricultural area (Nove, 1980, pp. 141–2).

The complementary effect of mechanisation was the creation of an entirely new occupational structure. On the one hand, traditional agricultural tasks were transformed by being split up into a number of part processes entailing varying degrees of mechanical sophistication; on the other, new occupations were introduced of an entirely industrial character such as the maintenance of the machinery associated with mechanised crop cultivation and animal husbandry, and the driving of agricultural and non-agricultural vehicles. As a consequence, the demand for non-traditional and skilled labour became more acute as 'new occupations' began to replace peasant ones. The concept of 'skilled worker', it should be added, refers in the literature exclusively to the new occupations, and implicitly degrades the traditional skills associated with peasant farming, shepherding and so on. This terminology is retained in the text since it is of some sociological significance in terms of labour type and occupational level. It should be stressed, however, that it bears little relationship to the intrinsic skill component of the jobs themselves. One theme implicit in this chapter is the breakdown of the all-round skill of the peasant farmer and its replacement by a plethora of isolated, specialised tasks.[2]

There are no continuous data available showing changes in the relative significance of occupational types within the co-operatives since 1961. Juhász, however, does provide figures indicating the rapidity of the change between 1967 and 1972 (Table 3.1). Over this period, the numbers of 'nightwatchmen' and 'others' increased from 7.7% of the total to 18.8%. Similarly, those employed in chemicals,

Table 3.1. *Change in occupational structure on agricultural producer co-operatives, 1967–72*

	1967		1972			
	No.	Per-centage	No.	Per-centage	Change	Per-centage Increase
Jobs requiring no specialist skills[a]	264	7.7	577	18.8	+313	+118.6
Cereal production	1655	48.5	993	32.4	−662	− 40.0
Animal husbandry	709	20.7	537	17.5	−172	− 24.3
Workers with machines and chemicals/ industrial workers	428	12.5	659	21.5	+231	+ 54.0
Administrative and commercial workers	101	2.9	143	4.7	+ 42	+ 41.6
Management	251	7.3	157	5.0	− 94	− 37.5
Unclear	13	0.4	n.a.	n.a.	− 13	n.a.
Total	3421	100.0	3066	100.0	−355	− 10.5

Note: a. Cleaners, porters, nightwatchmen, etc.
Source: P. Juhász, 1975, Table 5, p. 252.

machine work and other ancillary enterprises increased dramatically from 12.5% to 21.5%, while those employed in administration and other commercial workers increased from 2.9% to 4.7%. At the same time, manual workers in crop production and horticulture declined as a percentage of the total from 48.5% to 32.4%, as did those employed in animal husbandry and cart driving from 20.7% to 17.5%. Traditional 'peasant' jobs in animal husbandry and crop production thus fell from 69.2% of the total in 1967 to 49.9% of the total in 1972.

Collective farms in the Soviet Union in the late 1960s revealed a more or less similar division of labour as figures provided by Hill show. Managers and specialists comprise 5% of the membership and lower level administrative workers a further 6%. Amongst the manual workers, 12% of the total are machine operators, drivers and skilled workers; 4% are construction workers and 14% work with livestock. All these members are employed full-time. The remaining

59% of the membership are field workers who are not employed on a full-time basis (Hill, 1975b, p. 112; Wädekin, 1971b).

In Hungary, the growth in the proportion of 'new occupations' in comparison with the number of traditional peasant ones has continued since 1972. Simó, in a study published in 1977, reports as low a figure as 13% of the total labour force working in crop production, within which 5.5% is in horticulture. In addition, he found only 7.2% of the membership working in animal husbandry, while 37.3% worked in workshops, processing or as drivers of one sort or another, 6.1% worked in offices, 5.3% worked in store-rooms, and as many as 31.1% of the membership were retired (Simó, 1977, p.468). These figures seem out of the ordinary, and Simó presents in addition the results of the Co-operative Research Institute's survey of 30 co-operatives. In this sample 32.4% of the membership worked in crop production, 4.4% worked in market gardening, 17.5% worked in animal husbandry and 21.5% worked in machine shops or in other forms of industrial-type occupation. These figures are, perhaps, nearer the norm for the late 1970s.

This extended division of labour, with its new occupations of an industrial nature, and its sophistication of some agricultural ones, necessarily increased the demand for skilled labour. It is not surprising, therefore, that the proportion of skilled workers within the co-operative's labour force has consistently risen. In 1967 only 8.3% of the total labour force on co-operatives were skilled or semi-skilled workers (Vági, 1969, p.31), although, taking a proportion of active rather than total membership and including tractor drivers, Erdei manages to make this figure 20% (1969, p. 78). By 1970, Kulcsár and Lengyel report (1979, p.76), 19.1% of manual workers on co-operative farms were skilled. The *General Agricultural Compendium*, however, gives us the most precise data. In 1972 it reports a total of 24 069 skilled agricultural workers on co-operative farms, and 60 328 skilled industrial workers. The total of 84 397 accounts for 8.6% of total co-operative membership and 13.7% of members aged between 21 and 65, a rough estimate for the active membership. When added to the numbers of drivers, the proportion of those with some sort of skill rises to 15.2% of the membership, and 24.3% of the membership aged between 21 and 65. The skilled agricultural workers comprised 7596 workers in crop production, 9163 workers in animal husbandry, and 5496 workers in horticulture. The non-agricultural skilled workers consisted of 15 458 car or lorry drivers, 50 295 tractor or dumper drivers, 4089 motor mechanics, 5513 smiths, 11930 fitters (lock-smiths), 4511 electricians, 2841 joiners, 2705 carpenters, 9668 stone-masons and 16061 workers in the food supply industry (AMO, Vol. 12, p. 31).

These figures are cited in full not only to show the demand for skilled labour, but also to give a clearer picture of the variety of non-agricultural jobs to be found in agricultural co-operatives. Equally detailed figures for a period later than 1972 are not available; however, Mrs Tisza cites a different Central Statistical Office source for 1973, claiming that 13.3% of active manual workers in agriculture are skilled workers, and that the inclusion of drivers brings this figure up to 23.7% (Tiszáné Gerai, 1975, p. 548). Kulcsár and Lengyel offer the most up to date figure, when they claim that in 1976 26.6% of manual workers on co-operatives were skilled workers (1979, p. 76). Whatever the precise figures, the point is clear: there has been a very marked increase in the demand for skilled labour, agricultural or industrial, in a branch of the economy where the concept of skilled labour was previously more or less unknown. It should be noted, however, that the prestige of agricultural occupations overall remains low. Many studies of skilled worker trainees who have completed their studies have shown that over 50% of them leave agricultural employment within four to five years of graduation (Kulcsár and Szijjártó, 1980, p. 112), and Lengyel found in a study of 700 students in an agricultural training college that 50% of all students, and 60% of the girls, admitted that they did not want to get a job in agriculture (Lengyel, 1979, p. 59).

The new division of labour, not surprisingly, is associated with a differentiation in wage rates. This can clearly be seen from data taken from a study by Ferenc Kunszabó and from my own findings on the May 1st co-operative. Kunszabó, writing in 1970, found that those working with cattle earned between 2800 and 3000 forints a month, tractor drivers earned 2500, cart drivers earned between 1500 and 1800 a month while those in crop production earned only 1200 to 1400 forints a month (1970a, p. 12). Table 3.2, showing yearly earnings in the May 1st co-operative, fills in the intermediate levels of the hier-archy. The division between traditional seasonal workers in crop pro-duction and the full-time workers in animal husbandry and the new occupations is clear. These aggregate figures do not, however, reflect the very high wage rates which combine drivers, and those involved with the mechanised side of harvesting, can earn at harvest time.[3]

Table 3.2. *Annual earnings in May 1st co-operative, 1976 (forints)*

Mechanics for fodder works	48286
Full-time manager, independent leaders and administration workers	44384
Piggery	41897
Drivers and loaders	41635
Sheep and cattle (slaughter)	40685
Mechanised crop production	39872
Warehousemen	39615
Cattle (dairy)	36816
Workers in grass production	35869
Calf rearing	34541
Mechanics in general workshop	33909
Construction	30104
Traditional crop production	22000

THE LABOUR MARKET FOR CO-OPERATIVE FARM MEMBERS

The development of the agricultural producer co-operatives as large-scale socialist enterprises has resulted in the creation of a type of 'segmented labour market'[4] on which skilled labour for the new occupations within the farm's extended division of labour is scarce and in demand (as it is throughout the economy), but where unskilled labour performing traditional agricultural tasks is in plentiful supply and is inseparably bound by social factors to the farm. The standard approach in the Hungarian literature to these two elements in the farm membership juxtaposes 'mobile' and 'immobile' members, or 'workers' and 'peasants'.[5] The former have few ties to a locality because they derive the greater part of their income from wage labour on the farm and have a skill that can readily be used elsewhere. The latter have strong ties to a particular locality, partly because of age or marital status, and partly because of their position on the labour market. Having no skills other than traditional agricultural ones, they are constantly in over-supply. They therefore have to rely very heavily on 'peasant' aspects of membership to supplement their income, and this in turn creates a strong physical tie to the area. This approach could form the basis of an analysis of all occupations within the farm, relating degree of mobility on the labour market to the strength of associated 'peasant' ties; and an analysis of this type would be central to a full understanding of the class position of co-operative farm members. However, such refinements of analysis are as yet impossible, and we must here restrict ourselves to accepting the general division of the farm labour force into 'mobile' and 'immobile' sectors and consider the social attributes associated with the 'segmented labour market' that this implies.

In order to get a clear picture of this labour market, it must be stressed that there is no facile congruence between 'family labour'/ 'socialist wage labour' and 'immobile' labour/'mobile' labour. 'Mobile' labour and 'immobile' labour work as both 'family' and wage labour. (All members have the right to a household plot.) However, it does seem to be the case that those with a greater commitment to the 'family labour' of the household plot or share-cropping will be more likely to be 'immobile' in the labour market, their concentration on 'family labour' being either the reason for their immobility or the result of prior immobility. In order to consider this relationship and the nature of labour in the 'mobile' and 'immobile' markets, it seems reasonable to look first at the age and sex composition of those most committed to 'family labour' and then consider where these people stand on the communal farm's segmented labour market.

The *General Agricultural Compendium* is again the most complete source for information concerning the first of these questions. The statistics for ownership of household plots according to age and sex reveal an age limit above which members become more likely to own a household plot. This is clear from Table 3.3. Only 6.4% of household plots are owned by co-operative farm members aged under 30, and only 4.1% are owned by those aged between 30 and 34. On the other hand, 14% are owned by those aged between 35 and 44 and 18.7% are owned by those aged between 45 and 54. The ratios of ownership by age, at this stage, are roughly the same for both men and women although considerably fewer plots are owned by young women, the relevant percentages being 3.6%, 1.8%, 8% and 14% respectively.

Interestingly, there is a fall in the share of household plots owned by members in the 55 to 59 age range, only 7.9% of plots being owned by this age group, with roughly the same percentages for both men and women. The percentage share rises again in the next age group: 13.0% of plots are owned by those aged between 60 and 64, and in this age range the proportion owned by women (14.1%) exceeds the average for all members. Finally, those aged over 65 own 35.8% of all household plots, while 50.5% of the household plots owned by women

Table 3.3. *Household plot holders by sex and age (percentage distribution)*

Age	Men	Women	Men + Women
−30	7.4	3.6	6.4
30–34	4.9	1.8	4.1
35–44	16.2	8.0	14.0
45–54	20.4	14.0	18.7
55–59	7.9	8.0	7.9
60–64	12.7	14.1	13.0
65+	30.5	50.5	35.8
Total	100.0	100.0	100.0

Source: AMO, Vol. 14, pp. 32–3.

are owned by women aged over 65. The picture, then, is clearly one of household plots being predominantly the domain of pensioners, and especially of women pensioners. The practice of giving widows a household plot in order to supplement their rather low pension must be at least part of the explanation for the disproportionate share the over-65s have in female ownership of household plots. In addition, there seems to be a major dividing line in household plot ownership around the mid thirties, perhaps the age at which a family decides that it will stay in agriculture and the village rather than move to the town (AMO, Vol. 14, pp. 32–3).

If, on the other hand, we look at the figures for the age and sex of those who are attached to household plots, rather than who own them, we find a slightly different distribution. The potential labour force on household plots is distributed differently from their owner-ship. There are rather more individuals available to work in the younger age groups than there are in the elder groups, and, interest-ingly, in the age groups over 35 years, rather more women available (Table 3.4).

Since families are not typically multi-generational,[6] and therefore those of retirement age are relatively unlikely to have a younger relative living in who might help with the farm, it is not surprising that both the size of the plot and the numbers of animals kept on it vary with the age of the plot holder. This can be seen from Table 3.5. Those aged between 40 and 49 years, where there is a likelihood that both family members are capable of work and where it is perhaps also more likely that both are employed on the co-operative,[7] have a larger than average household plot. Pensioners, who are less likely to have a family member to help, have a smaller plot and also show a tendency to give up such time-consuming tasks as keeping cows. There is a clear indication too that younger members, under 30 years, who begin household plot farming also keep away from cows and additionally avoid specialist crops such as grapes. They concentrate rather on the easier options of pigs and, to a lesser extent, market gardening, and thereby exploit the possibility inherent in the household plot for part-time farming in its recently encouraged form (see chapter 2). It should be borne in mind that the younger members' commitment to arable land revealed in Table 3.5 does not indicate readiness to work in the fields since, as we saw in chapter 2, this can be commuted to direct income in cash or kind.

These figures indicate, then, that household plots are predominantly the preserve of the old, while reminding us visibly that they are not uniquely so. They have also given a rather imprecise indication that women, especially in their elder years, are more dependent on the household plot. Other sources substantiate the important role of women in the household plot. A survey of village households in Békés county in 1969 revealed the overwhelming importance of the wife in performing work on the family plot. In 65.1% of households the wife did the majority of the work on the plot. Where the women had no employment outside the home this ratio rose to 74.9%, but, even in

Table 3.4. *Persons attached to household plots by sex and age (percentage distribution)*

Age	Men	Women	Men + Women
−30	17.6	15.6	16.5
30–34	27.2	23.6	25.3
35–44	11.8	12.0	11.9
45–54	12.9	13.5	13.2
55–59	4.8	5.8	5.3
60–64	7.4	8.7	8.1
65+	18.3	20.8	19.6
Total	100.0	100.0	100.0

Source: AMO, Vol. 14, pp. 36–7.

Table 3.5. *Scope of household plot farming by age of plot holder, 1972*

Age	−30	30–39	40–49	50–59	60+	Total
No. of plots	49858	91518	141426	116895	381537	781234
% distribution	6.4	11.7	18.1	15.0	48.8	100.0
No. of people attached to plots	158428	362802	541945	369443	866918	2299536
% distribution	6.8	15.8	23.6	16.1	37.7	100.0
Per 100 plots						
Total no. of persons	318	396	383	316	227	294
Of which active earner	148	152	192	174	62	119
Of which inactive earner	26	21	24	34	91	58
Area of plot in hectares	67	71	77	74	61	67
Of which arable	60	61	63	59	47	54
Of which garden/ fruit	5	7	8	8	8	8
Of which grapes	1	2	4	5	5	4
No. of cattle	29	62	91	88	49	63
No. of pigs	340	466	495	438	234	346
No. of horses	1	1	2	2	1	1
No. of poultry	2688	3913	4350	4023	2606	3292
Per 100 plots which keep them						
No. of cattle	220	252	271	260	224	245
No. of pigs	557	621	632	582	444	541
No. of horses	126	121	128	128	116	122
No. of poultry	4044	4566	4732	4329	3063	3811
For every 100 plots						
Has arable land	97	97	97	97	96	96
Has garden/fruit	47	63	71	73	67	67
Has grapes	9	17	29	34	32	29
Keeps cattle	13	24	34	34	22	26
Keeps pigs	61	75	78	75	53	64
Keeps poultry	66	86	92	93	85	86
Keeps cattle, pigs and poultry	10	22	30	30	18	22
Keeps pigs and poultry	50	69	75	73	51	61
Has a stable	19	32	44	47	41	40
Has a pigsty	66	84	90	90	78	82

Source: AMO, Vol. 14, p. 125.

households where the wife also went out to work, in 55.3% of cases the wife did the majority of the work on the household plot (Sas, 1976, p. 113).

There is no reason to believe that Békés county is in any way exceptional in this. Nationally, whilst the average number of hours spent daily working on household plots for agricultural co-operative members was 3.3 hours, the time spent by women members was 4 hours. In addition, women spent daily another 3.4 hours doing other forms of housework (Andorka and Harcsa, 1973, pp. 103–4). In a further study carried out in 1973 in six Hungarian counties, Lengyel found that most household plot work was performed by women dependants and pensioners, and that even women who had full-time employment on the co-operative farm did one and a half times as much work on the household plot as men (1979, p. 16). Household plot work, however, was even more important for women who were unable to take on full-time work because of child-care duties, villages having many fewer kindergarten places than Budapest or other towns (Lengyel, 1979, pp. 17 and 26).

This form of segmentation within the collective farm's internal labour market is also present in the Soviet Union. Depending on the sources used, between 70% (Hill, 1974, p. 495) and 80.6% (Dodge and Feshbach, 1967, p. 274) of labour time spent on the household plot is accounted for by women. Women devote 30–40% of their working time to the household plot, whereas men devote only 10–13% of theirs (Hill, 1974, p. 495) and, according to a survey carried out in Soviet Moldavia, this means an average of 5 hours a day for women on the plot (Shubkin, 1969, p. 165). Hungary again appears to be simply following a socialist norm.

We should now consider where within the occupational structure of the co-operative farm those who exhibit a commitment to the household plot work. Unfortunately, there is no direct evidence to reveal where those aged between 40 and 49 years, with their larger than average household plots, work within the communal farm and we will have to restrict our analysis to the occupations of women and pensioners. Women work predominantly in crop production and, overwhelmingly, in seasonal labour. Thus Holács, in a study of 300 women in south western Hungary, found that 52% of women worked on a seasonal basis, and exactly the same percentage worked in crop production. Within the 39% who were permanently employed, 32% worked in animal husbandry and 7% in administration (Holács,

1971). That women tend to be employed in seasonal jobs, the majority of which are in crop production, can be seen from figures for the number of days worked. Table 3.6 presents figures taken from Gyenes (1973) for 1971. He found that while only 6.5% of women worked 300 ten hour days or more, 29% of men did; a further 21.7% of men completed between 250 and 300 days, but only 12.9% of women did. On the other hand, as the remaining sections of the table show, a greater proportion of women than men were employed on the farm for the shorter time periods. Women thus clearly predominate in seasonal employment, and Lengyel even states that the co-operative farms have become split into male and female branches on this basis (Lengyel, 1977a, p. 79).

The occupational structure of the Red Flag co-operative confirmed this picture. Despite the high level of mechanisation on the farm, 56 women were employed in crop production. More men than women worked in crop production overall, but 74% of them were either tractor drivers or lorry drivers. The overwhelming majority of the women employed in this sector were simply manual workers. Women in this farm were generally over-represented in agricultural occupations: 74.8% of women members were employed in agriculture, as were 66% of women employees, compared with 39.3% of male members and 46.1% of male employees, while the proportion of the whole labour force in agricultural professions was only 49.9%. Since women comprised only 18% of those employed in animal husbandry, their over-representation in crop production is clear. What is more, not only would women appear to be concentrated in traditional peasant jobs, the segment of the labour market where labour is in over-supply and where labour is 'unskilled', these are also the sectors of agricultural production which are most likely to retain share-cropping and thus utilise 'self-exploiting' 'family labour'. Thus, for example, on the Red Flag co-operative participation in onion production, which was carried out on the basis of a modified form of share-cropping, was dominated by female labour.

That pensioners are likely to be employed in traditional seasonal tasks in crop production is self-evident. Their employment must be seasonal – or unrealistically low paid – if they are to retain pension rights, while the only skills that the majority of members old enough to be pensioners have are likely to be those traditional peasant ones, classified as 'unskilled'.

Women, on the other hand, are not entirely restricted to the

Table 3.6. *Number of days worked in communal work by sex of member (percentage distribution)*

No. of ten hour days worked in 1971	Total	Men	Women
– 40	12	10.2	16.1
40–100	10	8.7	12.9
100–150	11	7.2	19.4
150–200	12	10.2	16.1
200–250	14	13.0	16.1
250–300	19	21.7	12.9
300+	22	29.0	6.5
Total	100.0	100.0	100.0

Source: Gyenes, 1973, Table 6, p.45 (recalculated) (based on Co-operative Research Institute figures).

'immobile' labour market. Certain of the new occupations on the co-operative farm have become feminised, and this is an entirely new phenomenon in large-scale agriculture.[8] To some extent this has been the result of legislation in that, as we saw in chapter 2, in 1968 regulations were passed banning the employment of women in areas considered dangerous to their health. Female jobs in the new occupations, the 'mobile' segment of the labour market, either resemble rather closely traditional 'peasant' tasks, or are the traditional female jobs that the co-operative farm, in all its new complexity as a relatively autonomous economic enterprise, has need of. Thus, women tend to be employed in fruit and vegetable production, with poultry, and in lower grade clerical jobs. In the 'B' agricultural co-operative studied by Gyenes (1977), for example, women exclusively worked in the fruit sector (p.74), while, on the Red Flag co-operative, women predominated in the farm's egg production and in its tree nursery, and 120 women were due to begin work in 1978 in its new glasshouse complex for vegetable production.

Women's over-representation in lower grade clerical jobs is confirmed by Meszticzky. Overall, 28% of those working in administration and management were women in his survey (1975, p. 284), but of these 84.7% were employed in administration and bookkeeping, and 50% of them were under 30. This picture too is confirmed on the Red

Flag co-operative. Although not employed in large absolute numbers, women were disproportionately highly represented in occupational categories such as 'health and cultural' and 'accounting and financial'. In addition, it is interesting to note that, on the Red Flag co-operative, a disproportionately large percentage of women performed jobs that were classified as semi-skilled: 65.2% of women members and 64% of female employees performed 'semi-skilled' tasks, compared with the co-operative average of 46.2%. Unfortunately, there are no figures showing how far this is the case in agriculture nationally, but it is of some significance in the light of women's high over-representation in 'semi-skilled' jobs in industry nationally (Kulcsár, 1975, p.980; Vajda, 1976, p.679). Lengyel confirms female predominance in semi-skilled occupations in agriculture, but again does not provide statistical material to support the case. She refers directly to women being 'squeezed out' of professions as they become mechanised, only to be 'let in' again if, for any reason, there is a shortage of male labour (Lengyel, 1979, p.49). Kulcsár and Szijjártó point to women's underrepresentation in skilled jobs even among the young: 50% of male manual workers under 30 on farms in 1976 were skilled, whereas only 13% of young female agricultural manual workers were (1980, p.111). They estimate that two thirds of the female labour force in agriculture work there because they cannot work anywhere else (1980, p.116). From the other side, virtually 100% of skilled workers in agriculture were men, and 90% of them have skills that can be used elsewhere in the economy (Lengyel, 1979, p.45). Women are also more likely to figure as temporary rather than full-time employees (Lengyel, 1979, p.45). Furthermore, the chances of such a situation changing radically in the future are diminished by the fact that girls are relatively underrepresented amongst students on agricultural worker training courses. In 1974/5 the percentage of girls on such courses was 27.4%; by 1977/8 it had fallen to 24.8%.

Given the fact that women tend to be employed in jobs with a lower 'skill' content and in seasonal jobs, it is not surprising that women's earnings from the co-operative are lower than men's. Table 3.7 taken from research by the Co-operative Research Institute shows this clearly.

These same sorts of divisions exist on the Soviet kolkhoz, while in China they are less obvious because the division itself is less developed. Nevertheless, women certainly earn less than men for this communal work. In 1973 the average work point differential between

Table 3.7. *Percentage distribution of the membership of agricultural producer co-operatives by yearly earnings groups and sex, 1973*

	–6000 Ft	6001–15000	15001–25000	25001–40000	40000+	Total
Members excluding pensioners and those						
receiving rent for land contributed to co-operative						
m	6.0	9.6	20.4	39.9	24.1	100.0
f	16.7	32.1	32.2	16.0	2.9	100.0
m + f	9.5	16.9	24.2	32.2	17.1	100.0
Pensioners and those receiving rent						
for land contributed to co-operative						
m	55.1	27.1	13.1	4.2	0.5	100.0
f	76.7	17.3	4.6	1.2	0.2	100.0
m + f	60.2	24.7	11.1	3.5	0.4	100.0
Total membership						
m	17.1	13.6	18.7	31.8	18.8	100.0
f	26.3	29.7	27.8	13.7	2.5	100.0
m + f	19.9	18.5	21.5	26.3	13.8	100.0

Source: Gyenes, 1975, p. 324 (based on Central Statistical Office figures).

men and women was 2.5 points, 7–9 against 10–11 (Selden, 1979, p. 123). In the Soviet Union, women are clearly concentrated in the more demanding, less skilled, and therefore less rewarding branches of the collective farm. Thus, Dodge and Feshbach discovered that 97% of women collective farm members were engaged in 'physical labour', of which 83% were employed in non-specialised and unskilled work compared with 66% of male kolkhoz members; 87.2% of kolkhoz women are employed in seasonal labour. In 1959 only 0.8% of tractor drivers and 1.4% of machinery handlers were female. On the other hand, 98.8% of milking personnel (unlike the situation in Hungary), 87.3% of field team workers, 80.6% of vegetable and melon growers and 93.4% of poultry workers were women (1967, p. 275); furthermore, in 1960 the prospects for a change in these ratios did not look promising. Only 1.7% of students entering courses related to mechanised agriculture were girls (1967, p. 279).

It is apparent, then, that within communal agriculture, women (and pensioners) generally work in traditional manual jobs in crop production, the traditional 'peasant' work. In addition, a number of new feminised professions have emerged, either in areas similar to traditional sectors, or in archetypal 'women's jobs' where lower wages are paid and where the work is classified as 'semi-skilled'. Women and pensioners are thus on the 'immobile' side of the labour market, and when women do enter the market for potentially mobile labour, they tend to end up in typically feminine, low 'skilled', low paid jobs. The greater commitment of both these groups to 'family labour' on the household plot is clearly associated with their being at the losing end of a 'segmented labour market'. Although it is not necessarily the case that commitment to 'family labour' indicates an overall low joint income from both sectors of the economy, in the case of single person households, such as pensioners, this is rather likely.

The corollary of this is that 'mobile' labour in the new skilled occupations of co-operative farms must consist of males below pensionable age. This was indeed the case on the Red Flag co-operative and is likely to be true elsewhere, if only because the majority of the new occupations on farms are traditional 'men's jobs'. However, no national figures relate age, sex, level of skill and economic branch within the co-operative labour force so that we might substantiate the point beyond doubt. The absence of such figures also prevents us from checking the intuitively attractive claim that, within the 'mobile labour force', elder workers predominate in more traditional sectors such as animal husbandry, while younger workers are more dominant in the new industrial-type jobs. A study in 1970 of five co-operatives in the Homokhátság region produced findings which support such a claim to some extent.

Although he did not divide the membership according to sex, Szijjártó found that, while the proportion of workers aged from 26 to 50 was the same for both workers in animal husbandry and those in the workshops, there was a larger percentage of workers aged over 50 in the former (14.8% compared with 6.0%) and a larger percentage of workers aged between 14 and 25 in the latter (28% compared with 17.6%). Tractor drivers, on the other hand, were highly represented in the age groups 14 to 25 (23.8%) and 26 to 50 (75%), but hardly at all in the group of those aged over 50 (Szijjártó, 1972, p. 13). Since these are predominantly male occupations the potentially confounding issue of sex can be discounted, thus giving weak evidence – on the basis of five farms – that workers in agricultural occupations tend to be older than those in the new industrial trades. If this is the case. it gels to some extent with the speculation above linking older members, with larger household plots, to the agricultural professions. Although the 40–49 year olds had the largest plots (Table 3.5), those aged between 50 and 59 years (whom we might compare with Szijjártó's figures) also had large ones, and it is conceivable that in the Homok-hátság study the agricultural workers were concentrated in the upper half of the rather broad 26–50 year old age range.

As mechanisation transformed the nature of the agricultural co-operative, and 'family labour' and 'socialist wage labour' were integrated within it, a segmented labour market developed on the farm in which 'mobile' and 'immobile' elements performed increasingly age-specific and sex-specific jobs. What is more, position on this labour market correlates to some extent with the degree of importance attached by the individual member to 'family labour' and 'socialist wage labour', although it should be remembered that almost all members of the co-operative farm use both types of labour to some extent. Younger members are more likely to concentrate on areas which gain from the increasing government support of 'family labour' production in their 'marginal labour time'.

THE SOCIAL COMPOSITION OF OCCUPATIONS ON CO-OPERATIVE FARMS

We can supplement the above examination of positions on the labour market in terms of members' age and sex with a consideration of certain additional social characteristics of those members who had experienced relative succcess on the labour market in the sense that they were employed full-time on the farm. The pattern of individuals' careers and their social origin in terms of their family's pre-collectivi-sation social standing constitute two further dimensions of relevance to the work-situation of members or groups of members within the co-operative farm in that both previous work experience and family background can be considered to have a direct bearing on the way individuals think and behave in their place of work. Social survey data from 1972 and 1973 provide evidence for both these additional social characteristics.

A survey of farm members by the Co-operative Research Institute compares the occupants of various posts on the farm in terms of their social status immediately before collectivisation, and a Sociological Research Institute study compares the respondent's present occupa-

Table 3.8. *Percentage distribution of occupational group by social origin*

Social status of head of household before creation of co-operative	Requiring no special skill	Crop production	Animal husbandry	Workers with machines or chemicals	Workers in administration and commerce	Management	Total
Unknown or started in co-operative	6.9	5.4	5.0	13.2	11.9	22.9	8.5
Agricultural proletarian or semi-proletarian	22.7	21.8	25.1	10.5	9.1	10.8	18.9
Small, middle or rich peasant	37.5	47.6	52.9	26.4	29.3	27.4	40.2
Artisan, trader or agricultural employee	3.8	5.0	2.8	9.6	4.9	5.7	5.4
Industrial worker	22.0	15.5	11.2	35.0	21.7	11.5	20.3
Employee	6.9	4.5	2.8	5.0	18.2	7.0	5.5
Intellectual	0.2	0.2	0.2	0.3	4.9	14.7	1.2
Total	100.0	100.0	100.0	100.0	100.0	100.0	100.0

Source: P. Juhász, 1975, Table 8, pp. 260–1 (N = 3066) (percentages recalculated).

tional category with that of his father (only male heads of households were surveyed).[9] The evidence of these two major surveys can be further supplemented by findings of less ambitious pieces of social research.

Table 3.8 presents those findings of the Co-operative Research Institute's survey which are of relevance to an analysis of career patterns amongst the farm membership. Because the table compares the status of heads of households in the respondents' families at the time of collectivisation with their occupation in 1972, this table does not compare the occupational status of given individuals at two points in their careers. However, we have already seen that the average age of the membership rose continually until the mid sixties, thus precluding the possibility of there being any significant influx of sons and daughters of these heads of households until then, and Juhász, who reports the Co-operative Research Institute findings, states specifically, in relation to this data, that the drop in the average age of the membership between 1967 and 1972 was not sufficiently large for it to have been the result of a mass of young people entering the labour market for the first time (P.Juhász, 1975, pp. 248–50). The majority of the movement between pre-collectivisation status and 1972 position on the co-operative farm reported in Table 3.8 must, then, reflect the changing career experience of the same individuals.

Comparing columns in Table 3.8 we see that those members who had been landed peasants before collectivisation predominated, in 1972, in all occupations except those of workers with machines and chemicals. Clearly, and unsurprisingly, most co-operative farm members had worked in agriculture all their lives, and this held for most of the occupations on the farm. More significantly, however, amongst workers with chemicals and machinery, the majority of members had worked in industry immediately before collectivisation; and those who had an experience of work in industry also formed a significant proportion of workers requiring no special skills and of workers in commerce and administration. Table 3.9 provides additional information indicating the extent of this movement into agriculture by workers with industrial experience. The table shows how many of those working in the same categories of farm occupation as in Table 3.8 joined in the preceding three, five and six years. It also indicates how the growth or concentration in occupations presented in Table 3.1 is related to the numbers of individuals actually joining those occupations between 1967 and 1972. If we discount the figures

Table 3.9. *Occupational group and period spent in the co-operative*

Joined co-op in previous		Requiring no specialist skills	Cereal production including gardening	Animal husbandry and cart drivers	Workers with machines and chemicals and industrial workers	Workers in administration and commerce	Lower level management	Branch managers and middle management	Total
0–3 yrs	No.	177	230	97	318	64	34	36	956
	%	30.7	23.2	18.1	48.3	44.8	43.6	45.6	31.2
3–6 yrs	No.	58	122	81	97	10	10	16	394
	%	10.1	12.3	15.1	14.7	7.0	12.8	20.3	12.9
6+ yrs	No.	342	641	359	244	69	34	27	1716
	%	59.2	64.5	66.8	37.0	48.2	43.6	34.1	56.0
Total	No.	577	993	537	659	143	78	79	3066
	%	100.0	100.0	100.0	100.0	100.0	100.0	100.0	100.0
Of which between 1967 and 1972	No.	216	312	151	382	71	41	46	1219
	%	37.4	31.4	28.1	58.0	53.0	52.6	58.2	39.8
Those who joined 1967–72 as % of increase/decrease in the size of each occupation group		+69.0	−47.1	−87.8	+165.4	+166.7	−42.6	−353.8	−337.7

Source: P. Juhász, 1975, Table 6, p.253.

for management and administrative workers (discussed in chapter 4), the extent of recent movement into industrial-type jobs is quite clearly greater than into the more traditional agricultural occupations, although it is perhaps surprising how great the movement has been in and out of all co-operative farm professions, including those in decline. The extent of movement into industrial-type professions on the farm is highlighted by the figures in the bottom row of Table 3.9, which show the numbers of individuals joining each occupational group between 1967 and 1972 as a percentage of the overall increase or decrease in the numbers employed in that occupational group over the same five years. Not only did 58% of those working with machines and chemicals join agricultural producer co-operatives within this five year period, their turnover was also very rapid, the numbers joining these professions being well in excess of the expansion in the number of job opportunities.

It is less easy to find reliable information concerning the pattern of career experience, since collectivisation, of those who work in the agricultural branches of the co-operative farm. Holács (1976, p. 93) reports, on the basis of a study of six villages and their co-operatives, that there was frequent interbranch mobility. Kunszabó, on the other hand, reports that the only mobility that took place in the agricultural co-operative at Heréd, northern Hungary, which he studies in some depth (1970a, p. 18) was that occasioned by mechanisation. It is likely that some interbranch mobility was the norm, if only because of the large contraction of employment opportunities in crop production, even in those years preceding the decline already documented since 1967 (Table 3.1). If workers in this field, who it is reasonable to assume had worked in agriculture rather than industry before collectivisation, did not, in the course of their careers, move into jobs requiring mechanical, chemical or administrative skills (as we have seen they did not), then they can only have gone into either animal husbandry or the jobs requiring no special skills. The latter is an occupational category which has increased in size since 1967; the former has decreased, but not at such a dramatic rate as crop production. Since the formerly landed peasants are rather less heavily represented in the occupations requiring no special skill than they are in animal husbandry (Table 3.8), it is tempting to deduce that members who had been landed peasants before collectivisation, and who had initially gone into crop production only to find that their manual labour was being replaced by machines, were more likely than the formerly landless peasant members in the same situation to go into animal husbandry rather than to take on a job which required no special skill. However, we could only state this with certainty if we knew the relative proportions of members with various pre-collectivisation experiences working in crop production and animal husbandry immediately after collectivisation. Landed peasants might conceivably have constituted such a large majority of workers in animal husbandry at this date, that the only avenue open for the crop production workers replaced by machinery, of whatever pre-collectivisation experience, was to go into jobs requiring no special skills. Unfortunately, there is no generalisable evidence available on this point. It should be noted, however, that, in his study of five farms in the Homokhátság area, Kunszabó found that, in animal husbandry and cart driving taken jointly, members who had owned sufficiently large plots before collectivisation to be more or less independent farmers were relatively more likely to work in animal husbandry and cart driving immediately after collectivisation than would be expected on the basis of the number of animal husbandry and cart driving jobs on the farm, although they constituted a minority within these occupations in absolute terms (1971, p. 35).[10]

The pattern of career mobility of members who remained in agricultural trades within the farm, then, remains unclear, while that of workers in industrial-type jobs is very apparent: they came to co-operative agriculture via industry. A second large-scale survey indicates the likely social origins of these and the other co-operative farm members. This study is based on a sample taken in 1972/3 from all villages in Hungary, with the exception of those immediately surrounding Budapest. It compares the occupational group of male heads of households in 1972 with that of their fathers. We can assume that the inclusion within these figures of state farm workers has not significantly biased the results because state farm workers are very much fewer in number than co-operative members and are not likely to have much of a statistical effect in any case.[11] If such an assumption is made, we can make the following inferences from Table 3.10.

The key figures to be considered are in columns one, two and four, and in the first three rows.[12] Taking 'inflow' figures (column percentages) representing the present (1972) social composition of occupations, we see that members from agricultural proletarian families are, very marginally, the largest group amongst unskilled agricultural manual workers, closely followed by the other landed peasants, with

Table 3.10. *Present (1972) socio-economic group of head of household of village population (excluding villages surrounding Budapest) by father's socio-economic group at head of household's birth (percentage distribution)*

Father's socio-economic group	Head of household							
	Unskilled agricultural manual	Skilled agricultural manual	Independent peasant	Industrial skilled worker within agriculture	Industrial/ construction worker	Non-manual	Other	Total
Agricultural proletarian	32.6	20.0	15.8	22.6	24.3	13.9	7.5	23.9
	33.7	2.7	1.1	5.1	48.0	8.3	1.1	100.0
Up to 2.9ha	12.8	11.4	10.5	17.7	11.4	13.0	35.0	12.5
	25.0	2.8	1.4	7.8	43.3	15.5	4.2	100.0
Over 2.9ha	32.3	40.4	52.8	22.6	24.2	24.7	22.5	26.3
	30.3	4.7	3.3	4.7	41.2	14.2	1.6	100.0
Other agricultural manual	5.7	8.5	—	9.7	4.3	3.5	2.5	5.3
	26.7	5.0	—	10.0	45.1	11.5	1.7	100.0
Industrial skilled	0.7	—	5.2	4.8	5.7	9.8	2.5	4.9
	3.6	—	1.8	5.4	56.9	30.5	1.8	100.0
Unskilled	7.1	2.9	10.5	8.1	13.7	9.8	2.5	11.7
	21.5	1.1	2.2	5.4	49.3	19.4	1.1	100.0
Artisan/ trader	7.1	8.6	5.2	9.7	11.4	13.8	15.0	10.6
	16.5	2.5	0.9	5.0	53.7	16.4	5.0	100.0
Intellectual/ managerial	0.4	5.7	—	1.6	1.2	7.7	—	1.9
	4.5	9.1	—	4.5	36.3	45.6	—	100.0
Other	1.3	2.9	—	3.2	3.8	3.8	12.5	2.9
	11.8	2.9	—	5.9	50.1	23.5	5.8	100.0
Total	100.0	100.0	100.0	100.0	100.0	100.0	100.0	100.0
	12.7	3.1	1.7	5.4	48.2	14.8	2.1	100.0
								(N = 1141)

Source: Hanák, 1978, Table 1, pp. 368–9 (modified with some recalculations).

poor peasants in the minority, except for the very few members from non-agricultural families. If poor peasants (with less than 2.9 ha) are included as semi-proletarians, however, as they were in the Co-operative Research Institute survey, then there is a clear predomi-nance of those of a poor family origin in unskilled manual jobs. On the other hand, there is a clear predominance of those from richer landed peasant families in the skilled trades within agriculture, and this predominance is maintained whether or not agricultural proletarians and semi-proletarians (poor peasants) are taken jointly or together. The picture is not so clear in the case of industrial skilled workers within agriculture. An equal proportion comes from families of both richer peasant and agricultural proletarian origin, while a minority (of those of an agricultural origin) come from poor peasant families. Again, if poor peasant origin is grouped together with agricultural proletarian origin, this group becomes the majority amongst skilled industrial workers in agriculture.

If, on the other hand, we examine 'outflow' figures (row percen-tages) and consider relative mobility chances, then an interesting distinction is revealed between the members of a poor peasant and agricultural proletarian origin. While members from poor peasant families are relatively over-represented in the skilled industrial pro-fessions within agriculture, their representation within unskilled agricultural manual jobs is at a level which we would more or less expect on the basis of the marginal (bottom row). Members from agricultural proletarian families, on the other hand, are clearly over-represented in unskilled agricultural manual occupations, and are represented at the more or less expected level as skilled industrial workers in agriculture. The trend would, therefore, seem to be for the newer, skilled, industrial-type workers to come from an agricultural proletarian and poor peasant background, with a relative over-representation of those from poor peasant families. Those working in jobs requiring no special skill, on the other hand, come from agri-cultural proletarian and poor peasant families also, but with a relative over-representation of those from agricultural proletarian families.

To these findings we might add some of the results of a survey of 4500 co-operative farm members and 500 state farm workers compar-ing respondent's occupation with father's social status in 1938, carried out by the Gödöllö agricultural university in 1973.[13] Lengyel, presenting the study's findings, claims that within the two most clearly agricultural professions on the farm, there is a tendency for members from both middle peasant (over 5.7 ha) families and poor peasant families (0.57–2.9 ha) in 1938 to be concentrated in animal husbandry, while members from small-holding families (2.9–5.7 ha) are concentrated in crop production (1977b, p. 86; Kulcsár and Lengyel, 1979, p. 67). She also notes that these relative concentrations in terms of family origin are maintained when skilled workers in these occupational groups are examined (1977b, p. 86). Kulcsár and Szijjártó add a further dimension to this when they state that landed peasants were slow in encouraging children to go on to further education because there was always work on the farm; the agricultural proletarian families, on the other hand, recognised the need to gain qualifications in the 1950s and they themselves, and their children, became skilled workers in greater numbers. They do not, however, produce figures to support their statement (1980, pp. 92–3). Such a picture is confirmed to some extent by Nándor Pálfalvi, who found that in a producer co-operative farm made up of peasants from both an agricultural estate and middle peasant background, 80–90% of tractor drivers with diplomas came from the poorer peasant background and the Party secretary admitted feeling encouraged by the growing number of children in the local general school from middle peasant families who wanted to join the agricultural co-operative (1975, pp. 105–6). But, again, no full figures are given.

Finally, we should consider whether members' social origin is related to the size and scope of their household plot and thus, by implication, to their degree of commitment to 'family economy'. There are no national figures concerning this question, but Kunszabó's Heréd study divides the membership according to its social status in 1957 and compares the size of household plot animal stock of pigs and cattle in 1962 and 1968 between these groups. The figures (Tables 3.11 and 3.12) reveal an interesting pattern of an initial clear advantage in terms of animal stock for one-time small-holders and middle peasants being mitigated over time so that, by 1968, the situation was considerably changed. Although there had been an overall fall in the number of cows kept by all groups, there was a clear indication that some members from small-holding and middle peasant backgrounds began to specialise in cattle and owned two or three cows if they kept any at all. Members of all other social origins exhibited a tendency to give up cows completely. In the case of pigs, however, the evidence indicates a democratisation in ownership rather than continued inequality or new specialisation. Both the

Table 3.11. Size of household plot animal holding in 1962 by land holding/occupation in 1957

	None		One		Two		Three		Total plots	Total animals	
	Cows	Pigs	Cows	Pigs	Cows	Pigs	Cows	Pigs		Cows	Pigs
0.57–2.9 ha	32	5	10	10	2	24	1	6	45	17	76
3.42–5.7 ha	18	2	4	5	5	17	2	5	29	20	54
6.27 ha+	3	1	3	1	5	6	1	4	12	16	25
Agricultural proletarian[a]	23	7	1	8	1	9	—	1	25	3	29
Co-operative member	15	—	2	9	4	10	1	3	22	13	38
Industrial manual	90	16	8	36	2	42	—	6	100	12	138
Industrial skilled	28	4	—	8	—	14	—	2	28	—	42
Other	27	6	—	7	—	13	—	1	27	—	36
Total	236	41	28	84	19	135	5	28	288	81	438

Note: a. 'Agricultural proletarian' includes those with up to 0.57 ha of land.
Source: Kunszabó, 1970a, Tables 23 and 25, p. 32.

Table 3.12. Size of household plot animal holding in 1968 by land holding/occupation in 1957

	None		One		Two		Three		Total plots	Total animals	
	Cows	Pigs	Cows	Pigs	Cows	Pigs	Cows	Pigs		Cows	Pigs
0.57–2.9 ha	42	7	3	13	—	20	—	5	45	3	68
3.42–5.7 ha	22	3	—	3	3	16	4	7	29	18	56
6.27 ha+	6	1	1	—	3	6	2	5	12	12	27
Agricultural proletarian[a]	25	4	—	8	—	9	—	4	25	—	38
Co-op member	17	—	2	8	3	10	—	4	22	8	40
Industrial manual	97	13	2	35	1	42	—	10	100	4	149
Industrial skilled	28	1	—	8	—	15	—	4	28	—	50
Other	27	2	—	8	—	15	—	2	27	—	44
Total	264	31	8	83	10	133	6	41	288	45	472

Note: a. 'Agricultural proletarian' includes those with up to 0.57 ha of land.
Source: Kunszabó, 1970a, Tables 24 and 26, p. 32.

former landless and the former industrial workers had increased their pig stock while former small-holding peasants had decreased theirs. It is tempting to conclude that government policies introduced since 1968 (see chapter 2) will enhance both these trends. Despite the generous aid for dairy cattle, it is possible that only former middle peasants will specialise in them. Cows are considered very time-consuming, and it is only former middle peasants who have any tradition of keeping them. On the other hand, the increased government aid for pigs and vegetable production, where there is a real possibility of part-time farming, is likely to accelerate the trend towards the democratisation of plots with respect to the member's social origin.

If we assemble all the information presented in this chapter relating to labour market position, the social characteristics associated with occupational groups and the relative importance to members of 'family labour' and 'socialist wage labour', we can characterise the labour side of co-operative farm membership in the following terms. Divisions can be made between an elite, the mass and a non-agricultural, unskilled, manual stratum.

The elite consists of skilled workers employed full-time on the farm. In the case of industrial-type jobs, they tend to have come into agriculture from industry and are likely to be of an agricultural proletarian or poor peasant origin. Because their skills are industrial, they are potentially very mobile, but they are still likely to be part-time farmers on their household plots and, once over 30, their commitment to that plot is likely to increase. Skilled workers in agricultural occupations are, on the other hand, slightly more likely to be older workers, from small-holding or middle peasant backgrounds, who have never left agriculture and who, because of their slightly greater likelihood of owning a plot specialising in cows rather than products more conducive to part-time farming, are likely to be less potentially mobile than workers in industrial-type jobs. Consonant with this trend, workers in animal husbandry, where the work pattern is most conducive to a heavy commitment to the household plot, are rather more likely to be of a middle peasant origin, although members from poor peasant families are also relatively over-represented in this occupational group.

The mass is made up of pensioners, older members generally, widows and married women. Such members rely much more heavily on their household plot and on seasonal share-cropping, although they also work as seasonal wage labour. They are employed mainly in unskilled agricultural tasks in crop production. Their low income from the communal farm and their commitment to their household plot render them immobile on the labour market. Because this discrimination operates overwhelmingly in terms of age and sex, members of all social origins are located in this group, although it must be added that there remains a residual trend for some members from middle peasant families to be committed to the more time-consuming varieties of household plot farming, and this relegates some of them to this immobile group, despite their slightly greater likelihood of possessing a skilled agricultural qualification which renders them relatively mobile between farms.

The non-agricultural unskilled manual stratum within the membership includes workers such as porters, doormen, loaders and office cleaners. These members come from all agricultural backgrounds, although there is a tendency for members from agricultural proletarian families to be relatively over-represented. As a consequence, they combine their low income from wage labour with a tendency to be less heavily committed to the household plot, although these members too benefit from government aided part-time farming on the household plot.

A more complete analysis of the class position of the co-operative farm membership would supplement the above analysis of labour market position, pattern of career experience and influence of social origin with an examination of labour behaviour on the co-operative. It might consider, for example, whether a relationship existed between a group's propensity to take 'industrial action' in the form of, say, a 'go-slow' and the likelihood of members of that occupational group having previously worked in industry, or in terms of the likely degree of their commitment to 'family labour' as a source of supplementary income. Unfortunately, neither my own researches, nor those of Hungarian sociologists, have generated sufficient evidence to do this. We should now therefore direct our focus to the social characteristics of managers within the farm membership before turning to the questions of the nature of managerial control over production generally and labour in particular.[14]

4

Professional management on agricultural producer co-operatives: genesis and social characteristics

In this chapter we flip the coin. The development of two types of labour on co-operative farms and its stratification into the broad groups outlined in the previous chapter were associated with the birth of separate groups of organisers of labour and an increasingly complex internal differentiation amongst them. The chapter considers the emergence of a concept of farm management out of the communal 'family economy' of the early co-operative farms and the growth of a management which became increasingly 'credentialist' (that is, restricted to those holding prescribed minimum educational qualifications) and technologically oriented. It documents this change and then focuses on aspects of the social background and work-situation of the new managers that set them apart from members employed in manual labour. Despite having similar social roots, this new professional management is highly educated, tends to be young because it consists of a new generation performing new jobs, and has a pattern of career mobility generally associated with hierarchical, administrative structures. In future years, when the new managers grow older and the overall membership grows younger as the 'bulge' of the generation which experienced collectivisation retires and dies, the particular form of 'credentialism' associated with managerial posts will ensure that the educational and political exclusiveness of management is maintained beyond any equalisation in age groups. This difference in career prospects between managerial and manual members has implications for their respective work-situations and, ultimately, their class position.

This development is not surprising, but it was not inevitable. Management within collectivised agriculture could have evolved differently. We have already seen that part of the success of estab-

lishing collectivised agriculture between 1959 and 1961 was due to the
readiness of the central authorities to let farms elect their own local
(often middle peasant) presidents[1] (see chapter 1). It is not on the face
of it absurd to picture the smaller co-operatives of the 1960s continuing to be managed by local peasant farmers based around
relatively flexible work groups such as the 'Complex Brigades' (see
chapter 6) and this despite, in fact complementing, the influx of
complex new machinery. Regional research agencies could have
provided the necessary scientific and technological advice without
farms employing large bodies of specialists of their own; indeed, the
evidence suggests that the increased size of farms in the 1970s did not
lead to any increase in their efficiency.[2] After all, many farmers in the
West use substantially the same technology as Hungarian co-
operatives without a university education and with a minimal division of labour even in a marketing and land ownership climate which
is increasingly dominated by 'agri-business' (Burbach and Flynn,
1980, pp. 30–1). More surprising, perhaps, is the insistence on political qualification and preference for technically oriented management, both of which will be shown below, in the period following
Hungary's New Economic Mechanism. It should be stressed that no
attempt will be made in this chapter to discuss the issue of whether
management, with its distinct social experience, actually has interests
of its own which are in any way at odds with those of the rest of the
membership. Nor will it consider whether, simply by virtue of the fact
that its job is to organise and plan production, management necessarily has final control over it. The theory of co-operative democracy
in Hungary combines planning by experts with democratic control
over the executive by the Leadership and other democratic forums.
The question of the reality or formalism of this system of democracy,
that is, of the nature of managerial control over production, must be
shelved until the following chapter.

In the very earliest co-operatives formed immediately after the war
in 1945, the leader of the farm was merely a first amongst equals.[3] He
came from the same background as the membership, that is, predominantly from those who had not owned land before the war and who
had seized it during the course of the land reform; and he performed
the same work as the other members, only taking time off when it was
necessary to go into the local council or county council offices or to
consult with one of the many parties eager, before 1948, to attract the
peasant vote (Kunszabó, 1974a, pp. 76–7). This conception of

egalitarian management changed radically when forced collectivisation began at the end of the 1940s. The typical farm president
became a political cadre of either 'worker' or 'intelligentsia' origin,
placed there by the local Party organisation to ensure that the farm
followed the correct line and delivered the required produce to the
state (Kunszabó, 1974a, p. 78).

After the debacle of 1956 and the introduction of the Agrarian
Theses in 1957, the conception of the co-operative president as head
of farm management changed. The majority of the new presidents
were elected from amongst the membership, usually from amongst
those who had owned land before the land reform and who had gained
a reputation for successful farming (Erdei, 1969, p. 83; Kunszabó,
1974a, p. 82). Although this procedure was not uniform throughout
the country, Kunszabó suggests that this readiness in the first half of
the 1960s to accept successful farmers as co-operative farm presidents
was of fundamental importance in explaining the success of the third
attempt at collectivisation (1974a, p. 83).

During the mid to late 1960s the conception of the co-operative
farm president changed once more. Investment calculations and
choice of farm profile became important management concerns and it
was questioned whether even successful middle peasant common
sense was adequate preparation for presidency. A new generation of
presidents, together with a new stratum of technical experts and
middle management, began to appear. Throughout the 1960s, as a
result of continued state aid, young technicians and experts moved
into the farms in increasing numbers (Erdei, 1969, p. 83).[4] Meanwhile existing presidents and officials also set about acquiring an
education via correspondence courses so that, by 1966, 34% of
presidents, 48% of agronomists, 49% of heads of animal husbandry
and 61% of heads of horticulture had at least middle school qualifications (Fazekas, 1976, p. 176). As a result, from 1968 onwards,
when co-operatives were officially considered autonomous socialist
enterprises, the president of the most dynamically developing farms
would no longer be a former successful peasant but someone with
university or technical college education. This transformation was
not uniformly rapid. Erdei refers to the importance of the new
'manager' type of co-operative president in 1969, but notes that in
1968 52.5% of presidents had originally been uneducated peasants,
17.5% had been workers and artisans, the same percentage had
been qualified agrarian engineers and 12.5% had come from 'other'

backgrounds (1969, p. 84),[5] while, even as late as the early 1970s, 23.3% of the upper leadership had come from political or local government organs (Bognár and Simó, 1975, p. 73). Although the ideal-type transformation in the conception of co-operative farm president might have moved from first amongst equals through political cadre and successful middle peasant to professional manager, there were clearly many exceptions.

This final conception of the farm president and other managers as a distinct group of professionals is encapsulated in the regulation concerning personnel work passed in 1974 (TRHGY, 19/1974 (VII.18) MEM), when the reaction against the liberalism of the New Economic Mechanism was at its height. This regulation, reinforcing a party decree of 1967 which encouraged the development of personnel work in all economic enterprises including agricultural co-operatives, specifically required the appointment of a personnel manager in every farm. While rejecting 'Western bourgeois notions' which had emerged amongst some leaders and introducing the 'triple requirement' for managerial posts of political suitability, necessary academic/political qualifications and management ability, it strongly reinforced the notion of a separate management endowed with specific political and educational qualifications not shared by the ordinary membership. By the early 1970s, the conception of co-operative farm management that had emerged was one of a separate body of carefully chosen professional individuals whose duty it was to organise the efficient running of the farm.

Parallel with this development in the conception of what co-operative farm management should be like and the growth in the average size of the farms, the managerial structure itself mushroomed. The early co-operatives had been divided into only two branches, animal husbandry and crop production, run by the triumvirate of the president, the chief agronomist and the finance manager (bookkeeper). This simple model was implicit in all the regulations concerning the structure of co-operative farms during the 1950s (TRHGY, 18010/1951 (I.20) FM IV; 1070/1953 (XI.12) MT VII). With mechanisation and an extended division of labour, management structure became more complex. Consonant with the co-operatives' new autonomy (see chapter 2), no single structure has been prescribed in government regulations since 1968. However, the scope for variety is not infinite, and the structure adopted by the Red Flag co-operative is not untypical of successful farms. It is presented here to document the management structure on a successful farm, and a farm where there is no additional complication of an ancillary industrial enterprise.

The farm is headed by the president, who bears overall personal responsibility for its performance. He also acts as representative for the co-operative in its dealings with other farms and other outside bodies. Directly responsible to him is the co-operative's lawyer and the personnel manager. Next in the managerial pyramid comes the vice-president, who replaces the president when he is absent and has overall responsibility, after the president, for all matters other than production decisions. It is the production manager, occupying a position one rank further down in the hierarchy, who retains overall charge of these decisions. At the same level in the hierarchy, and completely autonomous from the production manager, comes the finance manager (bookkeeper), who is in overall charge of financial matters and who heads a department made up of all those concerned with drawing up farm plans, obtaining credits, maintaining accounts and paying wages and social benefits. Directly responsible to the production manager are the heads of the four main branches of the farm and its three subsidiary branches. Thus, subordinate to the production manager there is an overall head of crop production, an overall head of horticulture and an overall head of the technical branch whose role is to provide and maintain machinery; there are also the heads of the three subsidiary branches: construction, transport and supplies.

Each of these branches is then further subdivided. Crop production takes place in each of the three villages on whose land the farm operates, and each village is a distinct unit with its own head. Animal husbandry is also split into three sub-branches, poultry, pigs and cattle, each of which is further subdivided into two or more sites, depending on what each animal is used for, beef or dairy, for example, and each of these is headed by a unit chief. Horticulture is divided into two branches, the nursery and the glasshouse, while the technical branch is divided into a maintenance and repair division. Each of these branches is run by unit managers who bear individual responsibility for the section which they run and who take no part in the productive activity itself. The labour force in each of these sections is then further divided into as many brigades as is necessary, each with a brigade leader whose duties are equivalent to those of a foreman in industry.

The managerial structure of a successful co-operative farm was clearly rather extensive by the mid 1970s. Seventy-four jobs on the Red Flag co-operative, out of a total of 1300 active members and employees, were full-time, direct supervisors of production. A further 33 worked in administration and 101 performed technical jobs of some description. Such a preponderance of managerial, technical and administrative staff is not unique to a successful farm like the Red Flag co-operative. Nationally these figures are replicated. By 1974, 65 113 people were employed in the management and administration of co-operative farms (TOT 1976, p. 72),[6] 11% of the total membership plus employees. This represents a 57% increase on the number employed in such tasks in 1967 (Fazekas, 1976, p. 238) and, when it is recalled that the number of individual co-operative farms dropped by 46% during this same period (Appendix I), indicates a very considerable concentration in the weight of these occupational strata within each farm. Mechanisation, economic autonomy and economies of scale might have saved on the demand for manual labour, but they also created a vast administration within the average co-operative farm.

The work-situation of this new professional management, and of the administrative workers, is necessarily different from that of the people who execute manual production tasks on the farm, and this in itself is of significance for management–labour relations. It is also possible that those who occupy these managerial posts have a different career experience from those who work as manual labour, and evidence from a variety of sources suggests that this is the case. For one thing, upper management of co-operative farms has very different educational qualifications from the ordinary membership. This might seem natural, but the issues are not straightforward for all that. What, after all, is the nature of these educational qualifications (we shall see that many consist of political education in marxism-leninism), and how great a superiority in the making of farming decisions does even a technical education give management over the membership (members apparently adapt well to the complex technology of modern farming which they are permitted to use on their household plots)? These educational qualifications require further examination.

Throughout the period of collectivised agriculture, the number of presidents and specialists possessing higher educational qualifications has grown. In 1955, only 1.1% of co-operative farm presi-

Table 4.1 *Growth in educational qualifications of agricultural producer co-operative management (per cent)*

	Higher	Middle	Basic
President and vice-president			
1960	4.0	7.3	41.8
1970	18.3	39.1	32.3
1974	43.4	31.5	20.3
Specialist management			
1960	28.0	36.9	31.2
1970	72.0	23.6	3.6
1974	75.2	21.5	2.7
Brigade leaders			
1960	0.2	1.8	26.3
1970	4.4	16.8	24.8
1974	7.7	25.4	25.2

Source: Gy. Nagy, 1976, p. 16.

dents had any sort of higher educational qualification and, by 1958, this figure had increased to only 2.9% (Fazekas, 1976, p. 117). In 1960, university or equivalent educated members still comprised only 4% of the total; but by 1970 they had quadrupled in significance to represent 18.3% of all presidents, as Table 4.1 shows, and, by 1974, they had increased still further to 43.3% of all presidents. Such a sudden rise in only four years is unlikely to have been the result of a wholesale re-election of a new generation of qualified management.[7] It may simply be due to existing presidents acquiring higher educational qualifications via correspondence courses in anticipation of the obligatory minimum qualifications for management introduced in 1977, although, as we shall see, these do not apply to presidents. An alternative explanation for this sudden rise might be in terms of the equally sudden acceleration of the rate of co-operative farm mergers in the early 1970s (see Appendix I; Swain, 1981). This would posit a scenario in which, after the merger, the more highly qualified of the two previous presidents took control of the new, enlarged farm, and the less qualified, perhaps middle peasant, president was given a token post in the new management structure. Educational qualification would seem a quite reasonable ground on which to choose

Table 4.2 *Educational qualifications of co-operative farm management (percentage distribution)*

| | 1972 | | | |
	8 years' General or less	Middle school/ technical school	University/ Technical college	Total
President	43.0	25.2	31.8	100.0
Chief agronomist	—	10.2	89.8	100.0
Finance manager (bookkeeper)	24.1	64.4	11.5	100.0
All higher management	23.0	33.6	43.4	100.0
Middle management	36.7	31.4	31.9	100.0
Chairman of supervisory committee	84.5	6.9	8.6	100.0
	1970			
	General school	Middle school	Higher education	Total
Unit managers	45.7	34.9	19.4	100.0
Brigade leaders	68.7	22.8	8.5	100.0

Sources: Bognár and Simó, 1975, p. 86, and Meszticzky, 1975, pp. 315 and 317.

between two former presidents, and certainly this is what happened on the Red Flag and Great October co-operatives, and it was the fate of the *gazdálkodó* president in Tázlár (Hann, 1980, pp. 126–38).

At the same time, the number of experts with higher educational qualifications increased from 28.0% in 1960 to 72% in 1970 and 75.2% in 1974.[8] Figures collected by Bognár and Simó relating to 1972, that is to a date before the end of the accelerated rate of mergers in the early 1970s, provide more detail (Table 4.2). The relatively poor performance of co-operative farm presidents is clearly associated with the peasant origin of many of their number; however, even this is considerably in advance of the educational level of the ordinary membership. Bognár and Simó do not give figures for the member-ship as a whole, nor are they available elsewhere; however, they can be assumed to lie somewhere between those of the brigade leaders and the chairman of the supervisory committee (see chapter 5). Brigade leaders are, perhaps, rather more likely than the average member to possess some technical school qualifications, while the chairman of the supervisory committee is usually a respected elder co-operative member, and therefore less likely than the average to possess paper qualifications. In the Soviet Union too, despite a drive to improve educational standards within management in 1955, the level of education at the brigade level remains low (Stuart, 1971, pp. 133–6). It should also be noted that the Hungarian finance manager is relatively underqualified by comparison with his production manager counterpart. Part of an explanation for this phenomenon will become apparent when we look at another dimension on which co-operative farm management differs from the membership, namely age. At this stage, however, it should be noted that if the sudden increase in educational qualifications of co-operative farm presidents reflects the farms' take-over by highly qualified managers, then these managers are likely to come from technologically oriented pro-duction, rather than financial, branches.

Before considering the question of age, however, it is appropriate at this stage to note that women are hardly represented at all in the upper reaches of the co-operative farm. Lengyel gives the following figures for the percentage of women at various levels of management in agricultural producer co-operatives. At the A leadership category, only 8.4% are women and at the president level only 0.6% (eight in all) are women; while at the B level, 7.7% are women, 3.3% at head of department level (Lengyel, 1979, p. 47). She also indicates that women's earnings in agricultural management are 10–15% lower than those of men (1979, p. 47) and suggests that women with technical qualifications are persuaded to change careers and enter bookkeeping and administrative branches (1979, p. 48). Stuart shows that the situation is very similar in the Soviet Union. Women are relatively underrepresented at all but the lowest levels of manage-ment and, in 1957, only 1.3% of kolkhoz chairmen in the Soviet Union were women (1971, pp. 129–30). Management on collective farms in both Hungary and the Soviet Union is very much a man's world.

Although, as we have seen (chapter 3), the average age of members overall has ceased to climb and is beginning to drop, there remains a very obvious discrepancy between the average age of those involved in management and the rest of the membership, and this is especially true of those who are heads of production aspects of management. Recent figures taken from a Co-operative Research Institute publication can be used as a basic source of information on this point, but we should note first that in 1964, while 78% of the farm membership was aged over 40, as many as 73% of engineers and technicians were under 40 (Fazekas, 1976, p. 176). Table 4.3 shows the situation as it had developed by the early 1970s. Within the overall age discrepancy, a number of further factors must be noted. First, as might be expected for such a prestigious post, co-operative farm presidents tend to be older than other managers. Second, chief agronomists are exceptionally young, 65.4% of them being under 40 years of age. Middle management too is very young, and the growth of both these strata clearly reflects the novelty of the posts themselves. Middle management posts especially did not exist prior to the 1960s and since such tasks imply a degree of specialised knowledge, it is hardly surprising that the posts were filled by new graduates.

Financial management, by contrast, is clearly older, as well as less qualified, than production management. This might simply reflect inertia within the management hierarchy, that is, existing members were simply not replaced so that the existing finance manager was retained, while the new production posts were filled with new blood. On the other hand, the chief agronomist was also part of the original management triumvirate of the 1950s, and older chief agronomists have clearly been replaced by more highly qualified juniors. A more plausible explanation might be in terms of the degree of seriousness, or lack of it, with which the economic orientation of the New Economic Mechanism era was taken. Either way, it is clear that the younger and more highly qualified members of the co-operative farm management are employed in production and technological branches of the farm. These figures also indicate that at the lowest levels of management, where experience rather than educational qualification is perhaps at more of a premium, and where it is more likely that members might have been promoted through the ranks, the average age rises again quite considerably. This fact, plus the traditional deference of peasant farmers and agricultural labourers to their superiors, might help explain the relative absence of tension between the work force and these brash young technocrats.

Table 4.3 *Age distribution of co-operative farm management and membership (per cent)*

	Age in years					
	−30	31–40	41–50	51–60	60+	Total
Management and administration	32.9	23.0	28.8	12.7	2.6	100.0
President	2.5	20.5	55.7	19.3	2.0	100.0
Chief agronomist	27.4	38.0	27.0	6.9	0.7	100.0
Finance manager (bookkeeper)	12.7	39.2	36.1	11.5	0.5	100.0
Middle management (chief engineers, heads of animal husbandry, etc.)	54.9	21.9	17.4	5.1	0.7	100.0
Unit manager	19.9	23.9	37.2	15.8	3.3	100.0
Brigade leader	16.4	18.3	38.8	22.0	4.5	100.0
	−26	27–39	40–49	50–59	60+	Total
Membership including pensioners	9.1	14.8	16.5	15.4	44.2	100.0
Membership excluding pensioners	14.6	23.5	25.5	21.3	15.1	100.0

Sources: Meszticzky, 1975, pp. 284–317, and TOT 1976, p. 68.

In addition to their higher educational qualifications and greater youth, co-operative farm managers are very mobile between farms. In this respect, they resemble the 'elite' of skilled workers amongst the co-operative's manual membership rather than the more numerous 'immobile' component. The high job mobility of co-operative farm management and especially its middle echelons is clear from Table 4.4, based on information collected by Meszticzky. A comparison of Table 4.4 with Table 3.9 in the previous chapter might be taken to indicate that mobility within the manual membership, even amongst these skilled workers, is less than that within management. Table 3.9 shows that 58.0% of workers in industrial-type jobs on co-operative

Table 4.4 *Career mobility of co-operative farm management (percentage distribution)*

	Years spent in present post				
	−2	2–5[a]	6–10[a]	11–20	21+
			1970		
President	15.6	30.8	34.2	18.0	1.4
Chief agronomist	30.4	35.1	26.4	7.8	0.3
Finance manager (bookkeeper)	22.8	27.1	33.6	15.6	0.9
Middle management (chief engineer,[b]	42.9	37.9	15.3	3.7	0.2
head of animal husbandry, etc.)[c]	13.7	34.7	26.1	20.7	5.1
			1973		
President	8.8	26.5	31.5	31.3	1.9
Chief agronomist	11.7	37.5	30.7	18.9	1.2
Finance manager (bookkeeper)	9.5	25.6	26.7	37.1	1.8

Note: Co-operative farm presidents are elected for a five year term.
a. For chief agronomists the figures refer to 2–4 years and 5–10 years.
b. Years in present post.
c. Years in a given field.
Source: Meszticzky, 1975, pp. 289, 303, 309 and 313.

farms joined their present farm between 1967 and 1972. This is a higher percentage than that of agronomists and middle managers joining their farms in the five years preceding 1970, but rather less, in the case of chief agronomists, than the percentage who joined in the five years preceding 1973. Now it is simply unclear whether it is more meaningful to compare workers in the five years preceding 1972 with management in the years preceding 1970 or 1973. The latter is closer temporally, but then non-agricultural jobs on the co-operatives developed very dramatically between 1967 and 1972 with the expansion of ancillary enterprises (see chapter 5) and this perhaps inflated artificially the number of 'mobile' workers at this period. The increase in management and administrative posts, on the other hand, began rather earlier.[9]

More important, in the case of management, is the fact that such job mobility is associated with career mobility progressing ever higher up the managerial pyramid. This is evident from the correspondence in Table 4.3 between the structure of the management hierarchy and the age distribution of the co-operative farm management. Such career mobility is clearly not available to even the 'elite' workers, or at least to only very few of them. Despite the generous provision for adult education in Hungary, the chances of the average co-operative member going on to obtain a university degree in agronomy or agricultural economics are not great, and the number of possible posts as brigade leader, which are accessible, is necessarily more restricted than the supply of labour. Even the most mobile of the co-operative farm membership, then, faces a very different market of labour opportunity from the new co-operative farm management. On the other hand, if we compare 1970 with 1973 in Table 4.4, there does appear to have been a degree of consolidation since the initial influx of new talent and this might place certain restrictions on the openness of the career structure.

This picture of a greatly expanded managerial structure with access restricted to those with a specific social experience clearly relates to the present, or more precisely to the middle 1970s when the studies cited were carried out. As the new occupations become less new and the incumbents grow older, and as the 'bulge' of original co-operative members retires or dies, a certain equalisation will occur in the age discrepancy between management and manual membership. As we have seen, there has already been considerable equalisation since the 1964 ratio cited above. It might be argued that this will diminish the distinctiveness of management from manual member. It is undoubtedly the case that ages will tend to equalise, but the different pattern of career mobility will remain and the 'credentialism' which, as we shall see, has been introduced into the managerial structure in recent years will ensure that the difference in social experience between manual membership and management will continue and that severe impediments will remain on the former graduating through the ranks to become the latter. The credentials needed for management should be considered in more detail.

During the early to mid 1970s, farms in the vanguard of co-operative development, such as the Red Flag and May 1st co-operatives, were already operating a system of minimum qualification conditions for certain managerial posts. In 1977, such compulsory minimum qualifications were established by government regulation (TRHGY, 31/1977 (XI.22) MEM). The regulations did not apply to those aged over 50,[10] and those who were already in a job where minimum regulations were introduced and who did not fulfil the requirements were given two years to acquire them. The requirements extended throughout management, from vice-president down to brigade leader, and it is instructive to cite some examples since they reflect a mixture of both political and academic qualifications. The full regulations are quite complex, however, and vary according to the economic category to which the farm belongs, the larger farms having more stringent requirements.

For the general vice-president, the obligatory qualifications introduced in 1977 were: university or technical college higher education; middle to upper level political education (that is attendance at a course or evening class session in marxism-leninism); and five years of experience. A chief agronomist, in charge of a whole branch of production, was required to have: a university or equivalent qualification in the relevant field of learning; middle level political qualifications; and five years' experience. Qualifications for the finance manager were analogous, although they allowed an alternative of lower academic qualification and a longer period of experience, much as might be expected from their generally greater age and lower educational achievements. At the lower levels of management, unit managers and brigade leaders either had to have a technical school qualification and three years' experience, or five years' experience, a completed middle school education and a relevant skill qualification obtained by attending a recognised course.

Such compulsory educational requirements are strict and, especially at the upper level of management, very demanding. A university degree is almost essential if a newcomer is to begin a career of co-operative farm management on either the production or financial side; and, without spending a period at this level of management, it is difficult to see how an individual might acquire the experience necessary to become a president, even though existing presidents are specifically excluded from this regulation. Promotion through the ranks from ordinary membership to management would seem to be excluded as a future possibility. While skilled workers might be able to work their way through to the lowest levels of management, it is unlikely that they would be in a position to obtain a university degree and thus proceed to the top. The difference in social background and experience between farm management and the manual membership is likely to be reinforced in future years.

The information given above on educational qualifications, age and career mobility, then, shows that management has developed as a distinct function on co-operative farms and that managers enjoy a distinct social background and experience which differs from that of the manual membership. This is not to say that management has wildly different social origins from the rest of the membership. This is far from the case. Bognár and Simó show that two thirds of co-operative management comes from a family which was involved in some way in agricultural production, as do 80% of co-operative farm presidents (1975, p. 39), and such a general identity of origin is scarcely surprising in a country where so many worked on the land until comparatively recently. On the other hand, in a study of co-operative farm presidents only, Simó found that, while they were generally more likely to be of small-holder or middle peasant origin than other managers (Simó, 1975, pp. 26–7) because of the compromise introduced during collectivisation in the 1960s, those with the best academic qualifications, and therefore those with the best chances of surviving in the 'credentialist' agriculture of the future were those whose parents had either had no land prior to collectivisation or had been poor peasants (Simó, 1975, p. 30). Thus, there is some indication that, whilst the elite positions within the co-operative farm's agricultural manual labour force belong to those with a landed background, top positions within farm management, like those within the farm's industrial manual labour force, are increasingly being occupied by those with a background in poor peasant agriculture who had needed to gain academic or industrial qualifications in order to succeed within collectivised agriculture at all.

The picture of a young, highly educated, highly mobile, 'credentialist' and technically, rather than financially, oriented management must be modified in one respect, however. Political criteria may not be as important in the 1970s as they were in the 1950s when presidents were primarily political cadres, but they still carry weight. Although presidents have on average lower academic qualifications than management as a whole, they are rather more likely than their colleagues to have completed a course of political education.[11] Such a course has been completed by 55.1% of farm presidents, compared with an average for management generally of 44.8% and an average for chief agronomists of 39.8% (Bognár and Simó, 1975, p. 96). One implication of this finding is that young agronomists will have to complete a course of political education in their middle age before they can be promoted further to president.

More important perhaps than the requirement of political education for final success in a management career is the nature of the work performed by personnel managers. This differs from the work of their Western counterparts only in terms of its overtly political aspects. The manager who, as we have seen, is directly responsible to the farm president keeps files on every individual employed in management and all other members of the farm who have a university or similar qualification. These files include details such as 'general moral behaviour' and visits made abroad in addition to a general political record and an evaluation of job performance. Management is assessed for promotion every three years on the basis of the 'triple requirement' of political suitability, professional expertise and management ability. On these occasions, in the case of upper management, the individual is confronted at a Leadership meeting (see chapter 5) with the official verdict on his past performance. While all three aspects of the 'triple requirement' are important, the first is openly admitted[12] to be the *sine qua non* of an individual's career in management. If management is becoming increasingly meritocratic and technocratic, it is clearly still a right-thinking and a right-acting one.

PART III

MANAGERIAL CONTROL IN AGRICULTURE

5

Co-operative management's autonomy

The aim of this chapter is to examine the constraints under which co-operative farm management operates so as to isolate the areas where it enjoys real autonomy. Labour in this chapter becomes again an economic category, a factor of production, a 'force of production' which management may, or may not, be in a position to control. The chapter falls into four sections: first, the relationship between the co-operative and the organs of local government with respect to economic planning is considered; second, the role of the Party machine within this relationship is examined; third, the areas in which management has scope for autonomous economic decision-making are delimited; and, fourth, the institutions of co-operative democracy are described and their performance evaluated. All four steps are necessary to establish who it is that exercises economic control on co-operative farms and the constraints, both from above and below, under which they operate.

The first question concerns the way in which plans received by the ministry are transmitted to individual co-operative farms. There is no need to repeat here the outline of the planning process, from national plan conception by the central planners to the receipt by the ministry of plan targets, presented in the introduction. The Ministry of Agriculture and Food Supply enjoys no special status in this respect. But agriculture does have some unique features which require comment. Unlike the situation in Hungarian industry where, until the most recent changes at least, oligopoly has reigned (Radice, 1981, p. 117) with each ministry being responsible for a handful of mammoth enterprises, in agriculture there is no oligopoly. The Ministry of Agriculture and Food Supply was responsible in 1980 for 1338 co-operative farms and over 130 state farms, almost as many as

133

the total number of industrial enterprises, state or co-operative, in the country (MSZS, 1981, p. 113). The minister cannot exercise control simply by chatting informally to the heads of key enterprises as is possible in state industry (Laky, 1976; 1979). At the centre, a more formal structure for suggestions is required; while, at the local level, the economic arms of the local government and Party machines come into their own.

In the 1950s, agricultural planning in Hungary had been quite straightforward and pyramidal in structure. Quotas for compulsory deliveries were passed down to the county level, which broke them down and passed them on to the district level, which broke them down and passed them on to the individual farms. The last steps in this process were performed by the agricultural departments of the local authorities at both county and district level, under the supervision of the respective local Party organisation. This sort of structure is still in effect in both the Soviet Union (Nove, 1980, p. 133; Stuart, 1972, p. 112) and, within the commune system, in China (Grays, 1982, pp. 175–7). Farms receive quotas in physical units which they are expected to meet. The events of 1956 and Kádár's honouring of the Nagy government's abolition of compulsory deliveries, however, made such a system of direct, hierarchical dependence unworkable in Hungary. The final level of compulsion disappeared. The district level, whether state or Party, no longer had legal authority to tell farms in its district what to produce.

Between 1957 and 1961, this caused some problems for agricultural planners and, despite continued interference from the local organs, farms tended to draw up too many contracts for too small an acreage with the representatives of state companies (Fazekas, 1976, pp. 172–4). Between 1961 and 1964, therefore, the agricultural departments of the district councils co-ordinated the contracts between enterprises and co-operatives. This change was presented as a form of help for inexperienced co-operative leaders but, in practice, operated as a form of subordination of the farms to local government, for the district council possessed crucial forms of economic leverage in that it controlled the supply of investment funds, technology and credits to the farms. Kunszabó describes this period as one of constant struggle between the farms and the district council and, responding to pressure from below, between the district and county councils (Kunszabó, 1970c, p. 265).

By 1965, it was recognised that this limitation on co-operative independence was having adverse and contradictory effects (Fazekas, 1976, p. 173; Keserű, 1966) and, from that year on, farms were free to make their own contracts with purchasing enterprises direct, without the intervention of the district council (Fazekas, 1976, p. 174). Henceforth, the government resigned itself to the spirit of the New Economic Mechanism which would follow in 1968 and developed forms of indirect control in agriculture. Indeed, after the introduction of the New Economic Mechanism, the local councils initially relinquished all control over investment. As we shall see below, originally the only arbiter of investment under the New Economic Mechanism was the fund giving body, the Hungarian National Bank, which made its judgement on financial criteria alone (TRHGY, 1/1967 (XII.1) OT–PM–MEM).

Indirect control of agricultural planning took the form of more or less yearly ordinances passed jointly by the Ministry of Agriculture and Food Supply and the Ministry of Finance. These specified, in effect, the contours of the artificial market environment in which the farms were to operate as profit maximisers. Price support, preferential terms for investment and so on were offered for the sorts of projects given priority by Party/government policy.[1] The formal role of the county and district administration was thus considerably reduced. With the new emphasis on market forces, the district administration was appointed as the body to institute the financial restructuring (receivership) of farms that could no longer meet their financial obligations (TRHGY, 29/1968 (X.25) PM–MEM; 32/1972 (XI.1) PM), and, from 1969 onwards, it re-acquired an increasing role in vetting, but not directing or initiating, investments, as we shall see below. But, further to this, the local organs simply advise and suggest to farms that their production plans really ought to follow government policy.

The role of the county and district organs of local administration, then, has gradually been reduced from one of active co-ordinator of all economic activity in the early 1960s, via a short-lived period of official impotence in the first years of the New Economic Mechanism, to one where their official role is to put moral pressure on farms within their area to follow official policy, but where, in addition, they have a certain amount of, albeit negative, economic power in the form of sanctioning investments.

We have so far referred to the county and district organs of local government because these are the bodies in which such powers as exist are formally vested. But, at this level, the role of the local Party organs is of considerable importance, although they have no constitutional authority. Merényi and Simon, in fact, stress that political control of the co-operatives is of central importance precisely because the local councils have so few powers of direction and control (1979, pp. 66–7). Written information on the Party's economic intervention in Hungary is generally hard to come by, but the abolition in the 1970s of the district level in local government and the consequent lack of symmetry between the organisational structures of the Party and local government apparatuses gave rise to some unusually frank discussion in Party journals. This change meant that the 'supervisory organ' of the agricultural producer co-operative, the body to which farms are legally responsible, became the agricultural department of the county, rather than the district, council.

The local Party apparatus, at both the county and district levels, operates similarly to the Party at a governmental level. It decides the basic policy outlines which are then adopted by the local government administration and which are binding on Party members; but it intervenes directly, and extra-constitutionally, in specific economic issues only in times of crisis. Under normal conditions, it relies for the implementation of these policies on its indirect control of certain key personnel, on the loyalty of its membership within the farms' economic leadership (who are bound by the Party line) and on a network of informal ties and interdependencies. It does not sully its hand with day-to-day economic policy; and neither does the Party committee within the farm.

Although it is the agricultural department of the county council which formally produces the 'guiding principles' for policy in that county, which all farms are pressed to follow, in practice, such directives are usually born in the Economic Secretariat of the county Party committee's Executive Committee. The county Party does not have a large independent apparatus which it can use to draw up these policy goals, but the resources of the county's agricultural department and the regional Producer Co-operative Union are at its disposal. In reality, these bodies are not separate (they are often in the same building) and the inspiration for policy direction comes from the Party. Although the district level of local government is no longer the 'supervisory organ' of farms in its area, district officers have been maintained (they are simply no longer legally responsible for the co-operatives in their area) and Horváth reports a high degree of integration between the Party district committee and the district agricultural office. The president of the district office always attends the district Party political committee and Executive Committee meetings (J. Horváth, 1976, p. 25). Similarly, group leaders of the Party committee and departmental heads of the district offices are both present at each other's group and departmental meetings (J. Horváth, 1976, p. 26). The independence of the two hierarchies is clearly minimal, but what does this imply about their ability to transmit instructions to the co-operative farm?

In addition to formulating in practice the 'guiding principles' which co-operatives and other economic agents in the county are encouraged to follow, the Political Committee of the county Party also issues an 'action programme' in line with Central Committee directives. The contents of this policy are binding on the Party organs within the county apparatus's sphere of authority and on all Party members working in economic and local government administration (Závondi, 1976, p. 29). And, since all Party members must give a report on their actions, the district Party organisation requires both village, industrial and co-operative Party committees within the district to report, especially on their economic policy and mass political work (I. Szabó, 1976, pp. 67–9). But this applies to Party members only. The only way that the local Party/government apparatus can apply sanctions constitutionally to ensure compliance with the 'guiding principles', if the farm president is not himself a Party member, is by its indirect control of appointments. Needless to say, at times of crisis, such constitutional niceties can be ignored, as they regularly were both during the period of co-operative farm formation and during the spate of farm mergers in the middle of the 1960s and early 1970s – and still are in cases of possible financial misconduct. On such exceptional occasions, the Party organisation, county or district depending on the severity of the case, sends out its men to form a new co-operative or convince the members that a merger is in everyone's interest (Pálfalvi, 1975, pp. 56–7, 100–2), or orders the offending president to resign (Kunszabó, 1978, pp. 5–6). When there is no need to go beyond its constitutional authority, the local Party/government apparatus has rather limited powers even in respect of personnel.

There is no *nomenklatura* in Hungary of the Soviet type.[2] The Party has no formal authority to control appointments directly, except those within the Party machine. Great importance is attached to personnel work, as we have already seen, but if informal pressure does not work, then the Party's power is relatively limited. The only individual whose appointment it can officially veto is the farm president, and then it can do no more than veto a candidate and make suggestions for an alternative, suggestions which will not necessarily be accepted by the farm membership. Each president must possess a 'certificate of trustworthiness' which is given by the President of the county council, after it has been sanctioned by the personnel department of the county Party committee; and the local authority/Party apparatus can refuse to issue such a certificate to individuals whom it does not want elected. The ultimate veto lies with the Party, but it is negative control by veto, not positive intervention. Its influence can be weak, as we shall see when we turn to consider the functioning of co-operative democracy and the members' 'ultimate sanction'.

Although the Party's formal right of veto only exists in relation to the president, at the May 1st co-operative the practice was for all candidates for co-operative farm office to be vetted by the county Party committee before election. Thus, while electoral theory allows for there to be more candidates than posts, and even allows for new candidates to be added to the list at a General Meeting itself if 50% of the meeting agree, the list generally consists of individuals who have already been vetted by the local Party. The indications at the May 1st co-operative were that this system of control over appointments worked satisfactorily for the Party; but Merényi and Simon, surveying the role of the Party generally, imply that the work of the local Party organs could be improved considerably (1979, pp. 102–3).

A further means by which non-constitutional influence can be brought to bear by the local government/Party organisation is simply by informal contacts. There are strong personal ties between co-operative management, especially co-operative presidents, and local party and government organisations. Bognár and Simó found that 29.0% of co-operative presidents had some sort of external post in either Party, local government or local co-operative council committees, 13.1% being members of the local council (1975, p. 126). When attending such meetings, the co-operative farm leadership is clearly susceptible to pressure from Party and other colleagues; on the other hand, it is also in a position to exert pressure itself. More important, perhaps, is the fact that the mere presence of an individual on both Party and co-operative leaderships indicates that the individual is not unacceptable to either, and is therefore likely to be the sort of individual who takes note of the 'guiding principles'.

The Party organisation within the farm itself exercises even less control. There is no single established pattern for Party behaviour at this level. Party secretaries usually attend Leadership (see below) meetings and encourage Party members within the Leadership to make decisions in line with Party policy. They also receive a report from the economic leadership on the farm describing future policy, irrespective of whether or not the leaders are Party members. The farm Party leadership debates these and passes the information up to the district Party apparatus and so on back up the hierarchy (Tiboldi, 1976, pp. 75–6). Farm Party groups are encouraged to create their own 'action programme' for the farm, which again consists mainly of ensuring that the farm's development strategy is more or less in line with government, that is Party, policy. It is normal practice for all important issues to be debated by the Party organisation, or a joint Party and Leadership meeting first, before being presented to the membership at a General Meeting (Pálfalvi, 1975, p. 103; also at Red Flag and May 1st co-operatives). This ensures that Party members are forewarned of the policy which they should be supporting in the unlikely instance of any real debate taking place.

However, even at the level of the Party farm committee, the official instructions are for the political cadres not to get involved in day-to-day economic decisions. Their role is to focus on political questions and to make sure that the right personnel are appointed. They are specifically instructed not to make economic decisions and to restrict themselves simply to ensuring that plans are more or less in line with the national plan, that they are realisable and that the membership has been properly consulted (Lantos, 1976, p. 20). From the sorts of economic information which Tiboldi lists as being those required by Party organs within the farm, two things are clear about these groups: first, they have a relatively low level of economic sophistication; second, they are interested primarily in the question of the ratio of funds being devoted to development and consumption respectively (1976, p. 76). So long as the farm does not appear to be squandering its assets and totally ignoring government policy, the Party committee is satisfied. It is not required to be interested in any detail in how the moneys in the various co-operative funds are spent; and to the extent that it is interested (because of the implicit imperative not to waste funds) it is likely to share management's values and be unwilling to see the co-operative pay excessive and unnecessary taxes. (The significance of this will become apparent in chapter 6.)

The Party organisation, then, at the local district level and within the farm, has rather limited control of economic decisions. It has the final say in matters of personnel, and it has the power to influence management towards certain preferred policies. But, unless a situation arrives that can plausibly be viewed as a crisis, the Party does not intervene. Party policy is to allow farm management considerable autonomy in day-to-day economic policy, but how real is that autonomy in relation to the economic environment?

Unlike those in China and the Soviet Union, Hungarian agricultural co-operatives enjoy some real autonomy in their economic planning, and it is an autonomy which might appear considerably greater than that enjoyed by Hungarian state enterprises. Whilst in the Soviet Union, despite the fact that since 1955 plans have only specified delivery obligations and not the structure of production itself (Nove, 1969, p. 335), collective farms are still subjected to such close control by local authority and Party organs that they cannot undertake reorganisation of their own volition (Zotova and Novikov, 1969, p. 214); and in China, Wheelwright and McFarlane report that the plan as passed by the local planning bodies sets the pattern of output and restricts the freedom of the commune and work teams within it to choose relative crop outputs (1970, pp. 50–1); in Hungary, the situation is rather different. The co-operative's autonomy of action regarding the method of plan fulfilment is not restricted to a single product or to a narrow product range. In consequence, the co-operative might be seen to possess greater autonomy of action with regard to investment and the acquisition of capital goods than the state enterprise. On the other hand, it could be countered that co-operative farm management has rather less autonomy of action in respect of labour because, unlike the industrial enterprise, the co-operative farm has a relatively tied labour force, for whom it is under a certain moral obligation to find employment. The co-operative is often the only employer in an area, its original members were put under considerable social and political pressure to join and the pensions it offers are rather low (Donáth, 1977a, p. 121). Thus, the position of agricultural producer co-operatives might appear to be the reverse in some ways of that of state enterprises. In fact, however, this is not the case. The obligation on the co-operative leadership to provide employment is not as strong as it might appear and, while the co-operative leadership does have somewhat more autonomy from government concerning production decisions, freedom is far from complete, and, once the investment market is entered, as it inevitably will be, the direction of that investment is administered by central government in ways similar to those employed in industry. Although they are considerably less controlled than Soviet or Chinese farms, the greater degree of autonomy that Hungarian agricultural producer co-operatives enjoy over state industrial enterprises can be exaggerated.

The duty of the co-operative to provide employment for its entire membership is a matter of genuine concern for the farm leadership. However, this concern is unimportant for the relative degrees of freedom which management experiences with regard to labour and capital for two reasons. First, because of household plots, co-operatives do not experience an overwhelming pressure from their membership to find jobs for them. The plot can act as a safety net for all members who are not employed, or only seasonally employed, on the farm. It can thus offer the farm a useful reserve of labour which can be drawn into production when necessary. A number of measures have been taken to increase household plot benefits for members who might be expected to work least regularly on the farm, in order to reinforce this safety net aspect of the household plot. Thus, widows and pensioners are charged less, and often nothing, by the co-operative for ploughing and other services offered to the household plot, while the state exempts them from income tax payable on its marketed produce (TRHGY, 51/1967 (XI.24) Korm 3§(b); 36/1976 (X.17) MT 2§(a)).

Second, we can examine the behaviour of co-operatives when setting up ancillary industrial or processing enterprises, whose express purpose was to help provide year-round employment for the farm membership, especially in more remote areas where there was no local source of alternative employment (Fehér, 1970, p. 100). The burgeoning of non-agricultural activities on co-operative farms between 1968 and 1971, and their subsequent restriction and vilification for poaching labour from industry, cannot be considered in detail here. However, an outline account of the events will be presented, since they are relevant to co-operative farm autonomy in respect of both labour and capital.

Ancillary enterprises were not in fact new to agricultural co-operatives in 1968. Both the 1951 and the 1959 regulations concerning agricultural producer co-operatives allowed a certain amount of processing or servicing activity to take place (TRHGY, 18.010/1951 FM I.15; 1959 évi tvr 7, 40§); until 1966, however, such initiatives were insignificant economically and only 1% of the farm membership nationally took part in them (Fazekas, 1976, p. 190). In 1966 and 1967, the regulations surrounding such enterprises were relaxed, permitting diversification into areas only marginally related to agricultural production.[3] This move has parallels in both the Soviet Union and China where kolkhozy, sovkhozy, communes and production brigades have all been encouraged to set up a range of non-agricultural plants (Aitov, 1969, p. 129; Grays, 1982, pp. 162–3 and 171; Nove, 1978, p. 11).

Because agricultural producer prices were still low, and profit margins from agriculture were small (M. Hegedűs, 1971; Szabóné Medgyesi, 1976), Hungarian farms immediately took advantage of this possibility of moving into profitable areas of production, and capitalised on their lower taxation of labour and less rigid taxation of incomes to offer higher wages than could be paid in equivalent branches of state industry. Consequently, between 1968 and 1970 there was a 113% increase in processing activities on co-operative farms, a 165% increase in construction, a 110% increase in other industrial activities and a 47% increase in the direct sale of produce via the farm's own shops (Csizmadia, 1971, p. 40). This rapid increase, and especially the 'labour poaching' associated with it, provoked a quick government response. In 1969, the crudest excesses, such as contracting out co-operative labour to labour-starved state enterprises, were restricted (TRHGY, 5/1969 (VII.23) MUM–MEM);[4] in 1971 a variable production tax heavily favouring agriculture-related activities was introduced as a rent equivalent on incomes from all non-agricultural sources (TRHGY, 35/1970 (XI.24) PM); and in 1972 the financial structure of farms where the majority of sales came from non-agricultural activities was reorganised.[5] As a result, the rate of growth of such enterprises was staunched after 1971. The number of ancillary enterprises increased more slowly until 1974 when their numbers began to fall off. Apart from a visible decline in the number of shops and an increase in the number of catering facilities, the commitment to activities unrelated to agriculture remained high until 1974. Since then, the proportion of enterprises devoted to activity connected with food supply has increased by comparison with other industrial activities, especially industrial services, but, even in 1977, they represented only 37% of co-operative farm non-agricultural units and, of the most clearly agricultural activities, only meat processing, baking and alcohol fermentation have increased in recent years (Appendix II).

The importance of these events for managerial autonomy of action with labour is the following. While the official justification for these non-agricultural ventures was to provide employment for those members who could not be employed full-time on the farm, the evidence available suggests that this was not the overriding concern of co-operative management. We have already seen in chapter 3 how the new skilled occupations on the farms tended to be staffed by those entering, or re-entering, agricultural employment from outside. Although it was stressed that these outsiders also went into industrial aspects of agricultural production, it is clear that many joined the ancillary enterprises. That is, while it is conceivable that processing and sales ventures could mop up some of the predominantly female (see chapter 3) membership of a working age who relied on seasonal employment and the household plot, it is less clear that construction and industrial ventures could; and we have already seen that the proportion of the total number of enterprises represented by meat and vegetable processing ventures is small. Furthermore, in 1975, 66% of the 26% of ancillary enterprises involved in industrial services were direct subcontractors to other enterprises (MAK, 1976, No. 2, p. 58). In fact, L. V. Nagy concluded, on the basis of Ministry of Agriculture and Food Supply figures for agricultural co-operative ancillary enterprises, that while in theory the aim had been to provide off-season employment for members, in practice the motivation behind the ventures was to increase the co-operative's overall income, and that the majority of those at work in the ancillary enterprises were outside employees and not the less employable members of the co-operative (L. V. Nagy, 1973).[6] Clearly, the duty of the co-operative farm to provide employment for its membership does not act as a very serious constraint on management's autonomy of action in relation to labour.

This episode of the flowering and relative decline of ancillary industrial production on the agricultural co-operatives also well illustrates the co-operatives' general autonomy from government policy. Farms enjoy a certain scope for action completely independent of government control if they ignore government exhortation and pursue their freedom of product choice. Gittings reports that even in

China some communes simply ignore state requirements, planting cash crops instead of grain which they then sell on the open market rather than direct to state purchasing companies (1975), and there is considerable evidence that, in Hungary too, farms ignore the somewhat milder pressure that they are under to follow state policy. Mrs. Szabó, for example, found that farms tended to increase production in the unsubsidised, but yet profitable, branches of agriculture such as wheat and maize at the expense of the subsidised, government supported, and yet still unprofitable branches such as animal husbandry (Szabóné Medgyesi, 1976, p. 1221 and Table 7). In fact, heeding government exhortation could have disastrous results. Analysing the bankruptcies of seven agricultural co-operatives in Nógrád county, Pál Juhász found that, in every case, the farms had responded to government pressure and initiated costly new investment in cattle shed complexes (P. Juhász, 1973).

It is, then, possible for agricultural co-operatives to ignore government, and even costly for them not to. However, as a growing branch of a growth-oriented economy, managed by individuals with strong Party connections, it is difficult for co-operatives to ignore investment for long and, once entered, the market on capital goods is greatly circumscribed by ministerial regulation. Government control of investment is not only visible in the types of price support offered for certain projects, it has also appeared in the growing administrative regulation of investment generally. This pattern of aided investment, together with the imperative for growth, jointly place severe restrictions on farm managers' freedom from central planning and their freedom of action in the capital goods market.

Before 1968, farms had no real autonomy in the acquisition of capital equipment. Investments were administered by the agricultural departments of the local councils and, with low agricultural prices, self-generated funds could at most cover the acquisition of cheaper goods such as tractors. The 1968 reform organised agricultural investment along lines similar to those in industry. Financial considerations were introduced into the evaluation of investment projects and into the allocation of funds for them, the arbiter of which was to be the Hungarian National Bank (TRHGY, 1/1967 (XII.1) OT–PM–MEM). However, a relatively unrestricted investment market did not last long. In 1969, the government insisted on requests for development loans being submitted in a fashion which all but required prior ministerial authorisation for the project, and gave the district council the task of reporting whether or not agricultural investments had been completed (TRHGY, 2/1969 (VI.20) OT–PM–MEM; 19/1969 (IV.20) PM–OT). Then, during one of Hungary's regularly occurring crises of over-investment (Bauer, 1981) – the result of a dramatic burgeoning of construction projects (Portes, 1972, pp. 655–6; Szabóné Medgyesi, 1976, p. 1217) – administrative control of investments was reintroduced more fully in 1971. The government first insisted that co-operatives should use their development funds and direct state support before applying for bank credit (TRHGY, 43/1970 (XII.13) PM–MEM); that is, it both imposed a credit squeeze and directed investment towards government sponsored projects. Then, in 1973, support for the investment in cattle sheds was made dependent on the sheds conforming to government specification (TRHGY, 37/1972 (XII.7) PM–MEM). In 1974, the state required investing farms to draft a 'base certificate' describing the project, the proposed source of finance, the method of construction and so on. This had to be submitted for approval to the Executive Committee of the county council which checked to see that it conformed to a list of specifications published simultaneously by the government. Central permission had to be obtained from the National Bank for any investment which did not figure on this list (TRHGY, 4/1974 (VII.7) OT–PM–MEM). In 1976, a dual system was introduced under which investment aid was more or less automatic for projects most favoured by the government, but had to be competed for in the case of others. In addition, the conditions of the competition consisted more of conforming to administrative preference than of maximising return on investment,[7] while aid for the purchase of agricultural machinery was henceforth forthcoming only at the discretion of the local administration (TRHGY, 42/1975 (XI.15) PM–MEM). These regulations have been tightened up subsequently (TRHGY, 6/1975 (XII.17) OT–PM–MEM; 2/1977 (V.27) OT–PM–MEM) and the right of the county apparatus to intervene directly has not been rescinded.

Lastly, parallel to Hungary's formal regulation of the investment market, certain informal, administrative channels have evolved for the distribution of capital goods. For example, part of the reason for the spectacular growth of 'industrial-type production systems' can be attributed to the fact that joining such a system gives a farm priority in the queue waiting to purchase Western tractors and harvesters (Swain, 1981; Tiszáné Gerai and Meszticzky, 1977). In a capital goods market subject to so many official and unofficial controls, the co-operative farm manager who invests at all does so with a severely restricted freedom of action.

It is perhaps worth noting briefly that this control by no means negates totally the freedoms introduced by the New Economic Mechanism. Soviet collective farms, for example, are held on an even tighter financial leash. The kolkhoz has access to three types of finance: short term loans, long term loans and trading credits (Millar, 1971, p. 287). However, stringent conditions for loans effectively exclude the kolkhoz from long term borrowing (Millar, 1971, p. 290); short term borrowing is of little use for financing significant investment and is, in any case, intended for funding advances on wages; and trade credits, advances on deliveries from procurement agencies, cannot be large and, if not tied to some specific use, are simply another form of short term credit, insufficient to fund investment. Farm management is therefore bound by short term horizons and is tempted to indulge in manipulations, rather than new investment, in order to maximise bonuses (Stuart, 1972, p. 109).

Nevertheless, despite farm management's full formal autonomy in policy decision-making, the co-operative farm in Hungary is subject to a system of indirect controls analogous in their effect to the industrial manager's relationship to ministries and planners.[8] Capital equipment is available only on a severely restricted market, as in industry, yet flexibility with regard to labour is possible irrespective of the farms' employment obligations to their members. In fact, the household plot, and the reserve labour force which this allows farms to retain, give management even greater flexibility in this regard.

Finally, we must turn to the question of the extent to which co-operative farm management is constrained from 'below' by the institutions of co-operative democracy. Agricultural producer co-operatives operate within a democratic framework and we must examine how this operates in practice before we can be in a position to state with certainty not only that co-operative farms enjoy a certain amount of autonomy as far as economic decisions are concerned but that, within the farm, it is management which commands that autonomy. First the institutions of co-operative democracy will be described and then evidence from a variety of sources on how they operate in practice will be considered. Good evidence concerning this latter question is hard to find. There has been little systematic research, and none to compare with the work of Héthy and Makó or other industrial sociologists. Evidence tends to be anecdotal, relying on community studies and ethnographic accounts which refer in passing to aspects of co-operative democracy. Nevertheless, an analysis of such published material as exists, together with my own observations, does allow some conclusions to be drawn.

The democratic structure for the organisation of decision-making on agricultural producer co-operatives in Hungary is not unlike that in any other co-operative organisation; and it is more or less identical to the formal organisation of the Soviet kolkhoz with its 'Management Board' or Leadership elected by the members, and a structure of General and brigade meetings (Stuart, 1971, p. 132; 1972, pp. 11–30). In Hungary, a General Meeting of the membership votes on fundamental issues of policy, and a Leadership, elected from all sections of the farm, looks after the day-to-day operation of the farm. Less typically in terms of co-operative theory, perhaps, the elected co-operative president bears personal executive responsibility for the direction of economic activity, for the accounts, and for adherence to the decisions of the General Meeting and Leadership. In addition to these bodies, there are regular meetings between working members and section management in every work group to discuss problems of immediate concern, such as working conditions and wages. The framework of democracy has, unsurprisingly, changed significantly as farms have grown in size, and in the farms of the late 1970s a much greater emphasis is placed on representative democracy. Since the organisation of co-operative democracy, unlike management structure, is regulated by statute, reference will be made to the relevant sections of the 1977 modification of the law on co-operative farm organisation (TRHGY, 1977 évi 9 tvr) rather than to the situation on a single co-operative.

The basic organ of co-operative democracy continues to be the General Meeting of the whole membership. This is the only co-operative-wide democratic forum, but with the growth in the size of co-operatives, the 1977 law allowed for the General Meeting to be split into 'Part Meetings' and for the creation of an additional institution of representative democracy, the 'Meeting of Representatives'. The General Meeting has exclusive jurisdiction in the election of all officers to the Leadership and various co-operative committees, as well as in the election of the president and the vice-president, and in their recall or expulsion from office. It approves medium term plans and the yearly accounts; it organises the election of representatives to the co-operative congress; and it sanctions the merging or disbanding of the co-operative. A General Meeting may be held as often as is required by the co-operative's 'Founding Statute', which itself has been passed by the General Meeting, but it is obliged to meet at least once a year, and if the co-operative has no 'Meeting of Representatives', it must meet twice a year. A General Meeting must also be held if 10% of the membership request it in writing, or if the chairman of the supervisory committee (see below) requests it, or if the legal state supervisory body requires it, or again if the co-operative fails, continually, to meet its financial commitments. The Meeting is only quorate if two thirds of the membership is present, and while a simple majority vote is usually sufficient, a two thirds majority is necessary for the election of officials and for decisions to change the 'Founding Statute' or to merge the co-operative. Elections and decisions on mergers must be made on the basis of a secret ballot.[9]

The 'Meeting of Representatives' is made up of representatives elected from the co-operative membership, according to their area of work. Members are elected for two years and are under an obligation to report back to their workplace community, and represent that community's views to the meeting. The duties of the Meeting consist of electing those officials whose election is not restricted to the General Meeting, debating in more detail and accepting the yearly plan and the previous year's accounts (but not passing them), setting conditions for the premiums of higher level management, approving the establishing of specialised groups[10] (see chapter 2), deciding on methods of payment and making decisions about joining other associations or about any other measure that affects co-operative property. The Meeting has to be called at least twice a year, and the same operational regulations apply as for General Meetings. The functioning of these meetings has not been studied at all, but they are worthy of mention because of their growing importance in co-operative theory in Hungary, and because of their relationship with the new 'Workplace Communities'.

These 'Workplace Communities' systematise and integrate the various types of production meeting and brigade meeting, which will be discussed below, and give them a new elective role in the organisation of representative democracy. They are allowed to meet whenever necessary, but are obliged to meet at least twice a year, and they consider matters concerning work as well as the election of representatives to the 'Meeting of Representatives'. They also consider the agenda for both the General Meeting and the Meeting of Representatives. If the 'Workplace Community' asks for clarification from, or offers a suggestion to, a manager, he is obliged to reply within a given time limit. This preparatory role for General Meetings was previously performed by other institutions, not regulated by co-operative statute, whose operation will be discussed in the context of the Red Flag co-operative below.

The co-operative membership also exercises indirect control over the running of co-operative affairs via its representation on the Leadership. The Leadership is the elected body which deals with the everyday running of the farm. Members are elected for a term of five years, and it has complete autonomy of action within the compass of the farm's 'Founding Statute' and the decisions of the General Meeting. It must consist of at least five members, but can be made up of more, and members may be re-elected without restriction. It meets as often as is necessary, but at least once a month; two thirds of its members have to be present for a quorum; and it votes on the basis of a simple majority with the chairman, the co-operative president, having a casting vote. The Leadership has authority over all co-operative members and managers, with the exception of the other elected committees within the co-operative.

Of the many supplementary committees a co-operative farm is entitled to elect, the compulsory ones are the supervisory committee, the arbitration committee, the women's committee and the household plot committee. The supervisory committee is the important one of these for the purposes of co-operative democracy, since its duties are to see that co-operative regulations are being adhered to. It is totally independent of the president and the Leadership, being answerable to the General Meeting alone, and obliged to report to it once a year. If the committee discovers irregularities, it is obliged to inform the Leadership in writing, and if this elicits no response it can ask the General Meeting to assemble. However, its role is essentially one of checking for misdemeanours and the abuse of power after the event rather than exercising positive member control.[11]

Finally, it should be mentioned that while trade unions do not operate amongst the co-operative membership, being considered unnecessary given the existence of co-operative democracy, the latest regulations do make provision for the formation of trade union branches where a co-operative, or association of co-operatives, has over 25 'employees'. If such a union branch is formed, it has the right to send a representative as an adviser to Leadership meetings, to General Meetings and to all other meetings except those of the supervisory committee.

But how do these institutions operate in practice?

THE GENERAL MEETING

The General Meeting is not a forum of direct participatory democracy and, in view of the present size of co-operatives, it is no longer considered that it should be. It is, rather, a theatrical event designed to show consensus and strength of purpose. If successful, it is unsullied by awkward questions, voices of dissent, and any sort of intervention other than the planned prepared speeches. The aim is to get business over as quickly and as smoothly as possible so that the ordinary members can be given their glass of *pálinka* (a form of schnapps) and sent back to their homes, while the management and Leadership repair to celebrations organised in their honour and strengthen their group cohesion through mutual congratulation. A 'good meeting' is one which goes without a hitch rather than one in which disputed issues are given a thorough airing.

Such an event, of course, requires careful staging, or prickly differences of opinion might emerge. Considerable groundwork has to be carried out first in order to achieve consensus, the main form of such preparation being the series of Party meetings and then meetings in all branches of the co-operative, where members are briefed about the content of the yearly reports and are asked for their questions and comments. At these meetings there is considerably more discussion. Constructive suggestions are made and grievances are expressed. From the records studied on the Red Flag co-operative, however, both sorts of comments were either personal in nature or concerned the household plot. No one seemed prepared to comment on issues of work organisation, although grievances in this area did exist. Perhaps more instructive for our concerns, the most that seems to have resulted directly from complaints and suggestions at these meetings is a record in the minutes to the effect that 'notice is being taken of the suggestion'. With the exception perhaps of winning a cryptic aside in the president's or vice-president's address to the General Meeting, this is as much as participation in the earlier meetings achieves.

'Notice' is of course taken of complaints and grievances, but it is the registering of problem areas where more effort might be necessary in order to achieve consensus rather than consideration on its merits of the members' suggestions. Significantly, the reports of these meetings include references to the atmosphere amongst the membership and notes as to whether 'they' were 'satisfied' and 'disciplined'. The General Meeting on the Red Flag co-operative was thoroughly prepared in the above manner and was a success. The contribution of the membership was minimal and, when it occurred, was disposed of with paternalist *bonhomie*. However, to some extent, such success is the luxury of a wealthy co-operative and meetings in other farms do not always proceed so smoothly (see below).

From meagre published literature concerning General Meetings, it appears that the experience of the Red Flag co-operative is not uncommon. Zám, in his study of the Bács Kiskun area, reports on a farm where the membership sat silent at the General Meeting even though it was known that there were issues on which membership and management did not agree (1973, p. 133), while Gyenes in his study of the 'B' agricultural co-operatives notes the election of an unpopular chairman being forced on the membership by the district council (1977, pp. 43–6). János Juhász has carried out a more systematic study of the management of the 32 co-operatives in the Co-operative Research Institute sample and he discovered certain 'worrying' features concerning the General Meeting. Managers, he found, were generally unclear about the scope of decisions which could be made uniquely by the General Meeting (1970, p. 47), while it was the president and the Leadership which made all the most complex decisions. Furthermore, 26.7% of General Meeting decisions concerned complex financial regulations about which the majority of the membership had no information (p. 46). He concludes that, under such circumstances, the membership cannot be making a real decision (p. 4) and thus that membership decisions within the General Meeting are purely formal (p. 86).

Further systematic research into the functioning of General Meetings has been carried out by Mrs Domé (see Table 5.1). Her study is based on research in 15 co-operatives, five strong, five middling and five weak, from various regions of Hungary. In response to the question 'Has there ever been a case of the membership voting out a Leadership initiative?', she received the results shown in Table 5.1. This is hardly a record of widespread membership initiative in, or

Table 5.1 *'Has there ever been a case of
the membership voting out a Leadership
initiative?' (percentage distribution)*

No	48.7
Once or twice	18.7
Many times	8.0
Unclassifiable	24.3

Source: Domé and Garancsy, 1973.

Table 5.2. *'What was the fate of suggestions made at the last General Meeting
to discuss the forthcoming plan?' (1972–3, percentage distribution)*

	Quality of co-operative		
	Good	Medium	Weak
Put into effect wholly	11.7	17.4	9.8
Put into effect partly	6.2	12.8	10.8
Accepted but not put into effect	3.7	5.3	5.7
Meeting formed no opinion	0.5	1.3	3.7
Rejected by meeting as not being good	1.5	0.5	0.4
Rejected by meeting as premature	0.8	0.8	1.3
Rejected because the mood of the meeting was against it	0.0	0.7	0.1
There were no suggestions	76.6	63.0	68.7

Note: The original is a rather curious table. Many of the percentages do not
add up to 100%. The original gives details of five co-operatives – one from
each of five Hungarian counties – officially designated 'good', 'medium' and
'weak', making a total of 15. The above table gives an average for the five
figures for the 'good' and 'medium' farms. In the case of the 'weak' farms only
four are averaged because the figures from the second farm in the group are so
wildly out of line with the others. For example, the figure for suggestions
partly put into effect was 67.9% compared with a range of 6–18% for the
other 'weak' farms. Whatever the true percentages, the low level of participation in General Meetings in unambiguous.

Source: Mrs Gy.-né Domé, 1976, Table 13, p. 102 (modified).

even veto of, decision-making. In only 8.0% of cases did respondents have a recollection of it being in any way a common occurrence for the membership to force through an opinion contrary to that of the Leadership. Table 5.2 is also based on Mrs Domé's work, and presents answers to the question 'What was the fate of suggestions made at the last General Meeting to discuss the forthcoming plan?' It both shows how uncommon it is for members even to make a suggestion and indicates how unlikely it is that suggestions made will be acted on positively.

THE LEADERSHIP

If the General Meeting is not an effective arena for direct participatory democracy, perhaps members can influence decision-making via their elected representatives in the Leadership. A preliminary point to make in this regard is that while there is no statutory obligation for anyone other than the president to be a member of the Leadership, it is very common to elect those involved in co-operative management to this body. It clearly makes sense for the most important decision-making body of the co-operative to include those responsible for the day-to-day running of the farm. It is not essential for them to be elected to the Leadership in order to do this, however, for the regulations insist on the invitation of all managers to Leadership meetings in an advisory capacity (TRHGY, 6/1967 (X.24) MEM 20§(2)). Nevertheless, Bognár and Simó found that 55.9% of upper management and 29.3% of middle management were coincidentally members of the Leadership. More specifically, one in two agronomists was on the Leadership, as was one finance manager in four (Bognár and Simó, 1975, p. 120). On the other hand, while there were no national figures indicating what proportion of the Leadership those with management posts represent, on the Red Flag co-operative they constituted about 30%.

While those in management posts may or may not predominate numerically within the Leadership, it is important to consider how Leadership meetings operate, and who takes most part in them. It would be wrong to say that debate and discussion are absent from Leadership meetings. An examination of the minutes of Leadership meetings on the Red Flag co-operative reveals that discussion and a divergence of views are as common as we might suppose in the management of an economic enterprise the size of the contemporary co-operative farm. However, three points must be made about the nature of the discussion at such meetings. First, it is dominated by managers, and especially by the farm president, who consider narrow production issues and are keen to defend their sectional interests. Second, major decisions entailing financial expenditure are passed without any debate; and, third, the contribution of those members who are not coincidentally managers consists of no more than requests for the clarification of items on the agenda or of other matters.

In a typical meeting on the Red Flag co-operative, the elected members would ask questions about items on the agenda. The relevant branch managers would then reply, whether they were members of the Leadership or not, and this might lead into a lengthy technical discussion. Alternatively, branch managers would have already submitted a written report, which would be discussed in the same manner. The farm president, as Leadership chairman, would then bring discussion to a close, decrees would be passed and reports accepted *nem. con.* and discussion would move on to the next business on the agenda. However, fundamental issues of policy, such as the merging of the farm's 'production system'[12] with that of another farm and choosing its manager, or the decision to build a new glasshouse, were simply presented to the Leadership as *faits accomplis* at the end of the meeting under the final general heading on the agenda equivalent to 'any other business', and with no record of there having been prior discussion of the matter. Even if such discussion had taken place, in private, the membership and their elected representatives received no indication as to what the issues were, and on what basis the final choice had been made. Again, the contributions of Leadership members who were not managers to 'any other business' were generally restricted to requests for clarification of additional matters. A worker in animal husbandry, for example, asked which sectors of the work force would be affected by a change in norms previously discussed. Unlike the farm president, they did not initiate any new matters of policy, although they did occasionally take issue with some of the answers given by management.[13]

It should be noted further that the agendas of Leadership meetings do not include a heading equivalent to 'acceptance of minutes of previous meetings', despite their extreme formality in other respects, and that the minutes are kept by a full-time secretary, not herself a member of the Leadership. In fact, the role of the minutes appears to be that of an unimportant record to be stored away until such time as farm affairs are submitted to internal or external examination. It is very obviously not that of informing the membership of the issues that were involved in decision-making which affects their everyday lives.

WORKPLACE MEETINGS

Since the Workplace Communities were established only in 1977, the end point of our period, the discussion below of democracy in practice at this level will be restricted to the less formal 'production meetings', 'brigade meetings' and 'work evaluations' (referred to below jointly as 'production meetings' for convenience) which have always existed and which continue to have a place in the new regulations. The novelty of the Workplace Community as such is simply its formal integrative and elective roles.

For management, 'production meetings' are seen explicitly as forums for winning over the membership to decisions that have already been taken. They are seen as areas of discussion, rather than the simple transmission of commands; some notice is taken of objections; but no institution exists to present an alternative to management's case,[14] and little notice is taken of such suggestions as are made by the members. Nevertheless, although management will almost invariably get its way, it experiences a genuine feeling of relief when members are persuaded to accept, for example, an increased norm, because, as is discussed below, the membership has a very powerful right of ultimate veto. What is lacking from discussion with co-operative farm management and the sketchy literature on co-operative farm production meetings is any feeling within management that the meetings should do more than this. As for the working members' attitudes to production meetings, the following points can be made. First, members are more likely to participate at such meetings than at the General Meeting; second, they are more likely to sit and listen than to take part actively; and, third, the information-transfer conception of co-operative democracy, of which this is the final stage, has had such little success that most members are not sufficiently informed about the co-operative and its economics to be in a position to make any contribution that is not job specific. Finally, it should be noted, the channels used by the membership to gain access to management are increasingly informal ones, including contacts via Party representatives.

Members are more likely to contribute to production meetings than they are to the General Meeting because the issues discussed are of more immediate concern. This can be illustrated from the May 1st co-operative by the young skilled worker who complained at a production meeting that shower facilities were not provided in the piggery. He was, however, the only member to raise the issue, and the complaint was ignored. The studies in the published literature reveal a similar situation. The fullest account is that given by Zám when he presents verbatim a tape recording of a production meeting among tractor drivers (1973, pp. 158–76). The overall direction of the meeting is dominated by the president and the chief agronomist. Their interest is in finding out what the members are thinking and in telling them what is planned for the following year. They are not concerned with acting on the members' suggestions unless they conform to their own plans. The president finally informs the members that his own suggestions are going to be taken up and, after aggressively dismissing complaints about inadequate payment with an attack on 'bad organisation' and 'lax labour discipline', he closes the meeting both before the issues have been fully discussed and without asking whether the workers have any further suggestions. Significantly, perhaps, he refers to the fact that minutes are not being taken as an indication that the members may speak their minds. He does not acknowledge that it might be in his interest that there is no official record of what was decided at the meeting. The members, it should be stressed, did forward concrete suggestions concerning work organisation, although these were allowed to lose themselves in the meanderings of the discussion.

The failure of the system of democracy, even as a system for information transfer, because it does not combine information with an ability to effect changes in the areas about which information is given, can be seen from a study of ten co-operative farms in the foothills of the Mátra and Jászság areas by Pál Szakál. This study is not representative, but the author ventures to suggest that his findings are not untypical. Only 25% of those asked in the survey could tell the size of the farm, that is its acreage, the size of the livestock holding, the number of members and so on, while fewer had a clear idea about its financial situation. As Szakál stresses, however, it is on major financial matters related to the standing of the farm that the General Meeting alone is competent to decide (Szakál, 1973, p. 294). Domé's study with Garancsy (1973) revealed that an equally low percentage of the membership in her 15 co-operatives knew the

Table 5.3. *'Do you know the major regulations in the Founding Statute?'* *(percentage distribution)*

Yes	26.0
No	26.2
Partly	34.0
Unclassifiable	17.7

Source: Domé and Garancsy, 1973.

main regulations in their co-operative's 'Founding Statute'. She received the answers presented in Table 5.3 to her question, 'Do you know the major regulations in the Founding Statute?'[15] Similarly, Kulcsár and Szijjártó found that 47% of younger farm members did not even know what the main targets of the long term economic plan were (1980, p. 124).

Additional evidence concerning the practice of co-operative democracy comes from Párkányi's work on the Co-operative Research Institute sample (1975). Comparing answers to questions about participation in democratic forums in 1967 and 1972, she found that the general willingness to participate had fallen. The proportion of those not wishing to participate in the co-operative's affairs had risen from 28.8% in 1967 to 44.2% in 1972, although members appeared to be rather more interested in particular issues and less interested in general ones in 1972 than they had been in 1967. Unskilled workers and those working in crop production were least likely to participate, and when workers in crop production did participate it tended to be in matters related to their household plots. Workers in animal husbandry and workers with machinery, on the other hand, were more likely to make contributions concerned with the organisation of the workplace and with the distribution of income. Unskilled workers exercised their right to participate at any sort of democratic forum less in 1972 than they had done in 1967, and they were the group within the membership most likely to think that this right was a pure formality. Skilled workers participated less in General Meetings in 1972 than they had in 1967, but they were more active in production meetings. This was especially true of skilled member households where another family member worked outside the co-operative. As a corollary to this diminishing involvement in co-operative democracy, Párkányi notes that while the real potential for certain groups in the membership, especially administrative workers and middle management, to influence decision-making had increased, the medium for this influence was personal informal contacts with management rather than the official channels of co-operative democracy (pp. 412–17).

Citing research carried out by György Lugossy on participation generally, Kulcsár and Szijjártó state that while 40% of younger members felt that notice was taken of their opinions, the majority felt that they were simply supposed to absorb what they were told and that the leaders did not like them to express an opinion (1980, p. 122). If they did participate, it tended to be concerning organisational and payment issues, usually reflecting a desire for further modernisation (1980, p. 123). The contributions of older members tended to focus on the position of the household plot and the possibilities of aid to it (1980, p. 144). Soviet materials point to a similar degree of non-participation in decision-making. When asked whether they had any influence over farm affairs, negative answers were received from only 9–10% of those in the management/specialist category, but from 60–75% of non-specialist workers (Arutyunyan, 1971, pp. 104–14). And the Grays refer to 'little or no democratic discussion' within agricultural units in China (1982, p. 169).

THE MEMBERSHIP'S ULTIMATE SANCTION

To compensate for this inability to contribute positively to co-operative management, the membership does have one ultimate, if negative, sanction – the right of dismissal. While in industry the use by the workers *in extremis* of the strike can lead to the temporary satisfaction of worker demands and perhaps to the replacement of management (Héthy and Makó, 1972a, pp. 258–61; Holubenko, 1975, p. 9), in the co-operative sector there is no need for such extreme 'industrial action'. The democratic structure itself provides an adequate forum for this albeit negative power. While industrial managers live with the fear that workers will down tools and ruin, or at least upset, their careers, the co-operative leaders are always aware that, not only do they have to seek re-election at regular intervals (every five years for the president), but that the General Meeting can force them to resign in mid-term.

As an example of this, we must turn to the events of the end of year

General Meeting at a farm considerably less secure economically than the farms referred to thus far. The co-operative concerned is of the 'specialised co-operative' type and is located in a small village on the Great Plain.[16] The General Meeting proved to be an adequate forum for calling the president to account so forcefully that he was subsequently obliged to resign, but it was incapable of proposing an alternative candidate, and at the following General Meeting an appointee of the local county organisation was elected, despite membership disapproval of the candidate. At the first of the two meetings, the professional and personal behaviour of the president was severely criticised. Objections were raised about his failure to inform the membership about decisions he had taken which impinged on the members' traditional rights, and exception was taken at his use, for personal reasons, of the co-operative's car. Feeling ran so high that when the district Party secretary intervened to try and smooth things over he was almost shouted down.

In the published Hungarian literature on agricultural co-operatives, it is Zám, again, who furnishes the only examples of the members' ability, *in extremis*, to influence who is to be leader. He recounts how a General Meeting decided, with little apparent pre-meditation, to reject their president who was standing for re-election and to vote in an outsider. It was reported, however, that the members took their own pencils with them into the voting booths, in case none were provided, so that they could write in the name of their desired candidate. In order to achieve this victory, the members had to walk out of the meeting *en masse* and stay out until the management allowed the election to take place (Zám, 1973, p. 126). In a less spectacular chapter, he recounts how, in a different co-operative, the death of a president in office led to a real debate about who would replace him. The issue between the two candidates was only finally decided when, after packing the meeting with bus loads of widows and pensioners belonging to his particular national minority, one of them achieved the necessary two thirds majority in the vote (Zám, 1973, pp. 142–9).

Occurrences similar to those described above, which have their parallels in the Soviet Union (Stuart, 1971, p. 132), are, if not uncommon, nevertheless not part of everyday 'industrial relations' on agricultural co-operatives. On the other hand, the evidence available provides no examples of informal bargaining over the production process between 'workers' and 'management', that is of 'go slows' or of tactical strikes similar to those reported by Héthy and Makó (1972a; 1972b) in Hungarian industry. There were, in the 1960s, refusals to work at all on many farms, but now that members have been persuaded to enter communal production, they do not seem to make systematic use of the strengths and weaknesses of their position within it to further their own ends. This could indicate that such behaviour is simply not reported, or it could be the case that it actually does not take place. Whether there are unreported examples of such behaviour or not, sound social and technological reasons preclude those engaged in agricultural production from having extensive recourse to such strategies. For one thing, there is no elite of elder skilled workers on the co-operative farm. As was mentioned in the introduction, these workers played a crucial role in both Héthy and Makó's and Kemény's accounts; but skilled workers on agricultural co-operatives, as we saw in chapter 3, are often young and, more important, have not worked as skilled labour in agriculture for very long. In addition, the nature of agricultural production, especially in cereal and vegetable production, calls for fluctuating work groups and therefore fluctuating methods of, and bases for, payment, depending on the season. So, while there may be a structural basis of conflict between hourly paid mechanics and tractor drivers who are paid a piece-rate, at harvest time – when the really big money can be earned – mechanics will be moved up on to the harvesters and paid a piece-rate too. With only semi-permanent work groups, it is difficult for an informal group strategy to evolve.

In animal husbandry, too, there are technological limitations on favourite types of 'industrial action'. Factory farmed dairy cattle, for example, can only be 'slowed down' by inflicting considerable suffering on the animals and, more important, cannot be speeded up again once new or revised rates have been won. It is more difficult therefore to catch up on lost income. Clearly more research is necessary to substantiate or refute these points, but it would seem fair to conclude tentatively, on the basis of the unsystematic evidence available and accepting the inadequacies of co-operative democracy, that the membership of the co-operative farm is marginally more able to influence decision-making negatively via formal channels such as the General Meeting than state industrial workers, who are, on the other hand, rather more able than co-operative farm members to exert informal pressure in the sphere of production.

Generally, however, we have seen that the General Meeting is not the sort of forum where real discussion takes place; the Leadership is dominated by management and by the co-operative farm president; and workplace meetings function more to gauge the membership's feelings and inform them of decisions already taken than to allow them to influence the organisation of work. As was suggested in the introduction is the case in socialist industry, it is management alone, rather than the membership generally or their elected (non-management) representatives or the Party organisation (internal or external), which makes day-to-day economic decisions on agricultural producer co-operatives; and management has most freedom exercising this decision-making power in respect of labour.

6

The exercise of managerial control in agriculture

The greater part of this chapter will examine what management actually does with the powers of control which we have seen it possess. But before we do this and go on to consider whether management has a group interest which it might be expected to pursue, it will be instructive to consider the issue of Complex Brigades as an illustration of the keenness of management's defence of its managerial prerogative. The extension in the 1980s to the state industrial sector of sub-contracting 'economic work partnerships' was accompanied in agriculture by a revival of forms of decentralised, sub-contracting work groups. Management's success in doing away with Complex Brigades in the politically less reformist 1970s nevertheless reveals how acutely sensitive it was to threats to its right to manage; and the evidence suggests that the current emphasis on decentralisation focuses very much more on increasing the effective autonomy of lower and middle management than on extending workplace democracy, which figures as a secondary, although desirable, aim (*Magyar Mezőgazdaság*, 1984, No. 6, p. 3).

Complex Brigades were first formed in 1964 on the Szekszárd state farm (Kunszabó, 1972, p. 260). They were based on new experiments in the Ukraine with the 'link system' (Juhász and Párkányi, 1977, p. 279), but this was a rather different form of 'link system' from that of the 1930s and 1940s (Pospielovsky, 1970) and it is perhaps better, if more clumsily, termed autonomous multi-purpose work teams operating on a profit and loss basis (Nove, 1980, p. 145; Zotova and Novikov, 1969, pp. 211–15). These were introduced in 1961, comprising 15–20 individuals, and were equipped with a full complement of machinery (Pospielovsky, 1970, p. 417). After their introduction in the Ukraine output increased threefold. In Hungary, they were similarly successful and, in 1965, the format was extended from cereal production to workers in animal husbandry and vineyards, extending from Szekszárd to neighbouring farms and then throughout the country. The Bátaszék agricultural producer co-operative even won a state prize for its use of the system (Kunszabó, 1975, p. 51), but then Complex Brigades went on the decline. The system was abandoned where it first began, without the consent of those who instigated it (Kovács and Kunszabó, 1974, p. 40) and, despite a call for 'Even more Complex Brigades' in *Népszabadság* on 27 February 1975, the theme disappeared from the press in 1976, and when Juhász and Párkányi decided to study the topic in 1976 they found that no groups existed in agricultural activity based on Complex Brigade principles (1977, p. 265).

What were the organisational principles of these groups which waxed and waned so dramatically in the late 1960s and early 1970s? The basis of the Complex Brigade was that it was an autonomous, self-accounting work unit which received the necessary machinery, land and technical materials and general instructions from the communal farm and was then left to organise its day-to-day work tasks by itself. Payment was not in terms of an hourly rate or piece-rate, but consisted of an advance plus a share in profits over a certain guaranteed rate (Kunszabó, 1972, p. 259). Organisation within the brigade was democratic:

'Morning or evening, but mainly morning we would get together and agree who should start off and who should finish which work. And then everyone went off on his task, everyone knowing that the others would work well because he was just as interested as I was' (Kovács and Kunszabó, 1974, p. 39);

and the brigades were democratically formed:

'This brigade was formed entirely democratically. We chose ourselves and my election as brigade leader occurred completely spontaneously.' (Kovács and Kunszabó, 1974, p. 43)

The organisation of the working day was entirely in the members' own hands:

'If it looked as if something had to be finished today because tomorrow things would be easier, then we would say to the others we are staying... We usually worked till five in the afternoon, but if things were tight we would work till six or seven – in the summer at harvest time for example we worked as long as the work demanded because we had to finish it.' (Kovács and Kunszabó, 1974, p. 42)

Complex Brigades certainly seemed to be an attractive proposition for those who favoured a non-hierarchical, rather democratic form of work organisation. Four detailed studies of their performance indicate that they were a success by both economic and social criteria, even if they were not entirely problem-free (Juhász and Párkányi, 1977, p. 316). Specifically, it was found that the combination of tractor driving and tractor maintenance could ensure a more efficient utilisation of machinery than the control group, and that the subcontracting group could adjust itself more efficiently to 'campaign work' than any other form of organisation (Juhász and Párkányi, 1977, p. 316). Complex Brigades were also successful in terms of other indicators. In Bátaszék, production of wheat was 11.8% higher in the Complex Brigade than other brigades; their superiority in maize was 59% and in winter barley 28.1% (Szomolányiné, 1970, p. 87).

The Complex Brigade system had further advantages. Between 1964 and 1969, members of the Complex Brigades acquired 2.6 skilled qualifications per head compared with 0.58 for other workers on the farm. Management was given more time to deal with technical problems and was less tied by the everyday concerns of running the farm (Kovács and Kunszabó, 1974, p. 41; Kunszabó, 1972, p. 259). This was all the more important since a study by Szakál found that top management spent 67% of its time doing things for which their qualifications were not necessary (1973, p. 303). Perhaps more important than this, though, was the improved in-group atmosphere within the brigade. In Bátaszék, while 67% of those in Complex Brigades were content with their relationship with their work mates, in the other groups only 42% were (Szomolányiné, 1970, pp. 53–4). On top of this, 'readiness to help' within the group was 69.9% higher than in the other brigades (Szomolányiné, 1970, p. 88). Workers in Szekszárd thought they worked 'more calmly' (Kovács and Kunszabó, 1974, p. 39) under the Complex Brigade system. The Complex Brigade was more of a 'small community' in private life as well, and might express a group opinion at co-operative General Meetings (Kovács and Kunszabó, 1974, p. 41).

The one real problem with the Complex Brigade was the disproportionately high incomes that their members earned. At Bátaszék, incomes of the Complex Brigade members were 30% higher than those of workers in other brigades doing similar work (Szomolányiné, 1970, p. 47). This not only resulted in tensions within the membership (Kovács and Kunszabó, 1974, p. 39), it also created problems for management in their control of wage levels.

However, this problem was not the central one referred to when agronomists explained the inapplicability of the Complex Brigades. The arguments used against them, arguments which were ultimately successful, were of a technological nature and, since they are fallacious, tend to suggest that a truer explanation would be in terms of a particular conception of who it is that should have power on the agricultural producer co-operative.

The first set of arguments against the Complex Brigades based itself around the extension of 'industrial-type production systems' to agriculture and the greater importance of sophisticated high performance agricultural machinery. It was argued that these new machines determined the nature of agricultural production (Kovács and Kunszabó, 1974, p. 43; Kunszabó, 1975, p. 52) and required such a degree of precision that there was no scope left for the independent decision-making of groups of independent producers. These arguments, however, do not take into account how the 'industrial-type production systems' operate in practice. A high degree of precision is required, but it is accepted that each farm will have to modify the requirements of the system and adapt them to the particular conditions on the farm (Tiszáné Gerai and Meszticzky, 1977, p. 622); indeed, with some systems, the systems chiefs do no more than suggest technology rather than prescribe it. In fact, as one of the agronomists associated with the Complex Brigade movement at its inception noted, such a pattern of suggested or prescribed technology fits in with the operation of Complex Brigades except that, in the latter case, it is the farm itself rather than a system chief which does the prescribing. The pattern is repeated at a lower level (Kovács and Kunszabó, 1974, p. 43).

The technological argument was taken a stage further to maintain that agricultural production was now too complicated for the average Hungarian agricultural worker (Juhász and Párkányi, 1977, p. 315). This was scarcely a powerful argument. The kind of knowledge necessary to be able to operate complex machinery is very different from that needed to invent it, and not so complex that it cannot be learnt on a short course (Kunszabó, 1975, p. 53). Indeed, the members of one Complex Brigade invented for themselves a mechanism to help them in production which has been taken over by many state farms and even displayed at the Hungarexpo exhibition (Kovács and Kunszabó, 1974, p. 42).

Further arguments against the Complex Brigades related to work organisation. The argument was that the Complex Brigade was in fact an 'area' form of organisation, that is, it required each territorial area within the farm to have its own equipment, while the future lay in 'branch' organisation, that is, where administration is centralised and there is no duplication within territories of each branch of farm activity, livestock, cereals and so on. This might be the conventional wisdom of the agricultural text book, but it can be dismissed as a simple confusion of terms. Organisation of production by economic branch does not require that the branch should not be split into sub-units, nor that there should be a strict division of labour between those who use a branch's machinery and those who maintain it. Complex Brigades could easily be part of 'branch' organisation. A second argument, that the organisation of Complex Brigades ties down machines when they might be needed elsewhere for 'campaign work', does have a certain force, but the findings on the utilisation of resources already cited indicate that 'campaign' periods might be less necessary if the machines were used more rationally throughout the year; and the opinions of members involved indicate that, within the Complex Brigade, if there was a period of 'campaign work', the members spared no effort to get it done:

'at the time of the Complex Brigade, we were so interested in work that time did not matter in campaign work... Not any more. Now tractor drivers try to earn their money in the appropriate work time and then go home...' (Kovács and Kunszabó, 1974, p. 43)

What is more, if 'campaign work' is necessary in another sector, the nature of Complex Brigade organisation itself does not exclude members from taking on jobs in other fields (Juhász and Párkányi, 1977, p. 317).

If the conventional Hungarian arguments against the Complex Brigades do not stand up, what other factors could be at work? An alternative explanation is that management was jealous of its authority and, feeling threatened, reasserted its relative monopoly of specialist knowledge. Such views have also been suggested about the fate of multi-purpose 'links' in the Soviet Union (Nove, 1980, p. 145). That Hungarian co-operative farm management did feel threatened can be seen from certain comments by management, for example that the Complex Brigade would pester it so as to be able to get on with the harvest if they thought it was time (Kovács and Kunszabó, 1974, p. 42), or by the fact that, in some cases, Complex Brigades forced management to behave as they wanted (Kunszabó, 1975, p. 54). Managerial attitudes can best be seen from their own words:

'We needed the industrial type production system like a starving man needs a mouthful of bread ... [now] I can say, "Come on lad, get on with it. It's not me who's saying so, it's the technology."' (Kunszabó, 1975, p. 53)

'[In the modern farms] decisions about work cannot be entrusted to, cannot be given to those who carry out the tasks ... The worker has only one task in this, the precise execution [of his allotted tasks]. The minute that we give them the possibility of deciding individually about when they work, at that very minute, the whole system explodes.' (Kovács and Kunszabó, 1974, p. 44)

Presumably, the extent of economic crisis by the 1980s convinced the government that whatever the interests of the management whose formation it had encouraged, national economic considerations should take precedence and new flirtations with decentralised, and sometimes self-regulating, subcontracting groups began.

Management, then, is strongly committed to its right to manage, but what does it do with its prerogative? In the introduction it was argued that part of the essence of 'socialist wage labour' is that it is an economic category susceptible to self-interested manipulation by those within a productive enterprise who control labour inputs. The introduction also outlined how industrial management might be seen as being guilty of such behaviour. In the remainder of this chapter we shall consider the question more closely in the specific context of the economic regulators which circumscribe Hungarian co-operative farms. The kernel of the argument presented in the introduction was that workers were most interested in maximising wages and hence, implicitly, in maximising the wage fund, while managers were interested in maintaining the level of the 'sharing fund' because of their greater interest in bonuses. The conflicting economic interests of management and labour on the agricultural co-operative are less clear cut, or rather they were so until the replacement of 'work payments' by 100% wages in 1977. With this latter reorganisation, the economic context of 'socialist wage labour' in those farms which adopted 100% wages became identical to that in industry. Workers/ members receive the great majority of their income as wages and, in addition, a rather small yearly profit share paid out of the 'sharing fund'. Management, on the other hand, which is not eligible for any overtime under the 1977 regulations, can receive a bonus of up to 50% of its basic wage from the 'sharing fund', provided co-operative funds have not been exhausted by those taxes, including the taxation of wage increases, which have to be paid before its formation (see Table 6.1). However, since our aim is to focus on behaviour within a functioning system, this chapter will consider the situation which prevailed between 1968 and 1977 while the system of 'work payments' (rather than 100% wages) was still the norm. And, under this system, it was not a question of management and labour being differentially interested in separate funds.

Because of the different economic regulators operating within co-operative agriculture, the conflict of management and labour interests between 1968 and 1977 was in some ways more straightforward than the complex relationships obtaining in industry. In co-operative agriculture it was a function rather of the relative size of income available to each group from the same co-operative fund. 'Worker' and 'management' bonuses, their profit shares, the supplementary 'work payments' (the additional 20%) and the basic 'work payments' themselves all came from the 'sharing fund'. Before the fund could be formed, however, tax obligations to the state had to be met, and before even these obligations had been met, the basic 80% element of work payments (treated as wage costs although nominally part of the sharing fund) had to be paid. This rather curious formulation was a hangover from the earlier days of co-operative agriculture when the 'remainder principle' was still in operation and members' incomes were simply a share of the final surplus. The whole of the co-operative membership therefore is interested in the same financial fund, although only management has the ability to affect its formation in any direct way, and management too has a much greater stake in it.

Although the regulations concerning management bonuses on the co-operative farm have varied in detail since 1968 and have become more strict, the general framework of bonus types has remained the same, and this is presented in Table 6.1 and the notes relating to it. As can be seen from the table, an additional income of 50% of the full wage payment (80% basic plus 20% supplement) is available to upper management as a bonus. In keeping with the relative administrative autonomy of the agricultural co-operatives, the farm itself can choose the indicator on which it wants these bonuses to depend, although this has to be determined at the beginning of the year and not *post facto*. It should be noted that, while the peculiarities of co-operative budget formation before 1980 required that 'worker' bonuses, 'management' bonuses and 'work payment' supplements all come from the same fund, co-operative farm management was able, in theory, to award itself bonuses for successful performance of its tasks without 100% 'work payments' being paid. All the indicators that are presented in Table 6.1 could be achieved without the payment of 20% supplements.[1] In 1972, the National Producer Co-operative Council recommended that farms should not award their managers bonuses unless 100% 'work payments' were met (TJ, 1/1972 TOT), but this recommendation has, as yet, not been translated into a government regulation and the 1980 regulations made it crystal clear that upper management's bonuses are formed before the formation of the farm's new R-funds which cover membership bonuses (TRHGY, 39/1979 (XI.1) MT).

If the higher leadership (management) is interested in bonuses, and the intensity with which production managers in the Red Flag co-operative requested that the following year's plan should be realisable suggests that the paper interest demonstrated in Table 6.1 is translated into fact, the ordinary member is so to a much lesser degree. The ordinary co-operative member is interested in receiving a full 100% 'work payment' from the post tax surplus, but his interest in an additional bonus is not strong. The extra profit share, paid out of post tax surplus in addition to the 'work payment's' 20% supplement, is very small, being rarely as high as 10% and usually 2–3% only. Indeed, both Kunszabó and Égető have found that this yearly profit share acts as a very weak incentive, while Kunszabó further suggests that the size of profit-share received depends more on factors such as length of service than on factors such as increasing productivity over which the working member might have some control (Égető, 1976, pp. 31–2; Kunszabó, 1974b, p. 78). On the other hand, because the payment of 100% wages depended, under the pre-1977 system, on a certain level of surplus being achieved, the situation is not straight-forward. Inasmuch as their total income increased by a quarter if the farm generated sufficient surplus for a 100% work payment, it was clearly in the members' interest for the farm to be successful. Consequently, if the end of year profit could not motivate workers to be interested in factors beyond the completion of the immediate tasks on which work payments were based, as Égető and Kunszabó suggest, the fear of losing a 25% wage supplement might.

Nevertheless, the actual bonus element from post tax surplus remains small, and its loss, provided 100% work payment is made, is

Table 6.1. *Leaders' bonuses and the 'increase in income' tax*

	1968	1971	1972	1976	1977
Leaders' bonus as % of salary	Maximum of 50%[a]				
Basis of bonus	Improving performance [b] indicators and carrying out specific tasks				
Source of bonus	Revenue[c] net of taxes and wage-costs				
Source of 'increase in income' tax, etc.	Revenue net of wage-costs and prior to fund formation				
Highest marginal rate of 'increase in income' tax, etc.	70%[d]	300%	300%	600%[e]	600%[f]
% increase in average incomes at which 'increase in income' tax begins	2%	2%	2%	4%	4%

Notes:

a. The 50% maximum on all kinds of bonus has remained since 1968, although regulations about particular kinds of bonus have changed over the years (see note b).

b. In 1968, the performance indicators suggested were gross production value, net production value, value-added, and improvement in the volume of consumption and investment. Suggested specific tasks in 1968 were the completion of a piggery or cattle-shed complex.

　The 1972 National Council of Agricultural Producer Co-operatives decree suggests value-added as an indicator for the performance-related bonus for upper leadership and makes no suggestion in relation to specific tasks. The ministerial regulations of 1976 suggest a bonus of 15% for maintaining either value-added, or net income, or production value at the same level as the average for the three preceding years, plus a further 15% if this level is improved on. A further 10% is available for unspecified specific tasks, leaving a further 10% from other sources. The 1977 ministerial regulations suggest a 20% bonus for increasing either production value, value-added or net income over its average value for the preceding three years. A further 20% bonus is related to the specific task of improving such areas as household plot production, animal husbandry or vegetable production, and the remaining 10% may be acquired from other sources.

c. Despite confusing wording in some of the regulations, it is clear that under all modifications since 1968 wage-costs cover the 'work payment' element of a member's income. It is only after the payment of these basic wages and other fiscal obligations to the state (including the 'increase in income' tax) that 'wage supplements' and bonuses may be paid. For example:

　– In 1968, it was suggested within the National Council of Agricultural

Producer Co-operatives that income be divided in the following order: (i) to cover previous years' losses; (ii) to pay income tax; (iii) to form the social-cultural fund; (iv) to form the development fund; (v) to fund 'wage supplements' (and presumably also bonuses); (vi) to form an income guaranteeing fund.

- In 1972, a National Council of Agricultural Producer Co-operatives recommendation stressed that a bonus can only be paid if there are sufficient funds to cover both 'work payments' and 'wage supplements'. Government regulations in 1968 refer to a specific order for the utilisation of income, but give no detail other than that taxes should be paid before the formation of bonuses.

- The 1976 ministerial regulations put the formation of funds for the payment of anything above 'work payments' sixth in order of uses to which income may be put after (i) town/village tax; (ii) income tax; (iii) 'increase in income' tax; (iv) formation of a reserve fund; (v) formation of a development fund.

d. Between 1968 and 1971 there was no 'increase in income' tax as such. The tax regulating the use of agricultural producer co-operative income introduced in 1968 performed effectively the same function. The much lower highest marginal rate reflects the weaker financial standing of agricultural co-operatives at this date. When the 'increase in income' tax proper was introduced in 1971, the weakest co-operatives (discounting those exempted from the tax altogether) paid a highest marginal rate of only 90% for increases in average personal income of over 7%. Average personal incomes under the 1968–71 tax were calculated in the same way as under the 'increase in income tax' before it was modified in 1976.

e. In 1974, exemptions to this tax were introduced for certain labour-intensive crops. The income levels constituting the various tax bands were subject to constant up-dating. In 1975, the highest marginal rate for the richest co-operatives was increased to 400%, and at the same time the marginal rates on weaker co-operatives were decreased.

In 1976, the base for calculating average per capita income was changed. The previous method of constructing an average worker from the total number of hours worked, divided by 2300 (a notional 230 ten hour days), and then using this from which to calculate average income, was abandoned, and the average monthly income of the actual active work force was adopted as the new base in average income calculations.

f. In 1977, modifications were introduced which discounted from the calculation of the average per capita income the income of those who had retired during that year. Measures were also taken to mitigate the effect on the level of the average per capita income of changes in labour inputs associated with the introduction of new technology.

Sources: Z. Kovács, 1969, pp. 21, 25 and 37; 1970, p. 14; 1967 évi Tv; 35/1967 (X.11) Korm; 6/1967 (X.24) MEM; 19/1968 (VII.20) PM; 36/1970 (XI.24) PM; 1971 évi 34 sz tvr; 46/1971 (XII.28) Korm; 15/1971 (XII.30) MEM; 1/1972 TOT; 31/1972 (X.13) PM; 18/1974 (V.28) PM; 40/1974 (XII.28) PM; 19/1975 (VI.18) MT; 40/1975 (XI.15); 1977 évi 9 sz tvr; 7/1977 (III.12) MT; 12/1977 (III.12); 19/1977 (V.25) MEM–MUM; 28/1977 (XI.5) PM.

clearly not so significant a loss for the manual membership as non-payment of bonuses would be for management. The extent of the ordinary member's interest in bonuses remains low when compared with that of management, despite the fact that it is in the overall interest of both groups to improve the economic fund from which bonuses come. In addition to the profit-share bonus, the ordinary working members do, of course, receive performance-related bonuses linked to their particular jobs. Such bonuses are, however, closely related to the tasks for which the members' normal 'work payment' is made and are best seen as forms of wage supplement.

Having established that farm management is very interested in receiving bonuses, and more interested in doing so than the ordinary membership, we are in a position to ask whether management exercises its control over production, over the method of plan fulfilment, in furtherance of that interest. The mechanism for income or wage regulation is central to our analysis, as it was in the discussion of wage regulation in industry in the introduction. Both the 'regulating tax' and subsequently the 'increase in income' tax, which were designed to control increases in the average membership income, were exceptionally progressive; and both had to be met out of post tax income prior to the formation of any fund, or the payment of any tax (although not before the payment of the basic – 80% – 'work payment'). This has continued into the period after 1977. Changes introduced in 1980 require that all taxes, including the new 'work payment' tax, also be paid before either management bonuses, or any other fund, including those covering members' year-end bonuses, can be formed (TRHGY, 39/1979 (XI.1) MT). Clearly it was, and is, in upper management's interest to avoid these taxes which might ultimately threaten the size of its bonuses.

The disincentive can be seen from the last three rows of Table 6.1: as co-operatives increased in size and scale of operations, the 'regulating tax', with its much lower marginal rates, was replaced first by the 'increase in income' tax in 1971, with rates almost on a par with industry's 'wage development payments' (see introduction), and then, in 1980, by the 'work payment' tax. There was an important interim change in 1976 associated with the change in the base value for income taxation from distributed income per head to per capita value-added (see chapter 2). The basis for calculating the average per capita income within the 'increase in income' tax was changed at the same time. Previously it had been based on the total number of hours worked by the whole membership divided by an artificial figure arrived at by multiplying the number of compulsory labour days per member by the standard agricultural ten hour day. After 1976, the comparative base became the real average monthly income of the actually active work force. This had important repercussions for management's flexibility regarding labour inputs (see below), but it did not alter materially the underlying relationship between bonuses and the taxes aimed at controlling increases in income and work payments.

The 'increase in income' tax, then, was highly progressive, as indeed is its successor, the 'work payment' tax, and the regulations expressly require that they be paid out of income before any funds, including that part of the sharing fund which covers bonuses and the supplementary (20%) part of work payments, can be made. Need payment of the tax necessarily affect the final sum that can be put towards bonuses and work payment supplements, however? Co-operative farm fund formation has been considerably less regulated than fund formation within state industry. If regulations concerning the other payments to be made out of income were sufficiently flexible, might not money be diverted from them to ensure the payment of bonuses despite the incurring of the work payment or 'increase in income' tax? The regulations did not allow as much flexibility as might be imagined, however, and they became decreasingly flexible as co-operatives gained in financial strength. Government decree regulated the size of a growing number of funds between 1968 and 1977, and in the case of those funds left to co-operative discretion, the nature of their use prevented any large-scale diversion of funds from them.

Between 1968 and 1970, the agricultural co-operative was obliged to form, in addition to the sharing fund, a social and cultural fund, a development fund and an income guaranteeing fund. Of these, the development fund left little scope for manipulation because co-operative investment depended on it and it is difficult to withdraw funds from an investment once started and keep on the right side of the local Party organisation. In addition, the farm was under an obligation to increase the fund at the same rate as the expansion in the sharing fund (TRHGY, 1967, III Tv 50§). The social and cultural fund was not strictly controlled either, but it had to cover certain obligatory social insurance contributions of a fixed value and its additional uses included the provision of sports and educational facilities which, once made, might prove embarrassing to withdraw (TRHGY, 35/1967 (X.11) Korm 64§). As we saw in chapter 2, in 1971 and 1973 two additional financial contributions had been demanded from the co-operative farm's budget, the town/village contribution, at 1% of value-added (TRHGY, 31/1970 (XI.15) PM), and the reserve fund (if incomes increased enough for the 'increase in income' tax to be due). Since this latter fund had to be maintained in a separate bank account (TRHGY, 35/1972 (XI.19) PM) and the town/village contribution was at a fixed rate, little manipulation could be associated with them. The 1976 modifications in co-operative farm finances placed a new requirement on the farms to form funds, and meet other commitments to the state, in a prescribed order. This in itself restricted the possibilities of manipulation. No new obligations were placed on the co-operatives, although the Reserve Fund was set at a fixed 4% of profit, but additional suggestions were made about the use to which the 'social and cultural fund' might be put, and an additional 'house-building' fund was suggested, both of which increased the pressure on how the surplus might be used (TRHGY, 40/1975 (XI.15) PM). The 1980 modifications introduced a number of special funds to cover certain credits and repair costs on improvement work for which farms had received special grants, but otherwise made no significant change to the regulations other than greatly increase the proportion of funds which were to be centralised rather than retained by the co-operative (TRHGY, 39/1979 (XI.1) MT).

On the other hand, under none of these regulations was the 'income-guaranteeing fund', a fund unique to agricultural co-operatives, very strictly controlled.[2] The purpose of this fund was to accumulate a reserve from which the supplementary (20%) 'work payments' could be met in years when they could not be covered by the year's post tax income. If, on the other hand, the farm was sufficiently successful not to have to draw on this fund for its prescribed purpose, it is conceivable that sums might have been diverted from it to subventing managerial bonuses. Their bonuses do, after all, come from the same source as the supplementary 'work payments'. Some of the negative effects of the income-regulating taxes might have been mitigated on some farms in this way between 1968 and 1977 when the adoption of 100% 'work payments' throughout the year rendered a specific 'income-guaranteeing' fund unnecessary. Unfortunately, no concrete evidence allows the corroboration or refutation of this possibility.

Thus, while the regulation of co-operative farm incomes does not perhaps affect managerial bonus formation in the same direct fashion as it does in industry, and while the interests of 'management' and 'labour' are not so clearly divergent, the structure of the relationship between managerial control and labour is analogous in essence. If the threat to bonuses is perhaps not so great, the underlying logic of the relationship is one in which, unless specific (and by its nature only short term) diversionary action is taken, managerial bonuses in particular, as well as co-operative funds in general, are at risk from the payment of the 'increase in income' and kindred taxes.

Does management act in order to protect its interests from this potential threat? Is there any evidence of forms of manipulation of labour inputs similar to the 'labour force dilution' referred to in the introduction; and is there evidence linking such manipulation, if it exists, to the self-conscious, self-interested behaviour of the management group? Unfortunately, there have been no surveys of management motivation for adopting particular economic strategies, and secondary analysis of the type cited in the introduction's discussion of analogous issues does not exist. Nor, indeed, has there been such a furore about 'labour force dilution' in this sector, partly because of the still extensive reserves of unqualified labour which farms possess, and partly because, since they can often offer rather higher wages, co-operatives are not suffering so much from Hungary's endemic shortage of skilled labour. However, there is clear evidence that management dislikes the 'increase in income' tax and avoids paying it when possible; and there is also evidence of a number of manipulations equivalent to 'labour force dilution', some of which capitalise on the farms' ability to address both the 'family labour' and the 'socialist wage labour' persona of the labour force.

Management's dislike of the 'increase in income' tax is very evident. The president of the Red Flag co-operative is known for contributions to radio and television criticising it, and he let it be announced with pride at the end of year General Meeting in 1977 that, again, the farm had not paid the tax. In fact, the farm had never paid it. The May 1st co-operative employed a woman full-time simply to keep a check on finances and ensure that wages paid throughout the year would not result in an increase in average income in excess of the tax-free limit permitted under the tax regulations.

Nationally the extent of the problems for management caused by the tax can be gauged by the fact that, in 1977, the government was forced to modify the system for fixing the comparative base for the tax. Henceforth, the incomes of all members earning lower than average incomes who retired during a given year were retroactively discounted from the previous year's average income when the base for comparing the two income levels was being calculated. Throughout 1976, there had been widespread demands for exemption from the 'increase in income' tax.[3] The new tax base of actual average income per active member, rather than a construct of total hours worked on the farm divided by a standard ten hour day (see above), had deprived the co-operatives of their ability to juggle as freely as before with labour inputs. They could no longer employ additional cheap labour, retired members, women and those who rely on 'family labour' generally, for a few days simply in order to increase the number of hours worked at a low wage rate, and thereby reduce the level of the average farm member's income. Without this manipulative device, the effect on the average income level of the retirement of large numbers of old, and therefore relatively low paid, members could no longer be camouflaged. The co-operatives had no alternative but to ask for exemption from the tax and demand its reform because this change in the membership's age structure was unavoidable. The speed of the government's response to the farms' appeals gives some indication of the strength nationally of opposition to the tax; and this strength of opposition itself suggests that something of more immediate relevance was at stake than a general increase in the co-operatives' costs.

Co-operative farm management, then, clearly dislikes the 'increase in income' tax and perhaps feels personally threatened by it, but does it manipulate labour inputs or resort to labour force diluting strategies in order to avoid it? That it does is implicit in the discussion of the previous paragraph. Up to 1976, the only way to camouflage the effect of retiring members on the level of average incomes was to ensure that the level was kept low by filling up the time sheets with numerous part-time, low paying jobs. This practice was noted by Huszár (1973, p. 536) and by the official historian of the May 1st co-operative, and Égető has noted that 'while state enterprises were encouraged [by wage-level regulation] towards "labour force dilution", agricultural co-operatives were encouraged towards "labour day dilution"' (1976, p. 158). Since the 1976 reorganisation of the basis of income calculation, co-operatives have had to employ cheap labour from within the membership full-time if they are to manipulate the figures successfully, although a clause in the new legislation permitting the employment of 'occasional employees' from outside the co-operative, perhaps on a share-cropping basis (as on the Red Flag co-operative), does allow a certain leeway for manipulation.[4] A commentator in 1977 referred, for example, to the unnecessary employment on many co-operatives of doormen, nightwatchmen and office assistants in order to keep the average income down (*Figyelő*, 1977, No. 18) and, writing in 1984, the president of the Pannonia co-operative farm at Bonyhád confessed to long years of 'diluting' the labour force by taking on low paid workers (*Magyar Mezőgazdaság*, 1984, No. 15, p. 3). The Red Flag co-operative provided further examples. The farm, according to one manager, maintained a 'reserve labour force' paid at a derisory rate of 6 forints an hour simply to keep the average down while, at harvest time, it employed a number of young girls as 'occasional employees' to sit in the sun and count how many truck loads of wheat left each field.[5]

The Red Flag co-operative also provides an example of a less sophisticated manipulation to avoid the 'increase in income' tax. The minutes of a Leadership meeting in 1976–7 record that performance-related bonuses, which are included within the sum on which the 'increase in income' tax was based and which had been promised to certain combine drivers, had had to be withdrawn because the 'real economic situation did not permit the payment of a further bonus'. Since the total sum involved was only 25 000 forints and the farm had a net income, after the payment of taxes and fund formation, of 44.5 billion forints, the 'real economic situation' clearly did not refer to any danger of bankruptcy. It must have referred to the danger that the 'increase in income' tax might be incurred. As we have already seen, no tax was paid under this heading in the financial year concerned.

In addition to these strategies in respect of 'socialist wage labour', the integration of 'family labour' within production on the agricultural co-operatives has resulted in further novel solutions to the problem of keeping increases in the average income low. For example, what are effectively very low hourly wage rates can be paid for 'family labour' in, say, the labour-intensive branches of crop production where share-cropping is still used. This is perhaps of most significance for the economy nationally in that it permits the production of crops which might not otherwise be grown. Nevertheless it has the significant effect for the co-operative itself of allowing correspondingly higher incomes to be paid to 'socialist wage labour' in mechanised areas of production.

However, one problem incurred by the growing use of monetary payments for the 'family labour' involved in share-cropping systems was the effect of fluctuating yields, and the fluctuating wages they produced, on income regulation. In response to this, while continuing to use share-cropping, the May 1st co-operative evolved a system of payment by results which was not tied directly to the actual quality or quantity of the crop produced and, in consequence, incomes from it did not fluctuate wildly from year to year in the way that yields inevitably did. Under this system, the achievement by members on the area of land under their cultivation of the average yield for that year resulted in an income based on the average income for the three or five previous years, plus the percentage increase allowed tax-free by the 'increase in income' tax. Deviations around the average yield resulted in the equivalent deviation around this income figure. Thus, members were personally interested in maximising production on the area under their charge where they laboured as 'family labour' with no costing of their own labour, but their final incomes did not fluctuate as erratically as the fortunes of nature and thereby inadvertently trigger the 'increase in income' tax obligations for the farm. Management's justification for this system was that it offered the members a more predictable income; but the keenness with which the leaders proffered it to the membership, its illogicality in strict cost terms (why pay more in a bad year when the farm's income from its part of the share is lower?), and the fact that the farm keeps an employee constantly checking what is happening to wage levels all suggest that the system worked to the benefit of managers as well.

Co-operative farm management can manipulate 'family labour' in other ways less directly related to the problems of wage-levels. High risk, low technology, labour-intensive crops can be farmed out to the household plot. As we saw in chapter 2, before 1977 the net benefit to management of such a strategy was that produce from household plots subsequently marketed by the co-operative counted (as it still does) towards overall value-added (TJ, 1/1972 TOT), which is one of the indicators on which managerial bonuses can be based, and in 1977 the improvement and encouragement of the household plot also became a factor for which a 20% bonus could be paid to higher management. What should be stressed here is that, because it is not produced by 'socialist wage labour', this additional income is achieved without there being any further risk of crossing the 'increase in income' tax threshold. Thus, by encouraging the use of 'family labour' on the household plot, co-operative management can initiate production which would not otherwise take place, reap at least some of the rewards, and incur none of the costs. If the crop itself is a failure, management risks nothing: the members themselves absorb the loss. This system was used for tobacco production on the May 1st co-operative. The co-operative charged a fee for the basic services associated with tobacco production and left the actual growing, tending and harvesting to the household plot. While a net income (disregarding labour costs) of 700 forints per day worked could theoretically be realised from this tobacco, roughly five times the fee charged by the co-operative, if the crop failed, there would be no income for the members at all and the co-operative would still have to be paid for its services.

It would seem, then, that management on agricultural co-operative farms does manipulate labour inputs and, although in an institutional and financial context which is distinct, does so using tactics analogous to those adopted by industrial management. The labour force was 'diluted', and both 'family labour' and 'socialist wage labour' were manipulated within the farm in order to avoid the 'increase in income' tax while it existed; and there seems to be no reason why this situation should change with its replacement by an essentially similar 'work payment' tax. What is lacking from our account, however, is an outright acknowledgement that management perceives its bonuses (rather than co-operative funds generally) as being threatened by the tax and manipulates labour inputs as a form of self-conscious, self-interested, evasive action. Nevertheless, managerial bonuses clearly are so threatened. If the evasive action taken really does not surface as the recognition of a self-conscious pursuit of group self-interest, it must surely be because the relationship between managerial bonuses and the non-payment of the 'increase in income' tax has become part of the unquestioned financial environment of the co-operative farm: the interests of farm management and the farm are seen as one and the same.[6]

On the basis of the above, then, not only has 'socialist wage labour' developed within co-operative agriculture over the 1960s and 1970s in the limited sense that the full cost of labour has become a production cost, it has also become a factor of production which, as in state industry, figures in management's equations for maximising its group interest. Agricultural producer co-operatives have not only taken on an industrial form, they have also reproduced the production relations of socialist industry. We saw in chapter 4 how the growth of a division of labour within the co-operative farm entailed the emergence of a separate group of professional managers. In this chapter and the preceding one, we have seen how, in the institutionally and financially different environment of the co-operative, management enjoys virtually monopoly control over production decisions concerning the method of plan fulfilment, especially with regard to labour, and makes use of that monopoly in its own interest, adopting strategies essentially similar to those adopted by industrial management when it exercises its monopoly powers. In addition, 'family labour' has been integrated both into the co-operative farm and into this management–labour equation. Management enjoys the added possibility of capitalising on the 'family labour' of the membership, and this, together with its 'diluting' manipulations of 'socialist wage labour', compounds the Hungarian economy's irrational use of labour generally.

As a final footnote to the possibilities for manipulation offered by 'family labour', we should note that economic commentators in the early 1980s pointed to the use by industrial enterprises of 'family labour' in their new 'enterprise economic work partnerships' as a means of circumventing wage-control regulations (*Figyelő*, 1984, No. 15, p. 6; 1984, No. 18, p. 4). After taking over its production relations from industry, agricultural management has repaid the compliment and shown industry how 'family labour' can be fitted into the equation as well.

Conclusion

This book has presented an account of Hungary's successful collectivisation of agriculture, the transformation in economic relations that this entailed, and the changes in the social composition of the agricultural labour force and management that accompanied it. In a sense, the book has been about Hungarian agricultural producer co-operatives as both a socialist success and a socialist failure: about an economic success, but a social and political failure, at least in the sense that these units have failed to create a workplace environment with intrinsically socialist features. The mechanisms which exist to promote workplace democracy do not function as such. We have seen how an agricultural sector based on collective and state production units can be made to work by devoting national resources to agriculture during the period of transition and by creating 'socialist wage labour' within communal production, while at the same time integrating with it an increasingly encouraged reliance on the 'family labour' of the work force, performed in its 'marginal labour time'. The success of this policy of symbiosis as a more general economic strategy can be seen in its extension, in the form of the 'economic work partnerships' of the 1980s, from agriculture to other sectors of the economy; and it is also evident in the fact that the two areas of significant difference between Hungarian and Soviet collective farms are Hungary's active encouragement of 'family labour' and its ability to put a competitive price on the 'socialist wage labour' of the collective farm. This economic success must be of relevance to any socialist country in the developing world.

But the process of Hungarian collectivisation has been characterised by certain social and political negatives. We have seen the breakdown of the peasant farm and its replacement by farms with an

181

extended division of labour where a 'segmented labour market' operates in which women, the old and, to some extent, the former agrarian very poor lose out. We have seen the replacement in co-operative farm management of the common sense of the successful middle peasant farmer by a body of young, highly qualified, techni-cally and politically educated managers. We have seen access to this managerial group from below impeded by increasing 'credentialism': managers are obliged to have technical qualifications which those who are already manual workers cannot be expected to obtain. This might not matter if all groups within the farm could influence equally the policy decisions made within it; but that this is not the case can be seen from the outline political economy which was sketched of both production relations within the co-operative farms, and the relation between the farms and the Party/government administrative system. The Party has considerable control over the selection of personnel; it has the ability to intervene at times of crisis; yet it has little positive control over day-to-day economic activity. Decisions concerning the method of plan fulfilment fall within the compass of management alone, and the factor of production with which it has most freedom – including the freedom to manipulate – is labour. No countervailing force from the workplace side can gainsay management's prerogative in this field. Co-operative democracy in agriculture is no less a mere formality than enterprise industrial democracy and scarcely even succeeds as a system of information transfer. Hungary has transplan-ted the non-democratic, technocratic production relations of socialist industry to agriculture.

This conclusion will follow up some of the implications of these findings for larger questions: the nature of 'soviet-type' societies, the administration of a socialist economy, the socialist organisation of the workplace, the political pluralism in 'soviet-type' society. This might seem to take the discussion far beyond the subject matter of this book, and in some respects it does. The larger issues listed clearly extend beyond the organisation of agricultural production; but the reverse is not true. The nature of 'soviet-type' societies, of socialist economies, and of political pluralism constitutes the very framework for agri-cultural production as much as for any other form of production. It might be permissible to relegate agriculture to the status of unimpor-tant marginal extra in Western Europe, but it is absolutely imper-missible to do so in relation to the socialist world. All of the socialist countries of the world were predominantly agrarian societies before their revolutions, and many of them still are. Changes in economic and social relations in agriculture, therefore, are likely to reveal the kernel of the larger social change. My excuse for using this conclusion to broach the larger issues of the nature of socialist society is simply to rescue agriculture and agrarian relations from their ghetto and place them centre stage.

Hungary's general economic success relative to other Eastern European countries cannot be doubted, despite the level of its indebtedness to the West. It is not so much a question of enjoying high living standards as reflected by statistical indicators for relative prices and incomes. Hungary's success manifests itself in two rather less easily measurable ways. First, goods, and especially fresh meat and vegetables, simply are available in shops. To anyone who has experience of searching in vain for anything other than tinned fish and packets of macaroni in the supermarkets of non-tourist areas of the Soviet Union, this advantage cannot be overemphasised.

Second, this has been achieved within a social climate which is relatively non-authoritarian. Hungarian 'dissidents' occasionally get coverage by the Western media, far less than they feel they deserve, but they rarely hit the headlines. And for good reason. The Hungarian political machine is sophisticated. There is repression of course. Hungary is no open society. 'Incitement against the Hungarian People's Republic and its institutions' can be a catch-all offence (Kellner and Sághy, 1978) for which workers can be imprisoned for such trivial crimes as showing dissident poems to fellow workers in areas where local police-chiefs are overly enthusiastic (Rakovski, 1978b, pp. 55–6). Psychiatric hospitals have been used as an alternative to political imprisonment in the past, and there is some evidence of the reintroduction of the practice (Haraszti, 1982). But the norm is 'repressive tolerance': little is prohibited, but much is impeded by bureaucratic obstructionism. Everyone has the right to a passport – but it can be withdrawn if to issue one is considered injurious to the state; and the right to seek clarification about what this means in individual cases does not exist. The only option is to try again: you might be lucky next time.

On the other hand, there are no mass arrests of workers or intellectuals. The dissident intelligentsia suffers little more for its pains than severely limited career prospects and the real, but personal, frustration of knowing that its thoughts will never circulate beyond the very restricted audience of its dissident colleagues and the police authorities who keep it under surveillance. It is kept under control by the carrot of just occasionally getting an article published in a major journal such as *Valóság* and the stick of, equally occasionally, being subjected to a house search, sacked or arrested. Economic success has meant that the government can afford to take a genuinely relaxed attitude to political dissent. So long as it provides the goods, it can be sure that the intellectuals will not get mass support and can restrict its judicial machine to the indiscretions of hapless, often drunken, unskilled workers venting their frustration against the regime (Rakovski, 1978b, p. 54). But, just in case, frequent and sophisticated public opinion surveys monitor the pulse of the population at large to ascertain whether mass support is likely.

The point is not that Hungary's economy and society differ in essence from other socialist economic systems. All the major features are there and, by common consent of students of its economic reforms, the reality of enterprise autonomy under its controlled market economy can easily be exaggerated. But general policy decisions in key areas of economic organisation have had genuinely humane consequences in social and political relations. Hungary under Kádár has made concessions in consumption rather than production, a process termed variously Hungary's 'tacit compact' or 'social compromise' (Kemény, 1978a; Schöpflin, 1977, pp. 137–54; 1979, p. 180). It has followed the spirit of Bukharin's, rather than Stalin's or Trotsky's, view of socialist industrialisation and has fostered social integration by giving the population something to use its often meagre rewards from the state sector for. The socialist sector has made a concerted effort to meet some of this need, in that a general improvement in the quality of consumer goods has been one of the undisputed successes of Hungary's economic reform, and, if the state sector has not been able to produce the goods for this consumerism, the private petty commodity production sector has been first permitted, and now encouraged, to provide them.

Hungary is not unique in having a 'black' or 'second' economy, in having worker-peasants or peasant-workers, in having workers who commute long distances to combine a wage-labour income from socialist industry with an income from 'family labour' on the household plot (Kolankiewicz, 1980; Wiles, 1974b). Such a combination is an inevitable consequence of the present level of development of soviet-type societies and their current organisation of production. What distinguishes Hungary is two things: first, its commitment to consumption and, second, its readiness to allow the private sector to provide the goods when the socialist sector is not forthcoming. We have seen this in some detail in agriculture, in the increasing proportion of national resources allocated to agriculture since 1957 and in the progressive incorporation of private agricultural initiatives throughout the 1960s and 1970s. A similar pattern is visible for another fundamental consumer good – housing. As Bauer *et al.* point out, although investment decisions in Hungary are less decentralised than the theory of the New Economic Mechanism would have us believe, there is real decentralisation in construction investment: only 20–30% of investment outlays in this area are subject to central regulation compared with a norm of around 70% in other socialist economies of Eastern Europe (1981, p. 170). Hungary's division of labour in the provision of essential consumer goods since 1957 might be summed up as follows: the private sector has provided meat and vegetables, the state sector wheat for bread; the private sector has provided houses, the state sector the fridges, washing machines and TVs to go in them. Pro-consumer policies began in the wake of 1956. The novelty added by the New Economic Mechanism of 1968 was that private sector integration was encouraged to an even greater extent and the consumer goods improved in quality – fridges are made under West German licence and are competitive in world markets.

Hungary's method of collectivisation and its approach to consumption and the private sector generally have all led to conspicuous economic success, a success that is all the more creditable because of the non-authoritarian social and political structure that has accompanied it and which it has helped create. But what sort of society is Hungary's socialism? The body of this book has taken at face value the claim that the economy is socialist in a fundamental sense but, in referring to 'soviet-type societies', has fought shy of committing itself on Hungary's political and class structure. In what remains of this conclusion I wish to draw together some threads which have run through the work to attempt to put forward a model of how the society hangs together and where socialist ideology and socialist social relations fit in.

Hungarian socialist society was characterised above as an economic success and a social failure; but in one sense even the economic success can be doubted. The degree of emphasis on the petty commodity producing private sector, which has helped economic success, is also, in part, an acknowledgement of failure in the socialist sector; and part of this failure must be attributed to inefficiencies which result from structural differences of interest between management and worker which have been built into the system. The 'irrationalities' of socialist economies are not simply due to the fact that there is no market to provide rationality in the distribution of resources. They are also due to real competing interests between administrators, managers and workers. An outline political economy of Hungarian socialism (and, by extension, other variants of existing socialism) might take the following form.

The Party, using its own political machine and that of government and local administration, imposes on both economy and society a structure that is informed by socialist values, values which are more or less genuinely held by the individuals who staff those machines. One-party rule is defended because, for most, it is accepted as an article of faith that rule by the socialist party equals socialism. This belief is axiomatic and unquestioned, in much the same way as Western politicians express commitment to the 'market' or the 'mixed economy'. Such faith is unshakeable, no matter how many academic, leave alone opposition political, publications show that market forces are not free, or that the mixture in mixed economies is one-sided; and it is genuinely held, requiring no greater dissimulation than that needed by all who embark on a political career. Eastern European politicians are equally impervious to arguments that socialism need not require one-party rule, or that, objectively, the economy does not function in the interests of the working class. If there is no longer a market in a planned economy to determine value, rather the security of its being determined by the Party, even if the Party occasionally makes mistakes, than the danger of anarchy or a return to capitalism. Under socialism, the Party must determine value and, once this step has been taken, acceptance of the occasional *realpolitik* dictates from Moscow, the mother of socialisms, is a simple progression.

The Party/government machine takes its socialism seriously, and it imposes economic policies which are inspired by genuinely socialist values. The economy must grow, but not at the expense of doing away with unprofitable but necessary sectors, or the social services; nor at the expense of uncontrolled inflation and unemployment. But here the contradiction between its commitment to socialism and its particular conception of socialism comes into play. Socialist forms have not been extended to the workplace. One-party rule by the value-determining party becomes translated at the enterprise level into one-man management by an individual whose actions can be regulated, although not directly controlled, by the Party machine. Dread of the unknown precludes faith in autonomous initiative.

However, it is regulation and not control, and, with nationalisation, the dual aspects of ownership – power and responsibility – are shared. The enterprise gets the power (but is responsible only to the controlled market and individuals within the controlling ministries), the planners and the controlling ministries get the responsibility (but not the power to influence day-to-day enterprise decisions). There is a structural difference of interest. The ministry is responsible to the Party and the people for how an enterprise performs, but it does not have the power to enforce its will absolutely. This would not be so bad if enterprises were working in the national interest. But, as we have seen, this is not the case. Enterprises and co-operative farms are under management control; management is materially interested in specific ends which differ from those of the work force and are contrary to the economic good; and there are clear indications that management, not surprisingly, follows its own group interest when managing its enterprise.

The Party machine has set up a socio-economic structure which, despite its socialist origins, objectively runs in the interests of managers whom it has appointed, and not, or not necessarily, of the proletariat in whose name it rules, nor indeed of the society at large which it administers. Administrators and 'bureaucrats' are also beneficiaries in the social inequalities of soviet-type societies in that they are in a position to award themselves a larger share in the distribution of the social cake; but it is management that structures the creation of that cake, the production of social wealth, in a way that serves its own, restricted interest.

What does this mean for the economy? That there is a labour shortage because labour is cheap and development has been labour-intensive is not in itself the result of conflicting interests in the economic hierarchy. It is the result of understandable socialist policy goals, rapid economic growth and the avoidance of unemployment. That the concomitant of such a pattern of development is some bourgeoning of a petty commodity production based private sector is also the consequence of 'normal' socialist development. What is not 'normal' in the Hungarian case (and in other socialist economies the details will differ depending on the systems of economic regulation and managerial reward), and what exacerbates the problems that this pattern of development entails, is the 'wasteful' use of labour resulting from direct management manipulation in order to avoid the taxation on increases in income. An in-built tension is exacerbated by managerial pursuance of its private interest, and the economy is further distorted. But, in Hungary, both the original tension and its exacerbation have been offset by the government's successful encouragement and incorporation of the private sector. The circle has been squared.

What are the implications of this outline political economy for the class structure of soviet-type societies? Does management or the Party/government administration constitute a class? Traditionally, writers who have looked for the existence of a 'new class' in Eastern Europe have concentrated on two areas: the unequal distribution of political power and the unequal distribution of socially produced wealth. Critics from the left have pointed to the enormous power of certain (usually imprecisely defined) members of the 'bureaucracy' and have located the 'new class' there. As Trotsky states, but in failing to amplify begs all the questions, 'The state, so to speak, belongs to the bureaucracy' (1967, p. 249). Western, and to some extent indigenous, sociologists point to the social stratification and social mobility surveys carried out in the 1960s which document inequalities in the distribution of socially created wealth and to inequalities in life-chances (Andorka, 1982; Ferge, 1969; Kolosi, 1974; Konrád and Szelényi, 1979; Lane, 1971). Depending on their political persuasion, they have been more or less willing to refer to these social groups as classes.

This book has, albeit obliquely, adopted a rather different approach to the vexed question of the 'new class' by concentrating on 'work-situation' elements of class.[1] To the extent that management uses its position of monopoly control over an aspect of the production process and influences the pattern of production to its own ends, it might be considered to be a 'class': the nature of its power is certainly 'class-like'. Under capitalist relations of production (in their ideal-type form), it is the ultimate power of capitalists as owners of the means of production to dictate what production takes place, or whether production takes place at all, which divides capital from labour. The question is not so much one of ownership *or* control in the class formulation of 1960s sociology as one of the various sorts of control that the ownership of assets, rather than their administration

on behalf of others, confers. The sorts of control conferred by ownership of the means of production do not exist in soviet-type societies,
and any attempt to find them will also fail.

On the other hand, if class is not defined *a priori* as a concept which
can only be used in connection with capitalist society (and this is
essentially a doctrinal question which it would be fruitless to attempt
to resolve here),[2] then a relationship of class inequality might be said
to exist between those whose position within the relations of production allows them control over the method of plan fulfilment and
those who simply implement production decisions. The contradictory
results of this 'class-like' inequality are less far-reaching than the
contradictions of capitalism, but they are real nonetheless. The
contradictions of capitalism (again, pictured in their ideal-type form)
lead to crises of overproduction (or insufficient demand), unemployment and, occasionally, radical social change. 'Class' inequality in
Hungary's particular variant of soviet-type society merely leads to an
exacerbation of the labour shortage and 'irrational' use of labour that
already exists. Management's manipulation (if not exploitation) of
labour acts to the detriment of the social good in that resources are
wasted needlessly.[3]

What implications follow from this for the socialist organisation of
production? If there is a contradiction between management and
labour in soviet-type societies which has society-wide consequences,
can it be resolved?

Brus (1975) has forwarded a powerful case for development
towards a model of socialism based on a combination of a regulated
market environment and enterprises run under workers' control. He
sees this as the real socialisation of the means of production which
must follow their mere nationalisation; and in his book he tries to
present an argument in favour of this type of socialism which is built
around criteria other than those of moral superiority. Working from
within an intellectual framework which is clearly informed by classic
historical materialism, he seeks to show not that workers' control is
superior in any moral sense to one-man management, but that there is
evidence of an objective, immanent, economically determined trend
within socialism towards workers' control. Pointing to the growing
evidence in organisational and managerial sociology that increased,
and genuine, worker involvement is good for increasing productivity,
while the selection of competent leading personnel in a strongly
hierarchical structure is increasingly difficult, he argues that there

exists a rational basis for democratisation and so, following dialectical logic, there arises an indispensable need for democratism, a need which is grounded in economic relations (p. 197).

One supplementary aim of this book is to make a similar point about socialist enterprises, but from a different intellectual tradition. The findings presented so far have indicated that there are reasons, again not based on the moral superiority of workers' self-management, for questioning one-man management in Hungarian enterprises and agricultural producer co-operatives. They do not demonstrate the necessity of a move towards the 'real socialisation' of the means of production, but offer the basis for a case for workers' control which is grounded on less insecure terrain than it simply being a moral good-in-itself. Although it is capable of mobilising people to political action, an argument based on moral grounds alone remains forever contested. A case which successfully demonstrates a relationship between certain forms of economic relationship and certain specific results cannot be contested. The significance and value of the finding can, of course; nothing can guarantee that notice will be taken of it; and if anything inspires political mobilisation it is more likely to be the objective results of the contradictory relationship demonstrated, as it was in a different context in Poland, than the logic of the argument which demonstrates it. But the relationship still stands and must be taken into account.

The question is, then, whether establishing that a 'class-like' relationship between management, labour and the wasteful use of economic resources exists also constitutes a case for arguing that there are sound economic reasons in favour of workers' control. The case cannot be entirely secure because there is no empirical evidence that worker-controlled socio-economic systems can work in practice. The option exists of simply countering *a priori* that such economies can never work and that the inefficiencies that have been isolated above are the necessary costs of having a workable system. Such an argument is unanswerable, however, and, putting it to one side, we can maintain that the only possible resolution to the conflict which does not negate the socialist advances already gained in Hungary is further industrial democracy, or workers' control. Chapter 6 of this book established that a combination of the existing method of wage regulation, management control of the method of plan fulfilment and the differential interests of management and workers within co-operative farms has resulted in a conflict of interest between management and the social good; and in the introduction evidence was presented of a similar relationship in socialist industry. Management wastefully manipulates labour inputs in its private group interest. There are two ways to approach solving this conflict of interest: via the wage regulation mechanism and via management. Is a purely technical solution to the problem of the wasteful use of labour possible via some tinkering with the wage control mechanism, or is more structural reform necessary? And if it is, should the different interests of workers and managers be transcended by shifting management up the hierarchy of control within the Party/government pyramid, or down to the workplace level? Or can bonuses perhaps be based on something else so that management self-interest does not distort the economy? It will be argued that only the workplace democracy solution is possible if the conflict of interest is to be resolved while key socialist goals such as full employment and low inflation, together with Hungary's socialist advances of limited consumer sovereignty and a relatively plentiful supply of consumer goods, are to be retained.

The last of the options listed above, that of changing the basis of bonuses, is a non-starter. If bonuses are to exist at all, they must be based on performance which the government wants to reward. At present, bonuses are adversely affected by large increases in the average wage because the government wants to control wage inflation and preserve full employment. If the economic environment were changed so that bonuses were influenced by some other factor, this would be because this was what the government wanted – it would be essentially the same as changing the method of wage control; we would revert to the first of the approaches above. And if bonuses were not supplied from, or affected by, the state of enterprise funds, this would necessarily restrict real enterprise autonomy and put one of Hungary's key achievements at risk; we would revert to the solution of reintegrating management into the administrative hierarchy. Bonuses could, of course, be abolished entirely and one-man management retained, but this is hardly a realistic option. If one-man management were introduced to ensure safe regulation of economic enterprises, it would be peculiar not to offer some reward to managers for behaving as expected. If this were in terms of political advancement rather than economic reward, it would simply be bonuses under a different name. If there were no bonus at all of any form, the government would risk losing its control altogether. If there were no managerial bonuses, there would be little point in one-man management.

So the options reduce themselves to the following: can wage regulation be modified without jeopardising Hungary's socialist achievements; and, if not, if the problem is that management has control, but has a private conflicting interest, should this conflict be resolved by integrating management up into the administration – so threatening Hungary's socialist advances – or by dissolving it into the work force?

Adoption of a different method of wage regulation, wage-bill regulation, for example, would threaten Hungary's achievement from two quarters, depending on the context in which it was introduced. If it remained part of a decentralised package, then the arguments which lay behind the infusion since 1976 of an element of wage-level regulation within the 'wage-bill' system would still apply. The 'average-wage brake' was introduced to avoid the twin risks of unemployment and wage-push inflation if enterprises, exposed to the rigours of the market, shed their accumulated reserves of labour, while skilled workers exploited their shortage in the labour market and pushed wages up. The arguments which prevented the introduction of a fully wage-bill based system within a decentralised market structure still stand: its introduction would threaten the commitment to full employment, and Hungary is proud that its market reform has not resulted in Yugoslav levels of unemployment.

Maintaining the existing system of decentralised market regulation combined with managerial control of the method of plan fulfilment and simply tinkering with the wage regulating mechanism, then, would not solve the problem, or, rather, it could only do so by threatening fundamental socialist principles. Management would still have a group interest in avoiding 'wage-development payments'. Abolishing managerial autonomy and its ability to control production in its own interest by reintegrating management into the traditional pyramid of power in a command economy would not threaten traditional socialist values; but it would simply be a return to the economic system which predated the 1968 economic reform (and if average-wage control were also abolished, the situation before 1957). It would negate, that is, Hungary's genuine advances in socialist organisation, its increase of consumer choice and its reduction of the level of general social control. This would be a retrograde step and one which no one but the hardest of hard-liners in Hungary is seriously considering.

The only way around the conflict of interest between management and labour which does not either endanger socialism or threaten a return to an outdated form of socialism is to do away with management as a separate entity and merge management and labour functions. Under such a system, the enterprise could decide whether or not it was going to incur 'wage development payments', or their agricultural equivalent, on the basis of how the enterprise as a collective viewed its economic prospects, not because the controlling management group perceived a threat to its source of a not inconsiderable bonus. The collective view might be that incurring the tax was worth it for larger economic reasons. Since the bonus fund would now have to be spread over the enterprise as a whole, and its per capita size would consequently be smaller, the financial cost per worker of using labour rationally rather than irrationally would be considerably less penal to the individuals concerned. The average-wage mechanism would still be there as a control, but because it did not penalise so inordinately those who control production, it would simply be one of the factors in a controlled market environment, not an overriding concern within the structural relationship between the controllers and executors of production.[4]

The snag is that this inevitably poses a threat to Party control. One-man management at the enterprise level, which can then be regulated and vetted by the Party/government organisation, was the simple solution to the problem of how Party definition of value could go unquestioned under socialism. The option of the abolition of management bonuses and the retention of one-man management discussed above made no sense because the Party was scared that by weakening its ability to influence at this level in the control pyramid, the consensus about value, which is a consensus amongst the political controllers and not a social consensus, might break down and anarchy, or a return to capitalism, might follow. The Party is even more concerned at the prospect of losing control altogether at this level if management functions were handed over entirely to the work force.

Consideration of an alternative political structure for soviet-type societies lies well beyond the scope of this work. Nevertheless, despite events in Poland which demonstrate yet again that in practice it is impossible to relieve the Party of its monopoly of political power, the rational grounds for fearing anarchy as the consequence of its removal are weak. Stable economies provide a host of examples of ways in which political opposition can be institutionalised; and Hungary's economy is stable. Dissent could be channelled into some sort of party system where all parties were as committed to the achievements of socialism as Western European parties are to the 'mixed economy'. There would be plenty of room for political dissent between such groups, yet none would seriously threaten to undermine the foundations of the socialist economy. The development of such parties would, in effect, merely institutionalise the fractions which already exist: the hard-liners and reformers. Ironically, the swings in fortune between these half-acknowledged groupings within Hungary's political structure appear to follow four–five year cycles similar to the lifetimes of parliaments in the West. Hungary's political leaders have learned to trust popular initiatives in the private sector of the economy; if they were not watching the Soviet Union so intently over their shoulders, they might have faith enough in their people to do the same in the socialist sector and in the field of politics.

Appendix I. The transformation of Hungarian agriculture

A. The structure of the agricultural population in 1941, 1949, 1957 and 1960

In millions

	1941	1949	1957[a]	1960
Agricultural worker	0.64	0.16	n.a.	0.37
Day labourer	1.12	0.43	n.a.	0.10
Co-operative member	—	—	n.a.	1.46
Independent peasants and helping family members				
−0.57 ha	0.24	0.16	n.a.	0.07
0.57–2.9 ha	0.99	1.38	0.74	0.55
2.9–5.7 ha	0.76	1.43	0.42	0.56
5.7–14.3 ha	0.82	0.82	0.18	0.26
14.3 ha+		0.13	0.04	0.01
Size of agricultural population (%)	48.97	48.99	n.a.	34.17

Notes: n.a.: not available.

a. The 1957 figures refer to the number of plots of various sizes, rather than the population farming them. They are included in order to give some indication of the agricultural structure after 1956, but before final collectivisation began in 1959. The 1957 figures are more precise with respect to the categories of peasant farm. The lower figure in each row is 0.1% higher than the upper figure in the previous one. The census material is unclear on this matter.

Sources: 1960 Népszámlalás (Census), Vol. 6, p. 71; MAR, Vol. 1, p. 9.

B. *The number of Agricultural Producer Co-operatives, their average acreage and their average membership, 1948–81*

	No. of farms	Agricultural land per farm (hectares)		Membership per farm (including non-active members)
1948	279[a]	n.a.		n.a.
1949	1290	86		26.4
1950	2149	147		54.9
1951	2406	184		76.9
1952	3632	230		80.1
1953	3307	290		58.4
1954	3239	239		54.0
1955	3759	224		67.3
1956	1617	262		59.4
1957	2557	200		46.9
1958	2755	220		50.8
1959	4158	368		132.0
1960	4507	747		211.9
1961	4204	966		265.2
1962	3720	1086		295.9
1963	3612	1113		301.0
1964	3413	1206		311.2
1965	3278	1249		316.7
1966	3181	1266		321.0
1967	3033	1336		336.3
1968	2840	1391		360.2
1969	2676	1543		382.7
1970	2441	1658		419.9
1971	2373	1702		423.5
1972	2314	1752		426.5
1973	2199	1842		439.7
1974	1917	2115		496.6
1975	1598	2583	2839[b]	585.1
1976	1470		3120	626.5
1977	1425		3224	644.5
1978	1369		3365	670.8
1979	1350		3441	680.6
1980	1338		3477	675.7
1981	1320		3525	676.2

Notes: n.a.: not available.
a. Based on official estimates.
b. Calculated on a slightly different basis from Fazekas' figures: 1975 is given using both methods to facilitate comparison.
Sources: Fazekas, 1976, pp. 293–4; MGSZS, 1978, p. 134; 1981 (1982), pp. 8, 28 and 31. (Although Fazekas (1976) is not a primary source, he gives the only accessible complete run of figures. He uses Central Statistical Office sources, including those unavailable in the West.)

C. *Gross and net production indices, 1950–81, and the percentage of agricultural workers in the labour force, 1949–81*

	Gross production index	Net production index	Agricultural earners as % of all earners	
1949	—	—	54.5	
1950	100	100	51.2	
1951	117	123	49.0	
1952	86	73	47.0	
1953	105	105	43.9	
1954	105	96	43.0	
1955	118	114	43.2	
1956	102	90	43.0	
1957	117	109	44.2	
1958	123	110	43.0	
1959	128	114	41.6	
1960	120	102	40.0	37.7
1961	118	96	37.3	33.8
1962	122	101	35.7	31.7
1963	128	107	34.0	30.1
1964	134	110	32.1	28.4
1965	127	99	31.2	27.4
1966	139	109		26.6
1967	144	110		26.2
1968	145	109		25.8
1969	155	123		25.0
1970	146	98		24.0
1971	160	108		23.3
1972	164	111		22.7
1973	175	119		21.9
1974	181	116		20.9
1975	183	117		20.4
1976	178	n.a.[a]		19.8
1977	197	n.a.		19.3
1978	201	n.a.		19.3
1979	199	n.a.		19.3
1980	207	n.a.		19.5
1981	207	n.a.		19.6

Notes: a. MGSZS, 1981 (1982), p. 153, gives a coy graph showing the net production index oscillating around 110 between 1975 and 1981. It takes 1960 as 100. The 1950 base in 1960 was 102.

Sources: Column 1: To 1972 (MAK, 1973, No. 2, p. 40); 1973 (MAK, 1974, No. 2–3, p. 1); 1974 (MAK, 1975, No. 2–3, p. 14); 1975–7 (MGSZS, 1978, p. 18); 1978–81 (MGSZS, 1981 (1982), p. 10). Column 2: To 1974 (see column 1); 1975 (Fazekas, 1976, p. 292). Column 3: To 1965 (MAR, Vol. 2, p. 3); from 1960 (MSZS, 1978, pp. 8–9; 1981 (1982), p. 7). Before 1960 workers in forestry and water supply counted amongst agricultural earners. The MAR figures are extended up to 1965 in order to facilitate comparison with the post 1960 series.

Appendix II

Ancillary enterprises within agricultural co-operatives:[a] number of units engaged in non-agricultural activity

	1968		1971		1972		1973		1974		1975		1976	
Food supply industry	916	(20%)	1681	(25%)	2273	(31%)	2790	(37%)	3116	(40%)	2481	(37%)	2279	(37%)
Milk processing	68	(7%)	472	(28%)	595	(26%)	434	(16%)	343	(11%)	255	(10%)	176	(8%)
Meat processing	71	(8%)	158	(9%)	179	(8%)	173	(6%)	185	(6%)	187	(7%)	190	(8%)
Chicken and egg processing	—		14	(1%)	24	(1%)	20	(1%)	21	(1%)	14	(1%)	22	(1%)
Wine production	5	(1%)	437	(26%)	486	(21%)	513	(18%)	475	(15%)	385	(16%)	363	(16%)
Alcohol fermentation	198	(22%)	235	(14%)	283	(13%)	267	(10%)	273	(9%)	257	(10%)	249	(11%)
Pickling	—		105	(6%)	113	(5%)	97	(4%)	80	(3%)	70	(3%)	55	(2%)
Baking	21	(2%)	48	(3%)	58	(3%)	57	(2%)	64	(2%)	60	(2%)	59	(3%)
Wood processing	346	(8%)	716	(11%)	914	(13%)	1028	(13%)	977	(12%)	931	(14%)	933	(15%)
Extraction and supply of building materials	920	(20%)	1131	(17%)	1158	(16%)	1093	(14%)	949	(12%)	821	(11%)	747	(12%)
Supply of other industrial products	628	(14%)	847	(13%)	809	(11%)	791	(10%)	707	(9%)	707	(11%)	712	(12%)
Industrial services	1745	(38%)	2309	(35%)	2164	(30%)	2137	(27%)	2131	(27%)	1748	(26%)	1459	(24%)
Total industrial units	4555	(100%)	6684	(100%)	7316	(100%)	7839	(100%)	7880	(100%)	6688	(100%)	6130	(100%)
Farms engaged in transportation	1853		2328		—		—		—		—		—	
No. of shops	1818		1509		1497		1507		1388		1365		1362	
No. of restaurants, etc.	409		710		752		779		823		843		1291	

Notes: The figures in brackets refer to percentages of all industrial units except for the subgroups of the food supply industry which are percentages of the food supply industry as a whole.
a. These figures refer to all co-operatives rather than 'producer co-operatives'. Very few ancillary enterprises are attached to looser co-operatives.
Sources: MGSZS, 1974–8; TOT 1976.

Notes

1 See, for example, Bauer (1970, 1975, 1981), Laki (1980) and A. K. Soós (1979). Rakovski (1978a, pp. 73–104) presents the argument in more lay terms, while Gábor and Galasi (1978, 1981; Gábor, 1979c) apply the argument to the specific case of labour policy.

2 Kemény (1982) emphasises that workers are active on two markets and their economic rationality when active in the private sector. He does not consider the relevance of 'family labour' to the latter form of activity, however.

3 Measures taken to restrict labour mobility can be divided into two groups: (a) those taken to redress imbalances and control wage levels; (b) those taken to restrict actual mobility.

(a) TRHGY, 1001/1973 (I.24) MT and 1007/1974 (III.6) MT both increased the incomes of those in state industry and increased differentials between skilled and unskilled workers. TRHGY, 6/1974 (II.22) MUM introduced a wage table giving the maximum and minimum rates to be paid for all jobs classified by degree of difficulty and level of skill required. Enterprises were required to adopt these limits by 1975.

(b) Compare TRHGY, 5/1967 (X.8) MUM, 11/1967 (X.20) MUM, 5/1969 (VII.23) MEM–MUM, 11/1971 (IV.29) MUM, 10/1976 (VI.24) MUM, 7/1976 (IV.10) MUM, and 18/1976 (XII.18) MUM. More important than these national regulations were initiatives by local labour offices, see MTA–KISZ (1971) and Gábor and Galasi (1981).

4 In addition to the traditional trade union rights in areas of social benefits and working conditions, the 1968 regulations gave the trade union organisation within the enterprise the right to express an opinion on the appointment of managers and on policy matters which affected the work force. Modifications in 1972 required the National Trade Union Council be consulted on drafting five year plans (MTVR, 1973, pp. 19–21 and 281). Since 1975, trade unions have been required to express an opinion on the distribution of profits (TRHGY, 28/1975 (XI.15) MT, 37/1975 (XI.15) PM). For a summary of trade union rights as they stood in 1977, see TRHGY, 1018/1977 (V.7) MT–SZOT. The right of veto is, in fact,

rarely used. Czippan (1973) documents only 150 instances of its use between 1968 and 1973. Since in 1970 5681 industrial sites in Hungary employed 1.5 million people within 812 state enterprises (SE, 1978, p. 141), it is clearly only a tiny minority of trade union bodies which feel the need to enforce this right.

5 Héthy and Makó (1972a, 1972b, 1978), Kemény (1978b) and Hegedűs and Márkus (1966) give evidence of informal groupings amongst workers. Simonyi (1978) reveals how closely the ability of informal groups to act successfully is related to technology and monopoly control of a key stage in production.

6 For a more detailed discussion of this topic see my PhD thesis: 'Collectivization and the development of "socialist wage labour" in Hungarian agriculture 1946–77', University of Cambridge, 1981, pp. 49–64. Marrese (1981) gives a brief summary of all systems of wage regulation in Hungary since 1950.

7 'Labour force dilution' is referred to in, for example, the following texts: I. Antal (1968a, 1968b, 1969); Botos (1970); Buda (1972, p. 93); Ferge and Antal (1972, p. 81); Kaltenecker and Horváth (1971); Lökkös (1978); Marrese (1981); Nemes and Bullányi (1973); Nemes (1976); Portes (1972, p. 655); Révész (1972, 1974); Richet (1981); and Wiles (1974a). The problem of wage-level regulation for the rational use of labour by enterprises was such that Balázsy (1978) could refer to it as an 'evergreen problem', while for Laky (1980) it had become the 'classical problem'. By 1984, an article had appeared in *Figyelő* (1984, No. 12, p. 4) sanctioning the hiring out of surplus labour on agricultural co-operatives to state enterprises as a means of getting round some of the problems associated with wage-level regulation. This practice had been prohibited in 1969 by one of the measures taken to restrict labour mobility (see note 3 above).

1. 'FAMILY LABOUR' IN THE ACHIEVEMENT AND CONSOLIDATION OF COLLECTIVISED AGRICULTURE, 1946–68

1 From 1957 onwards agriculture's share of the national budget oscillated between 18% and 20% compared with 17% in 1954–5 and 13% during the first five year plan (1950–4) (Berend, 1974a, p. 102).

2 See TRHGY, 1959 évi 7 tvr 11§ for further details. 'Kulaks' were excluded from independent producer co-operatives and type III producer co-operative groups in 1951 (TRHGY, 18010/1951 (I.20) FM; 1070/1953 (XI.12) MT 12). Previous regulations had not excluded them specifically.

3 Orbán (1972, p. 78) estimates that the 'kulak' list could have been halved if the dividing line had been taken at 19.9 ha instead of 14.25 ha. Erdei (1977) estimates that in Bács-Kiskun county a farm of 28.5 ha scarcely counted as a middle peasant farm because of the poor quality of the land.

4 For more details compare TRHGY, 18010/1951 (I.20) FM and TRHGY, 1959 évi 7 tvr 24§. In 1956 the sum was set at 10–20% (TRHGY, 1091/1956 (XI.11) MT).

5 Compare TRHGY, 18010/1951 (I.20) FM and TRHGY, 1959 évi 7 tvr 46§. The new regulations emphasised that the sum should be paid and

that members had a right of complaint if it was not. This right of complaint disappeared in 1960, however (TRHGY, 1960 évi 8 tvr).

6 This is still the case. See TRHGY, 133/1950 (V.7) MT; 18010/1951 (I.20) FM; 1959 évi 7 tvr 46§; 1967 III TV; 1977 évi 9 tvr.

7 Note also that in 1955 the distinction between type I and type II producer co-operative groups was abolished. Both became agricultural producer co-operative groups. Simultaneously, the notional distinction between the type III producer co-operative group and the independent producer co-operative was also abandoned.

8 Orbán considers this problem nationally (1972, p. 83) and K. Hegedűs (1972) provides one of the many farm histories which deal with it at a local level. The emotions aroused by collectivisation are best seen in literary sources such as Sánta (1964).

9 Subsequently two main types of looser co-operative were permitted: the agricultural producer co-operative groups (which did not specialise in any particular product), and the specialised co-operatives where members concentrated on a specific crop – usually fruit or viticulture – for their joint production. In addition, there existed 'hill groups' in certain hilly regions with poor soil. In 1968, all looser co-operatives were termed 'specialised co-operatives' (TRHGY, 50/1968 (XII.31) MEM; Gyenis, 1971).

10 For details of aid to co-operative farms, see the 3004 series of government decrees, also TRHGY, 1024/1964 (IX.13) Korm; 17/1964 (XII.30) FM; 10/1967 (XII.27) FM. The commitment to agriculture can be seen from the following figures. In 1964, 22% of all Hungarian investment went into agriculture, as did 21% in 1965 (Feher, 1970, p. 21). There were five broad types of aid: investment credits and grants; price reductions on new machinery; the training of qualified agronomists and bookkeepers; the provision of facilities for the further training of existing leaders and the establishment of research and advice centres at universities and colleges; and the supplementing of incomes of agronomists and other specialists who were sent out to the economically weaker farms.

11 TRHGY, 3004/1/1959 (II.1) Korm offered no price reduction and prohibited the purchase of combines. TRHGY, 3004/2/1959 (XI.15) Korm offered a price reduction but prohibited the purchase of combines. TRHGY, 3004/3/1960 (XI.17) Korm offered a price reduction and placed no restrictions on the type of equipment purchased. A new preamble also stressed the independence of the co-operative farms. Szilágyi (1969) gives a full account of the mechanisation of Hungarian agricultural producer co-operatives.

12 In 1961 there were 235 machine stations and 2 repair shops; in 1963 there were 215 machine stations and 18 repair shops; in 1965 there were 63 machine stations and 110 repair shops; in 1967 there were 20 machine stations and 131 repair shops (*Figyelő*, 1969, No. 22).

13 The age limit for these benefits was a further five years higher for both sexes: 70 for men and 65 for women.

14 Referred to in TRHGY, 6/1953 (II.8) MT. TRHGY, 1065/1955 (VII.19) MT extended family allowances.

15 TRHGY, 13/1966 (VI.23) FM and TRHGY, 10/1966 (IV.16) FM also

initiated regulations concerning industrial accidents and their avoidance on co-operatives.

16 In 1951, when this system was made compulsory on type III co-operative groups and independent producer co-operatives (TRHGY, 1022/1951 (VII.8) MT), a universal value for the work unit was established throughout the country. Later, individual co-operatives could fix their own value for the unit.

17 Bango (1974–5, pp. 184 and 191) documents the aid given for the employment of specialists and bookkeepers, but fails to mention that those doing manual jobs were also taken on as employees. TRHGY, 1073/1953 (XI.12) MT permitted the payment of wages only to specialists; TRHGY, 1959 évi 7 tvr was silent on the matter. Employees only have the right to 'stipend land', which is limited to half the area of members' household plots. Although the guaranteed wage paid to employees initially gave them a higher income, by the 1970s the situation had changed. With relatively high 'work payments' for most members, the relative advantage associated with employee status diminished and now it commonly serves as a form of apprenticeship. Those wishing to join a farm are taken on as employees for a year or more before being allowed to upgrade to full membership.

18 The notion of 'unskilled labour' in the context of traditional agriculture is considered critically in chapter 3.

19 Lázár (1976) reports that István Szabó, later chairman of the National Producer Co-operative Council, almost lost his Party membership for initiating the Nádudvar system.

2. 'FAMILY LABOUR' AND 'SOCIALIST WAGE LABOUR': FROM INTEGRATION TO SYMBIOSIS, 1968–77

1 In 1965 there was a revaluation of capital goods used in agriculture. The depreciation fund was henceforth to be counted as a production cost, 30% of its value being payable in the June and the remaining 70% in the December of each year.

2 In 1973 the tax on incomes was increased (TRHGY, 31/1972 (X.13) PM) and in 1974 the maximum marginal rate was increased to 400% (TRHGY, 40/1974 (XII.28) PM).

3 In 1975, as a temporary measure, farms with an average income of under 3000 forints per member were allowed to pay at a rate one tax band lower than the rate which theoretically applied to them (TRHGY, 27/1975 (VI.30) PM).

4 This imbalance in actual money incomes led to tensions between workers and 'peasants'. The centrally introduced wage increases of 1973 and 1974 (TRHGY, 1001/1973 (I.24) MT; 1008/1974 (III.6) MT) were presented as an attempt to redress this imbalance.

5 Some areas of potential conflict are considered very briefly in chapter 5. Workers interviewed by the author resented changes in norms. Those who had previously worked in industry used rather more sophisticated criteria when comparing the value of various jobs and judging whether piece-rates

were fair. Other members were more concerned simply with the size of the final income.

6 See TRHGY, 35/1967 (X.11) Korm, modified by TRHGY, 46/1971 (XII.28) Korm. From 1972 co-operatives were allowed to pay overtime, but no rates were suggested.

7 See TRHGY, 20/1976 (V.27) MEM. Days spent working on the household plot could count towards the work days necessary in order to qualify for benefit. Under TRHGY, 6/1976 (II.18) MUM, members could henceforth store up periods of unused benefit.

8 See variously TRHGY, 41/1967 (X.22) Korm; 1/1970 (II.15) SZOT; 2004/1972 (III.28) MT; 1970 évi 34 tvr; 32/1972 (XI.2) Korm. The 'pension supplements' introduced in 1960 for those who had not completed ten pension years were continued. Their average value was two thirds of the pension proper (Fazekas, 1976, p. 279). The 1975 reorganisation of the system of social benefits nationally had no specific effect on agricultural co-operative pensions.

9 Figures not in Appendix I are taken from MGSZS, 1978, pp. 34, 53, 115–16 and 126.

10 See TRHGY, 51/1967 (XI.24) Korm; 33/1967 (XII.22) PM; 47/1970 (XI.24) PM; 39/1970 (XI.12) PM; 25/1972 (VII.30) MT; 37/1973 (XII.24) MT; 42/1973 (XII.28) PM.

11 See TRHGY, 33/1967 (XII.22) PM. Incomes of 50 000 forints per year were subjected to taxation if there was 'regular' employment of outside labour, whereas the tax threshold was 70 000 forints per year if labour was only hired occasionally, and 100 000 forints per year for those who hired no labour at all. In addition, the tax rates themselves were higher for those who employed outside labour. The 1976 reform of the tax structure, among other things, introduced a more generous definition of the 'regular' employment of outside labour.

12 This prohibition does not extend to specialised co-operatives.

13 This does not mean that no produce is sold at all. It is likely that these figures are underestimates. Simó (1977, p. 487) also reports that 18.1% of members either had no plot or the plot contributed an insignificant amount to their income.

14 Égető does not indicate precisely which period she is referring to. The figure accepted by most reasearchers in this field is 40–50% and was the figure reported by many of the co-operative farm members interviewed by the author.

15 This was reported by all those involved in co-operative agriculture and was the motivation behind the forms of aid discussed below in this chapter. See also the figures presented in Tables 3.11 and 3.12.

16 Rosenfeld (1979) gives a brief summary of some of these measures.

17 The wholesale market in Hungary is not entirely free. Tobacco, paprika, bread grains, sugar, pork and beef can only be purchased by the appropriate monopoly state enterprise. The free market is restricted to fruit, vegetables and 'mixed products' (honey, rabbits, geese, etc). On this market, the County Foodstuff Centres (which have GCMC representation within them), the GCMCs themselves and the state purchasing and

processing enterprises all compete. Since the state enterprises are the strongest forces on this market, and since they prefer to deal with large suppliers, it is the GCMCs which are the major purchasers from small-scale farmers (M.-né. Hegedűs, 1975, pp. 212–13).

18 The 'specialised groups' concentrate on the 'mixed products', although pig rearing for marketing via GCMCs has been introduced in some counties (M.-né. Hegedűs, 1975, p. 211).

19 Since this aid is dependent on adherence to specific regulations concerning, for example, the size of the building for which investment aid is offered (Győry and Tiszolczy, 1975, pp. 58–9), its real value might be questioned. The specialised groups do not operate on a sufficiently large scale for such aid to be taken up.

20 In 1977 additional measures were introduced regulating the activity of the specialised groups (TRHGY, 1977 évi 8 tvr; 32/1977 (IX.22) MEM). The groups were obliged henceforth to keep proper accounts, and it was recommended that they become an integral part of the GCMCs (Villányi, 1977, p. 702).

21 See TRHGY, 12/1977 (III.12) MEM 74§. The prohibition on horse ownership had long been both irrelevant (given the level of mechanisation on the co-operative farms) and ineffective. It did not extend to other small agricultural producers (who were subject to taxation for their horses) and most co-operative families could find a relative or friend who was not a co-operative member to act as nominal owner of a horse if one was required.

22 It is not clear from the statistics whether the figures for services (660 million forints) include services such as the ploughing of household plots when it is provided free for pensioner members.

23 This is referred to in the literature as a 'traditional duty' and it had a precursor on the pre-war agricultural estates (Illyés, 1967, p. 149). It has presumably existed since the early 1960s when the co-operatives acquired sufficient tractor power to make it possible.

24 Certain exemptions to this prohibition on the payment of 'household plot money' were permitted. It could be paid to retired members, members incapable of work due to illness and in other 'exceptional cases'. It remained very easy to get round the restriction. The farm could simply buy the produce back from members at the state purchase price. Produce need not actually change hands, although an additional stage of paperwork was necessary.

25 Unfortunately, there are no recent figures for the extent of the use of share-cropping and similar methods of payment on co-operative farms. Kalocsay (1970) considers the use of such methods at the end of the 1960s on the basis of a survey of 89 farms in 13 counties. At that time, share-cropping and kindred forms of payment were used in 5% of wheat production, 62% of maize production, 44% of potato production and 42% of sugar beet production. Payment in kind was most common in maize, potatoes and sugar beet production (in 29%, 27% and 30% of cases respectively) (Kalocsay, 1970, p. 16). Since Kalocsay was writing, maize production particularly has been fully mechanised and the use of share-cropping will have declined to the level of other cereals.

3. THE SOCIAL COMPOSITION OF THE AGRICULTURAL PRODUCER CO-OPERATIVE LABOUR FORCE

1 Since 1967 the minimum number of labour days necessary in order to qualify for membership (and the household plot rights which go with it) has been 150 for men and 100 for women (TRHGY, 1967 évi III TV). In the 1959 regulations it was 120 for men and 80 for women (TRHGY, 19/1959 (VII.12) FM).

2 Galeski (1975, pp. 33–53) discusses peasant farming and the concept of an occupation.

3 Monthly incomes of 8000–10 000 forints a month are possible for the brief period of the harvest on successful farms like the Red Flag co-operative. This should be contrasted with the upper limit of 10 000 forints a month (and lower limit of 4700 forints a month) for presidents' salaries in 1977 (TRHGY, 19/1977 (V.25) MEM–MUM). In 1977 the level of average earnings for full-time manual members and employees was 3027 forints a month, while that for non-manual members and employees was 4031 forints per month (MGSZS, 1978, p. 127).

4 The terms 'segmented' and 'dual' labour markets were first coined by economists (Doeringer and Piore, 1971). For examples in the British literature of sociological applications of the concepts see Barron and Norris (1976), Rubery (1978) and Friedman's (1977) account of 'centre' and 'periphery' workers. While not wanting to get involved in the debates this approach has fostered (especially about the explanatory powers of the terms), this book will make use of the term 'segmented labour market' to refer to the peculiar labour market on agricultural producer co-operatives where 'family labour' and 'socialist wage labour', following their distinctive logics, coexist and in some senses compete.

5 Gyenes (1968, 1973) distinguishes between 'workers' and 'peasants'. The distinction between 'immobile' and 'mobile' workers was also made by Dr Iván Novobáczky, then Secretary of the National Producer Co-operative Council, in a personal interview in 1976.

6 Szabady (1971) presents figures showing the near universality of the nuclear family in Hungary. However, A. Hegedűs (1971, p. 113) warns that this does not always mean that generations live apart. Before 1968, each separate household had the right to a household plot and consequently families would declare themselves separate households even if they shared the same dwelling. Since 1968 this has become unnecessary because individual members, not individual households, have the right to a plot.

7 Co-operative farm members from this generation are more likely to have two family members in the farm because, once the decision has been made in their mid thirties to remain domiciled in the village, both are likely to seek a job locally. Older generations, on the other hand, are more likely to contain a family member who has retired.

8 It is worth noting here that Illyés describes how women on the pre-war agricultural estates worked as day labourers and share-croppers (1967, pp. 154 and 221). Jobs in these areas could scarcely be termed 'mobile', however, in the sense of this chapter.

9 Both surveys only consider those employed full-time on the farms. The Co-operative Research Institute survey was based on a random selection from a blank map of 1% of farms in 1967 and a selection of every third name from the list of working members on the farm (P.Juhász, 1975, p. 243). Only workers who had performed at least 80–100 days were included in the sample, thus discounting the majority of pensioners. As we have seen, a large proportion of occasional workers, especially in crop production, are women; nevertheless, a large number of women must have been included in this survey (see Table 3.6). Published sources do not reveal how the Sociological Research Institute's sample was chosen, although Ladányi informs us that it was a representative one (1977, pp. 28–40). The majority of those included in the sample must have been employed full-time simply because the survey was of male heads of household who, if they are not pensioners, are more likely to be employed full-time (see Table 3.6).

10 Although Kunszabó compares the individual's status in 1938 with that in 1962 in this table, it can be assumed for a number of reasons that the occupational and landholding structure did not change very radically between 1938 and the period immediately prior to collectivisation. The Homokhátság area is one in which there was very little industrial development before the 1960s and where the land reform had minimal effect because of the absence of large estates. Furthermore, land in the area is so poor that few were able to survive on the basis of the small parcels which were received under the reform. The former landless failed as farmers, sold up to their slightly richer neighbours and returned to the life of the day labourer. Because of the poor quality of the land, Kunszabó increased the acreage which was necessary to qualify as a 'middle peasant' in his study. Despite the fact that we can discount the significance of changes which took place between 1938 and the late 1950s, it remains true that Kunszabó's sample is a very limited one. Because the main concern of his study lies elsewhere, the sample only includes individuals who were old enough to have a child of working age by 1970, but who were themselves working in both 1938 and 1962.

11 Since there is likely to be an over-representation in all occupations within state farms of those who came from landless and poor peasant backgrounds, any error induced by the inclusion of state farms would be in the opposite direction to the clearest findings in the survey concerning the location of the former middle peasantry.

12 Columns five and six are 'collapsed' from the original table. This 'collapsing' was performed on the percentage figures since the raw data were not available. Although this is bad statistical practice, the 'collapsed' figures are not the ones of relevance to the main concerns of this chapter. They are included simply to give some indication of the proportion of the village population which is employed outside agriculture.

13 No information has been published concerning the nature of this sample.

14 The Co-operative Research Institute carried out a further repeat study in 1977. This survey did not repeat questions on social origin and does not indicate that any unexpected changes took place between 1972 and 1977.

The only novel feature is that there has been a fall in the number of members performing jobs which 'require no special skills'. This is presumably a consequence of continuing mechanisation in all fields. Despite the decrease in the number of occupations in this category between 1972 and 1977, there remained a net increase when 1977 is compared with 1967 (P. Juhász, 1979).

4. PROFESSIONAL MANAGEMENT ON AGRICULTURAL PRODUCER CO-OPERATIVES: GENESIS AND SOCIAL CHARACTERISTICS

1 The term 'president' rather than 'chairman' (both of which are possible translations of the Hungarian) is used for two reasons: (i) because its connotations with large corporations fit better the scale of co-operative farm ventures; (ii) because it avoids possible confusion with the chairmen of the various committees within the co-operative farm.

2 Donáth suggests that: production value per hectare does not increase in larger farms; capital equipment is used less efficiently; unit costs are no cheaper than on smaller farms; and profits per hectare are lower on the bigger farms (1976a, p. 664).

3 See Gyenes (1968) and Pál (1977). Pál reproduces the documents authorising the functioning of the first 558 producer co-operatives and producer co-operative groups. They include a description of the farms, their members and the equipment they have available.

4 For more details on the aid given to weaker farms to employ qualified personnel see TRHGY, 32/1960 (XII.22) FM; 11/1963 (XI.10) FM; 1024/1964 (IX.13) Korm; 16/1964 (XII.30) FM; 10/1967 (XII.27) MEM; 2/1971 (III.20) MEM.

5 Erdei's results are based on a 'representative sample in some counties'.

6 Unfortunately, no national figures on co-operative agriculture distinguish between workers in management and workers within administration.

7 There is no conclusive evidence in favour of either explanation. It should be noted, however, that nothing in the literature indicates the re-election of newly qualified presidents.

8 The slower overall growth in the proportion of qualified managers (for whom compulsory minimum qualifications were introduced in 1977) compared with that of presidents (for whom no mandatory minimum qualifications apply) tends to reinforce the view that, on the occasion of two farms merging, it was the more highly qualified of the two former presidents who took charge of the enlarged farm.

9 Because of this career mobility, it is unusual for the new generation of presidents and managers to be locals. Kunszabó (1970b, p. 1299), for example, found that in one village, of the 17 'new intelligentsia' domiciled there, only 1 had been born in the village and only 3 had lived there for more than three years.

10 See TRHGY, 31/1977 (IX.22) MEM. Those already in jobs were required to gain the necessary qualifications within two years. Men aged over 40, and women aged over 45, were exempted from acquiring the general educational and political qualifications, but not the professional

ones. All those aged over 50 were exempted from the regulations altogether.

11 Bognár and Simó (1975, p. 95) take this to mean attendance at any establishment of political education which gives a certificate to pupils on completion of the course (marxist middle schools, evening universities and Party schools).

12 This section is based partly on TRHGY, 19/1974 (VIII.18) MEM, and partly on interviews with personnel managers.

5. CO-OPERATIVE MANAGEMENT'S AUTONOMY

1 See the 3004 series of government decrees and TRHGY, 1028/1967 (IX.8) MT; 1041/1969 (XII.7) MT; 1045/1970 (XI.17) MT (plus subsequent amendments); 1030/1975 (XI.15) MT (plus subsequent amendments).

2 It should be noted that the formalism of the Soviet *nomenklatura* as it relates to the lower levels in the administrative hierarchy can itself be exaggerated, and this in turn exaggerates the degree of difference between the Hungarian and Soviet systems. Schapiro (1965, p. 127) emphasises that it is a series of documents and procedures rather than a single entity, and Churchward (1975) stresses that, at the local level, it is simply a vetting process which ensures that those appointed to certain posts are acceptable to the Party organisation. See also Fainsod's study of Smolensk in the 1930s when dealing with the appointment of lower level managers (1959, p. 64).

3 In 1966 co-operatives were allowed to set up shops to market their own produce (TRHGY, 7/1966 (II.5) FM) and to provide transport services (TRHGY, 1/1966 (VI.30) FM–KPM). The following year, this was extended to the provision of marketing, purchasing and processing activities subject to the approval of the local council's Executive Committee.

4 Ministerial permission was still required before certain kinds of processing activity could be undertaken (TRHGY, 19/1969 (XII.31) MEM).

5 There had been certain exemptions in the 1971 regulations which were subsequently changed. TRHGY, 48/1971 (XII.31) PM increased the rates of production tax on industrial activities and decreased those on agriculture-related activity. TRHGY, 1048/1971 (XII.14) Korm decreed that from June 1972, new engineering, light industrial and chemical operations could be undertaken only if the farm concerned had a contract with a state enterprise. Farms where 30–50% of the value of sales came from engineering, light industrial or chemical operations were obliged to pay the production tax for that industry and were renamed Agricultural-Industrial Producer Co-operatives. Farms where over 50% of the value of sales came from the above sources were obliged to pay the production tax, a 5% charge on assets and an 8% wages tax, bringing them into line with the state industrial enterprises. These co-operatives were to be renamed Industrial-Agricultural Producer Co-operatives. In 1974, there were only 34 Agricultural-Industrial Producer Co-operatives in the country, of

which 16 were in Pest county; and there were only 5 Industrial-Agricultural Producer Co-operatives, all of them in Pest county (MAK, 1975,
No. 4). In 1975, the number of Agricultural-Industrial Co-operatives had
increased to 46 (24 in Pest county), and there remained 5 Industrial-
Agricultural Producer Co-operatives.

6 This was officially recognised in a government decree (TRHGY,
1025/1969 (VII.1) Korm), which acknowledged that the areas of new
employment had not always coincided with areas of surplus labour in
agriculture. It should be noted that diversification into non-agricultural
activity did not generally take place at the expense of agriculture. In fact,
it often stimulated a faster growth in agricultural production as well
(M. Hegedűs, 1971, p. 809).

7 Financial considerations were not abandoned altogether. The Hungarian
National Bank was given the power to determine whether a co-operative's
development fund was capable of covering a given investment project. A
credit squeeze was also introduced for all construction and refitting
projects. Twenty per cent of the cost of such projects had to be lodged in a
separate fund in the National Bank. Farms were additionally obliged to
use all other possible sources of finance before turning to the Bank for
credit. In addition, investment credits for certain types of project were
occasionally cut completely (TRHGY, 26/1975 (XI.3) PM–MEM;
19/1977 (X.31) PM).

8 The following additional points should be noted. At the 1976 Producer
Co-operative Congress, Mrs Attila Zámori, lawyer of the Kunság People
agricultural producer co-operative, commented that in the four years
since 1971, 219 official, but not legally binding, directives or circulars had
been issued in addition to 308 legal documents (A. Balogh, 1977,
pp. 118–21). The reverse of this coin is that the local level administration
is sent copies of the farms' yearly plans, while the ministry, the National
Bank and the Central Statistical Office receive copies of the farms'
quarterly accounts (B. Szabó, 1974, pp. 35–44).

9 If the General Meeting is split into 'Part Meetings' because of the size of
the membership and their dispersal over many villages, the agenda for
each Meeting must be the same, an overall two thirds majority of the
whole of the membership is required to change fundamental legislation,
and a member of the supervisory committee (explained below) is required
to be present at each meeting.

10 In 1984, the right to establish a 'specialised group' was transferred to the
Leadership from the General Meeting or Meeting of Representatives
(*Magyar Mezőgazdaság*, 1984, No. 10, p. 26).

11 The supervisory committee is entirely independent of the Leadership and
the president and is directly responsible to the General Meeting alone. It
must consist of at least five members who are elected for a period of five
years. The chairman of the supervisory committee has the right to attend
Leadership meetings and must report to the General Meeting at least once
a year. The committee reports any irregularities it uncovers first to the
Leadership; if the error is not rectified, it is then required to call a General
Meeting to discuss the matter.

12 For a discussion of 'production systems' see Tiszáné Gerai and Meszticzky (1977) and Swain (1981).
13 For example, the working members pointed out that the problem of untidiness in the cowshed could not simply be blamed on 'lax labour discipline'. It was also the result of shortages – in this case, a shortage of pipes.
14 It was noted above that since 1977 trade unions have been permitted to organise amongst the employees of co-operative farms. There is no reason to believe that they will be more successful in defending worker interests than the industrial unions discussed in the introduction.
15 She does not explain why the total is 103.9%.
16 These events are described in more detail by Hann (1980).

6. THE EXERCISE OF MANAGERIAL CONTROL IN AGRICULTURE

1 This is even true of net income (until 1977), since only 80% of work payments count as wage costs.
2 In 1971 it was suggested that it be set at between 30% and 35% of distributable income, however (TRHGY, 1045/1970 (X.17) Korm).
3 It has been estimated by a rural sociologist in Hungary that 40% of co-operative farms requested exemption from the tax in 1976 (personal report).
4 See TRHGY, 40/1975 (XI.15) PM. Because of the nature of agricultural production, the regulations have to allow for seasonal labour to be incorporated somehow into the calculation of the average labour force as a base for the subsequent calculation of the average per capita income. If sufficient 'occasional labour' is employed at a sufficiently low wage rate, this can reduce the value of the average income. A relatively low rate can be paid to such workers because they have their own, or their spouse's, household plot to fall back on.
5 Essentially similar ploys aimed at minimising increases in the value of the average income were reported in two other farms visited, one financially secure, the other officially 'bankrupt', that is, its finances were being restructured by the local council.
6 It is of incidental interest that management – or at least 'non-manual' employees – tend to have larger household plots than the rest of the membership. In 1972, 26.1% of non-manual employees had a larger than normal plot of between 1–1.9 ha, compared with only 22.1% of members generally (AMO, Vol. 14, p. 263). In addition, Simó found that higher level managers are relatively more likely to live in council or service accommodation than lower level managers (1975, p. 101). For the significance of this, see Szelényi's discussion of housing classes in Hungary (1972, p. 281).

CONCLUSION

1 'Work-situation' is used here in the stronger sense suggested by Mackenzie (1974). Such a view can be linked to Braverman's focus on the controls individuals have over their own labour (1974), to Wright's study

of the extent of middle management's control over others (1978), and Garnsey's stressing of the importance of an individual's labour market position to class analysis (1978). Traditional 'class' and social stratification studies of Eastern Europe have focused on consumption of the social product and the relative shares of that product obtained by households defined in terms of the, usually male, head of household's occupation.

2 Calvert is probably correct when he categorises 'class' as an 'essentially contested' concept (1982, pp. 209–16). My concern is to isolate the sorts of control certain individuals have over the production process in an economy which, as I have explained, I see no reason not to term 'socialist'. But perhaps 'socialist' too has become an 'essentially contested' concept.

3 Szymanski also insists on looking for people who 'in leading roles operating the means of production exercise control over the production process in ways which benefit themselves at the expense of the actual producers' (1979, p. 199) when discussing class in the Soviet context. His conclusion is the reverse of the one given here because he fails to locate any such group.

4 Since completion of the manuscript for this book, the Central Committee of the Hungarian Socialist Workers' Party resolved, at its session on 17 April 1984, to extend reform of Hungary's economic mechanism in 1985. The need to modify the method of wage and income regulation has been a prominent topic in the press discussion which followed this decision, but, at the time of writing, no firm proposals have yet been forwarded in this area. The indications are, however, that the new system of wage regulation will resemble experiments already under way in selected areas of the economy (*Figyelő*, 1984, No. 24, pp. 1 and 4). Whilst these experiments offer enterprises rather more flexibility with regard to wage increases in that there is no separate tax on yearly increases in average wages within the enterprise, control by regulation of the average has not been abandoned entirely. Under both experimental systems currently in operation, a progressive tax is levied from enterprises based on the average earnings of its workers (*Figyelő*, 1984, No. 24, p. 4). For all the discussion of the need for reform in the area of wage regulation, concrete proposals to date are concentrated in the fields of capital mobility and financial reform generally (*Figyelő*, 1984, No. 20, p. 3; No. 28, pp. 5–6). Proposals concerning labour focus either on permitting increased differentials or increasing the overall costs of labour to the enterprise (*Figyelő*, 1984, No. 27, pp. 1 and 3; 1984, No. 28, p. 6). In addition, there have been calls for improved retraining programmes and for enterprises to hire out to others temporarily unwanted labour (*Figyelő*, 1984, No. 22, p. 11). There has been no indication that the income tax on average earnings within the enterprise of the experiments will be abolished in any new national system, and, in view of the stark alternatives presented on pages 192–3, such abolition is unlikely. The equation of socialism with full employment remains too strong to be put at serious risk. The only change so far has been a new emphasis on full employment being the concern of state, and not enterprise, economic policy (*Figyelő*, 1984, No. 22, p. 11).

References and bibliography

STATISTICAL SOURCES CITED AND ABBREVIATIONS USED TO REFER
TO THEM

AMO: *Általános Mezőgazdasági Összeírás 1972 (General Agricultural Compendium)*, Budapest, Központi Statisztikai Hivatal (Central Statistical Office).

EA: *Építőipari Adatok 1972–75 (Construction Industry Data 1972–75)*, Statisztikai Időszaki Közlemények No. 297, Budapest, Központi Statisztikai Hivatal (Central Statistical Office).

H. *Háztartásstatisztika 1975 (Household Statistics 1975)*, Statisztikai Időszaki Közlemények No. 383, Budapest, Központi Statisztikai Hivatal (Central Statistical Office).

IA: *Ipari Adatok (Industrial Data)*, Statisztikai Időszaki Közlemények (various), Budapest, Központi Statisztikai Hivatal (Central Statistical Office).

KSE: *Külkereskedelmi Statisztikai Évkönyv, 1972 (Foreign Trade Statistical Yearbook)*, Budapest, Központi Statisztikai Hivatal (Central Statistical Office).

KSH 214: *A Keresetek Szóródása és Szerepe a Munkás-alkalmazotti Háztartások Jövedelmében (The Dispersal of Earnings and their Role in Worker-employee Households)*, Statisztikai Időszaki Közlemények No. 214, Budapest, Központi Statisztikai Hivatal (Central Statistical Office).

LJF: *A Lakosság Jövedelme és Fogyasztása 1960–75 (The Income and Consumption of the Population 1960–75)*, Statisztikai Időszaki Közlemények No. 391, Budapest, Központi Statisztikai Hivatal (Central Statistical Office).

MAK: *Mezőgazdasági Adatok (Agricultural Data)*, Statisztikai Időszaki Közlemények (various), Budapest, Központi Statisztikai Hivatal (Central Statistical Office).

MAR: *Mezőgazdasági Adattár (Agricultural Databank)*, Budapest, Központi Statisztikai Hivatal (Central Statistical Office), 1965.

MGSZS: *Mezőgazdasági Statisztikai Zsebkönyv (Pocket Book of Agricultural Statistics)*, Budapest, Központi Statisztikai Hivatal (Central Statistical Office).

MKA: *Magánkisipari Adattár 1938–71* (*Databank on Small-scale Private Industry 1938–71*), Budapest, Központi Statisztikai Hivatal (Central Statistical Office).

MSZS: *Magyar Statisztikai Zsebkönyv* (*Hungarian Statistical Pocket Book*), Budapest, Központi Statisztikai Hivatal (Central Statistical Office).

SE: *Statisztikai Évkönyv* (*Statistical Yearbook*), Budapest, Központi Statisztikai Hivatal (Central Statistical Office).

SPB: *Statistical Pocket Book 1973*, Budapest, Central Statistical Office (published in English).

TOT 1976: *Mezőgazdasági Szövetkezetek Gazdálkodása a Számok Tükrében* (*Agricultural Co-operative Farming in Figures*), Budapest, Termelőszövetkezetek Országos Tanácsa and Központi Statisztikai Hivatal (National Council of Agricultural Producer Co-operatives and Central Statistical Office), 1976.

TT: *A Társadalmi Mobilitás Történeti Tendenciái* (*Historical Trends in Social Mobility*), Statisztikai Időszaki Közlemények No. 343, Budapest, Központi Statisztikai Hivatal (Central Statistical Office).

LEGAL AND OFFICIAL DOCUMENTS CITED AND ABBREVIATIONS USED TO REFER TO THEM

MK: *Magyar Közlöny* (*Hungarian Gazette*), Budapest, Lapkiadó Vállalat (Newspaper Publishing Enterprise).

MTVR: *A Munka Törvénykönyve és Végrehajtási Rendelete* (*Book on the Labour Law and the Ordinance Putting it into Effect*), Táncsics Könyvkiadó (Táncsics Book Publishers), 1973.

TJ: *Termelőszövetkezeti Jogszabályok 1972* (*Agricultural Producer Co-operative Laws 1972*), Budapest, Közgazdasági és Jogi Könyvkiadó (Economic and Legal Book Publishers), 1975.

TRHGY: *Törvények és Rendeletek Hivatalos Gyűjteménye* (*Official Collection of Laws and Ordinances*), Budapest, Közgazdasági és Jogi Könyvkiadó (Economic and Legal Book Publishers), yearly.

OTHER ABBREVIATIONS USED

AT: 'Agrár Tézisek' ('Agrarian Theses'), *Társadalmi Szemle*, 1957, No. 7, pp. 54–79.

MTA–KISZ: A Magyar Tudományos Akadémia Közgazdaságtudományi Intézet KISZ Szervezetének Munkaközössége (Work Group of the KISZ (Young Communist) Organization of the Economic Science Institute of the Hungarian Academy of Sciences), 'A munkaerővándorlás indítékai és hatásai az új mechanizmusban', *Közgazdasági Szemle*, 1971, No. 7–8, pp. 805–21.

PHI: Party History Institute of the Central Committee of the Hungarian Socialist Workers' Party, *History of the Revolutionary Workers' Movement in Hungary 1944–62*, Budapest, Corvina, 1972.

SWB: *Summary of World Broadcasts*, BBC, Caversham Park, Reading.

NEWSPAPERS CITED

Figyelő (*Observer*): the economic weekly.
Magyar Mezőgazdaság (*Hungarian Agriculture*): an agricultural weekly.
Magyarország (*Hungary*): a current affairs weekly.

JOURNALS CITED

Acta Oeconomica
Actes de la Recherche en Sciences Sociales
Beszélő (*News from Inside*): a *samizdat* journal published in Budapest.
Cambridge Journal of Economics
Canadian Journal of Economics
Economie Appliquée
Gazdálkodás (*Farming*)
Gazdaság (*Economy*)
Journal of Peasant Studies
Kortárs (*Contemporary*)
Közgazdasági Szemle (*Economic Review*)
Látóhatár (*Horizon*)
Magyar Füzetek (*Hungarian Notebooks*): a dissident journal published in Paris.
Munkaügyi Szemle (*Labour Review*)
New Hungarian Quarterly
Pártélet (*Party Life*)
Pénzügyi Szemle (*Financial Review*)
Social Science Information
Sociologia Ruralis
Sociological Review
Sociology
Soviet Studies
Statisztikai Szemle (*Statistical Review*)
Szakszervezeti Szemle (*Trade Union Review*)
Szociológia (*Sociology*)
Társadalmi Szemle (*Social Review*): the theoretical journal of the Hungarian Socialist Workers' Party.
Társadalomtudományi Közlemények (*Social Science Papers*): the journal of the Social Science Institute attached to the Central Committee of the Hungarian Socialist Workers' Party.
Ungarn-Jahrbuch (*Hungary Yearbook*)
Valóság (*Reality*)
Vezetéstudomány (*Management Science*)

BOOKS AND ARTICLES CITED

Adam, J. (1974) 'The system of wage regulation in Hungary', *Canadian Journal of Economics*, Vol. 3, No. 4, pp. 578–93.
Agonács, G. and Mészáros, S. (1977) 'A szövetkezeteken belüli érdekviszonyok hatása az áfészek politikájára, szervezetére és vezetésére', in

Szövetkezeti Kutató Intézet Evkönyv 1977, Budapest, Közgazdasági és Jogi Könyvkiadó (Economic and Legal Book Publishers), pp. 9–59.

Aitov, N. A. (1969) 'An analysis of the objective prerequisites for eliminating the distinctions between the working class and the peasantry', in G. V. Osipov (ed.), *Town, Country and People*, London, Tavistock, pp. 120–39.

Andor, M. (1974) 'Konfliktus vagy harmónia a munkaszervezetben', *Látóhatár*, No. 4, pp. 162–72.

(1979) *Az Üzemi Demokrácia Feltételei és Érvényesülése egy Szállítási Vállalatnál*, Budapest, Népművelési Intézet (Popular Education Institute).

Andorka, R. (1979) *A Magyar Községek Társadalmak Átalakulása*, Budapest, Magvető Kiadó (Sower Publisher).

(1982) *A Társadalmi Mobilitás Változásai Magyarországon*, Budapest, Gondolat Könyvkiadó (Thought Book Publishers).

Andorka, R. and Harcsa, I. (1973) *A Községi Népesség Társadalomstatisztikai Leírása*, Budapest, Magyar Tudományos Akadémia Szociológiai Kutató Intézet (Sociological Research Institute of the Hungarian Academy of Sciences).

Andrle, V. (1976) *Managerial Power in the Soviet Union*, Farnborough, Saxon House.

Antal, I. (1968a) 'Vállalati érdekeltség és létszámstruktúra', *Közgazdasági Szemle*, No. 7–8, pp. 925–35.

(1968b) 'Vállalati érdekeltség és munkaerő-gazdálkodás', *Közgazdasági Szemle*, No. 9, pp. 1072–86.

(1969) 'A vállalati érdek és a jövedelemszabályozás néhány problémája', *Közgazdasági Szemle*, No. 12, pp. 1438–50.

Antal, L. (1973) 'Az élőmunka és a lekötött eszközök költségterheinek szerepéről', *Pénzügyi Szemle*, No. 12, pp. 1018–31.

Arutyunyan, Yu. V. (1969) 'Rural social structure', in G. V. Osipov (ed.), *Town, Country and People*, London, Tavistock, pp. 234–48.

(1971) *Sotsial'naya Struktura Sel'skogo Nasilenia*, Moscow, MYSL.

Aubert, C. (1975) 'People's communes – how to use a standard visit', *New Left Review*, No. 89, February, pp. 86–96.

Balassa, A. (1975) 'Central Development Programmes in Hungary', *Acta Oeconomica*, Vol. 14, No. 1, pp. 91–108.

Balassa, B. (1959) *The Hungarian Experience in Economic Planning*, New Haven, Conn., Yale University Press.

(1973) 'The firm in the New Economic Mechanism in Hungary', in M. Bronsteim (ed.), *Plan and Market*, New Haven, Conn., Yale University Press, pp. 347–72.

Balázsy, S. (1978) 'A keresetszabályozás "megoldhatatlan" dilemája', *Közgazdasági Szemle*, No. 2, pp. 154–73.

Balogh, A. (ed.) (1977) *A Mezőgazdasági Szövetkezetek III Kongresszusa*, Budapest, Kossuth Könyvkiadó (Kossuth Book Publishers).

Balogh, J. (1975) 'Az üzemi demokrácia vizsgálatának néhány tapasztalata', *Szakszervezeti Szemle*, No. 3, pp. 33–6.

Bango, J. F. (1974–5) 'La stratification dans le village de Hongrie', *Ungarn Jahrbuch*, No. 6, pp. 175–213.

Bánki, P. (1969) 'A részesedési alap felosztásának új rendszere', *Munkaügyi Szemle*, No. 11.

Barron, R. D. and Norris, G. M. (1976) 'Sexual divisions and the dual labour market' in D. Barker and S. Allen (eds), *Dependence and Exploitation in Work and Marriage*, London, Longman, pp. 47–69.

Bauer, T. (1970) 'A bankhitelek szerepe a beruházások allokációjában', *Pénzügyi Szemle*, No. 10, pp. 865–72.

(1975) 'A vállalatok ellentmondásos helyzete a magyar gazdasági mechanizmusban', *Közgazdasági Szemle*, No. 6, pp. 625–35.

(1981) *Tervgazdaság, Beruházások, Ciklusok*, Budapest, Közgazdasági és Jogi Könyvkiadó (Economic and Legal Book Publishers).

Bauer, T., Deák, A. and Soós, K. A. (1981) 'Investment decision making in Hungary', in A. Bohnet (ed.), *Gesamtwirtschaftliche Investitionssysteme. Eine Vier-Länder-Studie*, Berlin, Duncker and Humbolt.

Berend, I. T. (1974a) *A Szocialista Gazdaság Fejlődése Magyarországon 1945–68*, Budapest, Kossuth Könyvkiadó (Kossuth Book Publishers) and Közgazdasági és Jogi Könyvkiadó (Economic and Legal Book Publishers).

(1974b) 'Development strategy and urbanisation in Hungary', in A. Brown, J. A. Licari and E. Neuberger (eds.), *Urban and Social Economics in Planned and Market Economies Vol. 1*, New York, Praeger, pp. 271–86.

Berend, I. T. and Ránki, G. (1974) *Hungary: A Century of Economic Development*, Newton Abbot, David and Charles.

(1982) *The European Periphery and Industrialisation 1780–1914*, Cambridge University Press.

Berend, I. T. and Szuhay, M. (1973) *A Tőkés Gazdaság Története Magyarországon 1848–1948*, Budapest, Kossuth Könyvkiadó (Kossuth Book Publishers) and Közgazdasági és Jogi Könyvkiadó (Economic and Legal Book Publishers).

Berkovits, Gy. (1972) 'Bezártak egy bányát', *Valóság*, No. 5, pp. 64–74.

(1976) *Világváros Határában*, Budapest, Szépirodalmi Könyvkiadó (Literary Book Publishers).

Bognár, L. and Simó, T. (1975) *A Termelőszövetkezeti Vezetők Társadalmi Mobilitása*, Budapest, Szövetkezeti Kutató Intézet Közlemények (Cooperative Research Institute Papers), No. 101.

Botos, K. (1970) 'Miképpen hat a jövedelemszabályozás a műszaki fejlesztésre és a munkaerőgazdálkodásra', *Pénzügyi Szemle*, No. 7, pp. 547–58.

Braverman, H. (1974) *Labour and Monopoly Capital*, New York and London, Monthly Review Press.

Bronson, D. W. and Krueger, C. B. (1971) 'Revolution in farm household income' in J. Millar (ed.), *The Soviet Rural Community*, Urbana, Ill., University of Illinois Press, pp. 214–58.

Brown, A., Fennell, J., Kaser, M. and Willetts, H. T. (eds.) (1982) *Cambridge Encyclopedia of Russia and the Soviet Union*, Cambridge University Press.

Brown, E. C. (1966) *Soviet Trade Unions and Labor Relations*, Cambridge, Mass., Harvard University Press.

Brun, E. and Hersh, J. (1976) *Socialist Korea*, New York and London, Monthly Review Press.

Brus, W. (1972) *The Market in a Socialist Economy*, London, Routledge and Kegan Paul.

(1973) *The Economics and Politics of Socialism*, London, Routledge and Kegan Paul.

(1975) *Socialist Ownership and Political Systems*, London, Routledge and Kegan Paul.

Buda, I. (1972) 'Wage regulations and manpower management', in O. Gadó (ed.), *Reform of the Economic Mechanism in Hungary 1968–71*, Budapest, Akadémiai Kiadó (Academy Publishers), pp. 91–108.

Burbach, R. and Flynn, P. (1980) *Agribusiness in the Americas*, New York and London, Monthly Review Press and North American Congress on Latin America.

Calvert, P. (1982) *The Concept of Class*, London, Hutchinson.

Chayanov, A. V. (1966) *The Theory of Peasant Economy*, Homewood, Ill., Irwin.

Churchward, L. G. (1975) *Contemporary Soviet Government*, London, Routledge and Kegan Paul, 2nd edition.

Collier, J. and E. (1973) *China's Socialist Revolution*, London, Stage 1.

Coulson, M., Magas, Branka and Wainwright, Hilary (1975) 'The housewife and her labour under capitalism', *New Left Review*, No. 89, pp. 59–71.

Cox, T. (1979) 'Awkward class or awkward classes? Class relations in the Russian peasantry before collectivisation', *Journal of Peasant Studies*, Vol. 7, No. 1, pp. 70–85.

Csizmadia, E. (1971) 'A Mezőgazdasági termelőszövetkezetek profilja', *Társadalmi Szemle*, No. 12, pp. 39–47.

Csizmadia, E.-né. (1963) 'A munkadíjazás fejlesztése és a pénzdíjazás a termelőszövetkezetekben', *Közgazdasági Szemle*, No. 12, pp. 1297–409.

(1966) 'A munkaegységtől a garantált munkadíjazásig', *Társadalmi Szemle*, No. 11, pp. 17–29.

(1978) 'A háztáji termelés új vonásai', *Valóság*, No. 2, pp. 78–86.

Czippan, Gy. (1973) 'Vétójog', *Magyarország*, No. 36, p. 45.

Davies, R. W. (1980a) *The Socialist Offensive: the Collectivisation of Soviet Agriculture 1929–30*, London, Macmillan.

(1980b) *The Soviet Collective Farm 1929–30*, London, Macmillan.

Dodge, N. T. and Feshbach, M. (1967) 'The role of women in Soviet agriculture', in J. F. Karcz (ed.), *Soviet and East European Agriculture*, Berkeley, University of California Press, pp. 264–302.

Doeringer, P. B. and Piore, M. J. (1971) *Internal Labour Markets and Manpower Analysis*, Lexington, Mass., D.C. Heath.

Domé, Gy.-né. (1976) *Demokrácia a Mezőgazdasági Termelőszövetkezetekben*, Budapest, Kossuth Könyvkiadó (Kossuth Book Publishers).

Domé, Gy.-né. and Garancsy, M.-né. (1973) *A Közvetlen és Képviseleti Demokrácia Formái és Mechanizmusa az Ipari és Mezőgazdasági Üzemekben*, Budapest, Magyar Tudomanyos Akadémia Állam és Jogtudományi Intézet (State and Jurisprudence Institute of the Hungarian Academy of Sciences).

Donáth, F. (1949) 'A falu szocialista fejlődésének kérdései', *Társadalmi Szemle*, No. 2, pp. 106–21.

(1976a) 'A kollektivizált Mezőgazdaság iparosodása Magyarországon', *Közgazdasági Szemle*, No. 6, pp. 661–78.

(1976b) 'Gazdasági növekedés és szocialista Mezőgazdaság', *Valóság*, No. 9, pp. 18–32.

(1977a) *Reform és Forradalom*, Budapest, Akadémiai Kiadó (Academy Publishers).

(1977b) 'Economic growth and socialist agriculture', *New Hungarian Quarterly*, Nos. 65 and 66, pp. 33–42 and 107–23.

(1981) 'István Bibó and the fundamental issues of Hungarian democracy', in R. Miliband and J. Saville (eds), *The Socialist Register 1981*, London, Merlin.

Égetö, E. (1976) *Felhalmozás és Jövedelmezöség a Termelőszövetkezetekben*, Budapest, Kossuth Kiadó (Kossuth Book Publishers).

Ellman, M. (1975) 'Did agricultural surplus provide the resources for the increase in investment in the USSR during the first five year plan?', *The Economic Journal*, Vol. 85, December, pp. 844–64.

Erdei, F. (ed.) (1968) *Information Hungary*, Oxford, Pergamon.

(1969) 'A Mezőgazdasági termelőszövetkezetek néhány társadalmi kérdése', *Valóság*, No. 2, pp. 74–89.

(1973) 'Agrárfejlődésünk a felszabadulás után', in F. Erdei, *Válogatott Irásai és Beszédei*, Budapest, Kossuth Könyvkiadó (Kossuth Book Publishers).

(1977) *Futóhomok*, Budapest, Akadémiai Kiadó (Academy Publishers).

(1980) 'A magyar paraszttársadalom' in F. Erdei, *A Magyar Társadalomról*, Budapest, Akadémiai Kiadó (Academy Publishers), pp. 83–252.

Fainsod, M. (1959) *Smolensk under Soviet Rule*, London, Macmillan.

Farkasinczky, T. (1973) 'A vállalati belső munkaerőtartalékok vizsgálatának tapasztalatai', *Munkaügyi Szemle*, No. 4, pp. 5–10.

Fazekas, B. (1976) *A Mezőgazdasági Termelőszövetkezeti Mozgalom Magyarországon*, Budapest, Kossuth Könyvkiadó (Kossuth Book Publishers).

Fehér, L. (1970) *Agrár-és Szövetkezeti Politikánk 1965–9*, Budapest, Kossuth Könyvkiadó (Kossuth Book Publishers).

Fejtő, F. (1974) *A History of the Peoples' Democracies*, Harmondsworth, Penguin.

Fél, E. and Hofer, T. (1969) *Proper Peasants*, Chicago, Viking Fund Publications in Anthropology, No. 46.

Ferge, S. and Antal, L. (1972) 'Enterprise income regulations', in O. Gadó (ed.), *Reform of the Economic Mechanism in Hungary 1968–71*, Budapest, Akadémiai Kiadó (Academy Publishers), pp. 59–89.

Ferge, Zs. (1969) *Társadalmunk Rétegződése*, Budapest, Közgazdasági és Jogi Könyvkiadó (Economic and Legal Book Publishers).

(1979) *A Society in the Making. Hungarian Social and Societal Policy 1945–75*, Harmondsworth, Penguin.

File, J. (1977) 'A tervszerű kistermelés', *Figyelő*, No. 21, p. 11.

Fischer, L. A. and Uren, P. E. (1973) *The New Hungarian Agriculture*, Montreal and London, McGill–Queens University Press.

Flakierski, H. (1979) 'Economic reform and income distribution in Hungary', *Cambridge Journal of Economics*, No. 3, pp. 15–32.

Fodor, L. (1973) *Falvak a Nagyváros Árnyékában*, Budapest, Kossuth Könyvkiadó (Kossuth Book Publishers).

Földvári, T. and Zsille, Z. (1978) 'Hát maguk nem tudták ezt', *Mozgó Világ*, No. 2, pp. 52–76.

Friedman, A. (1977) *Industry and Labour*, London, Macmillan.

Gábor, I. R. (1979a) 'The second (secondary) economy', *Acta Oeconomica*, Vol. 22, No. 3–4, pp. 291–311.

(1979b) 'A második (másodlagos) gazdaság', *Valóság*, No. 1, pp. 22–36.

(1979c) 'Munkaerőhiány a mai szocialista gazdaságban', *Közgazdasági Szemle*, No. 2, pp. 171–87.

(1979d) '"Relatív bérszínvonal" – ösztönzés – munkaerőkínálat (I)', *Pénzügyi Szemle*, No. 8–9, pp. 663–74.

(1979e) '"Relatív bérszínvonal" – ösztönzés – munkaerőkínálat (II)', *Pénzügyi Szemle*, No. 11, pp. 856–72.

Gábor, I. R. and Galasi, P. (1978) 'A "másodlagos gazaság": a szocializmusbeli magánszféra néhány gazdaságszociológiai kérdése', *Szociológia*, No. 3, pp. 329–44.

(1979) 'Munkavállalói státusz és a dolgozók racionális gazdálkodása a munkaerejükkel', *Közgazdasági Szemle*, No. 9, pp. 1030–41.

(1981) 'The labour market in Hungary since 1968', in P. G. Hare, H. K. Radice and N. Swain (eds), *Hungary: A Decade of Economic Reform*, London, Allen and Unwin, pp. 41–53.

Gadó, O. (1976) *The Economic Mechanism in Hungary – How it works in 1976*, Budapest and Leyden, Akadémiai Kiadó (Academy Publishers) and Sijthoff.

Gál, L. (1975) 'The veto and its use', *Hungarian Trade Union News*, December, pp. 8–9.

Galasi, P. (1976) 'A községekben élő ipari-építőipari munkások mint a munkaerő sajátos csoportja', *Közgazdasági Szemle*, No. 3, pp. 293–301.

(1978a) 'Megjegyzések a munkaerőallokáció szabályozáshoz', *Munkaügyi Szemle*, No. 6, pp. 22–5.

(1978b) 'A fluktuáló munkaerő néhány jellegzetessége', *Munkaügyi Szemle*, No. 8, pp. 6–9.

Galeski, B. (1975) *Basic Concepts of Rural Sociology*, Manchester University Press.

Gardiner, J. (1975) 'Women's domestic labour', *New Left Review*, No. 89, pp. 47–58.

Garnsey, E. (1978) 'Women's work and theories of class stratification', *Sociology*, Vol. 12, pp. 223–43.

Gervai, B. (1968) 'The role and situation of private artisans in Hungary', *Acta Oeconomica*, Vol. 3, No. 4, pp. 441–8.

Gittings, J. (1975) 'Workers arrive on China's 26th birthday', *Guardian*, 1 October.

(1979) 'Workers and Management in China', *Journal of Contemporary Asia*, Vol. 19, pp. 53–66.

(1982) 'The long march from famine', *Guardian*, 12 March.

Gough, K. (1978) *Ten Times More Beautiful*, New York and London, Monthly Review Press.

Granick, D. (1975) *Enterprise Guidance in Eastern Europe*, Princeton University Press.

Gray, J. and M. (1982) 'China's new agricultural revolution', in S. Feucht-wang and A. Hussain (eds.), *The Chinese Economic Reforms*, London, Croom Helm, pp. 151–84.

Gurley, J. G. (1976) *China's Economy and Maoist Strategy*, New York and London, Monthly Review Press.

Gyenes, A. (1968) '"Munkások" és "parasztok" a mezőgazdasági termelő-szövetkezetekben', *Valóság*, No. 4, pp. 26–35.

(1973) 'The restratification of the agricultural population in Hungary', *Acta Oeconomica*, Vol. 11, No. 1, pp. 33–49.

(1975) 'A termelőerők és a termelési viszonyok összhangja a mezőgazda-sági termelőszövetkezetekben', *Közgazdasági Szemle*, No. 3, pp. 314–31.

(1977) *A B-i Mezőgazdasági Termelőszövetkezet (Monográfia) Vol. 2*, Budapest, Szövetkezeti Kutató Intézet Közlemények (Co-operative Research Institute Papers), No. 124/II.

Gyenis, J. (1971) *Az Egyszerűbb Mezőgazdasági Szövetkezetek*, Budapest, Mező-gazdasági és Kossuth Könyvkiadó (Agricultural and Kossuth Book Publishers).

Győry, L.-né and Tiszolczy, Gy. (1975) *Az Áfész-ek Keretében Működő Mező-gazdasági Szakcsoportok Gazdasági Tevékenysége Jogi és Közgazdasági Feltétel-rendszere*, Budapest, Mezőgazdasági Kiadó (Agricultural Publishers).

Halmos, F. (1978) *Illő Alázattal*, Budapest, Szépirodalmi Könyvkiadó (Literary Book Publishers).

Hanák, K. (1978) 'Vázlatok a mai falusi munkásságról', *Szociológia*, No. 3, pp. 361–77.

Hann, C. M. (1980) *Tázlár: a Village in Hungary*, Cambridge University Press.

Haraszti, M. (1977) *A Worker in a Workers' State*, Harmondsworth, Penguin.

(1982) 'Illyesmi nálunk nem fordulhat elő', *Beszélő*, No. 1, pp. 35–45.

Hare, P. G. (1976a) 'Industrial prices in Hungary – Part I', *Soviet Studies*, Vol. 28, No. 2, pp. 189–206.

(1976b) 'Industrial prices in Hungary – Part II', *Soviet Studies*, Vol. 28, No. 3, pp. 362–90.

(1981) 'The investment system in Hungary', in P. G. Hare, H. K. Radice and N. Swain (eds), *Hungary: A Decade of Economic Reform*, London, Allen and Unwin, pp. 83–106.

(1982) 'China's system of industrial economic planning', in S. Feuchtwang and A. Hussain (eds), *The Chinese Economic Reforms*, London, Croom Helm, pp. 185–223.

Hare, P. G., Radice, H. K. and Swain, N. (eds) (1981) *Hungary: A Decade of Economic Reform*, London, Allen and Unwin.

Harrison, M. (1975) 'Chayanov and the economics of the Russian peasantry', *Journal of Peasant Studies*, Vol. 2, No. 4, pp. 389–417.

(1979) 'Chayanov and the Marxists', *Journal of Peasant Studies*, Vol. 7, No. 2, pp. 86–100.

Hegedűs, A. (1949) 'Termelőszövetkezeti mozgalmunk helyzete és fejlesz-tésének kérdései', *Társadalmi Szemle*, No. 6–7, pp. 461–70.

(1960) *A Munkabérezés Rendszere Iparunkban*, Budapest, Közgazdasági és Jogi Könyvkiadó (Economic and Legal Book Publishers).

(1971) 'A falusi család gazdasági funkciójában bekövetkező változások és következményeik', in P. Lőcsei (ed.), *Család és Házasság a Mai Magyar*

Társadalomban, Budapest, Közgazdasági és Jogi Könyvkiadó (Economic and Legal Book Publishers).

(1972) 'Az érdekeltség dilemmái', *Figyelő*, No. 32, p. 3.

(1977) *The Structure of Socialist Society*, London, Constable.

Hegedűs, A. and Márkus, M. (1966) *Ember, Munka, Közösség*, Budapest, Közgazdasági és Jogi Könyvkiadó (Economic and Legal Book Publishers).

(1976) 'Free time and the division of labour', in Andras Hegedus, Agnes Heller, Maria Markus and Mihaly Vajda (eds), *The Humanisation of Socialism*, London, Allison and Busby, pp. 106–23.

(1978) 'A kisvállalkozó és a szocializmus', *Közgazdasági Szemle*, No. 9, pp. 1076–96.

Hegedűs, K. (1972) *Rákóczi Mezőgazdasági Termelőszövetkezet Rákóczifalva*, Szolnok, no publisher.

Hegedűs, M. (1971) 'A mezőgazdasári termelői árak és a termelés összefüggése', *Statisztikai Szemle*, No. 8–9, pp. 800–15.

(1974) 'Some factors influencing urban development in Hungary', *Acta Oeconomica*, Vol. 12, No. 2, pp. 171–89.

Hegedűs, M.-né. (1975) 'Az ÁFÉSZ-ek élelmiszergazdasági szerepének néhány gyakorlati kérdése', in *Szövetkezeti Kutató Évkönyv 1975*, Budapest, Közgazdasági és Jogi Könyvkiadó (Economic and Legal Publishers), pp. 199–240.

Hegedűs, Zs. and Tardos, M. (1974) 'A vállalati vezetők helyzetének és motivációjának néhány problémája', *Közgazdasági Szemle*, No. 12, pp. 162–73.

Héthy, L. (1977) 'A szakszervezeti bizalmiak megnövekedett szerepe és az üzemi pártirányítás', *Társadalmi Szemle*, No. 11, pp. 80–7.

(1978) '"Bérvita" az építkezésen', *Valóság*, No. 1, pp. 76–88.

(1979a) 'Az üzemi demokrácia és a munkások érdekeltsége a részvételben', *Társadalomtudományi Közlemények*, No. 1, pp. 21–36.

(1979b) 'Üzemi demokrácia, érdekegyeztetés – üzemi párt-és szakszervezet', *Társadalomtudományi Közlemények*, No. 4, pp. 38–51.

(1980) *Az Üzemi Demokrácia és a Munkások*, Budapest, Kossuth Könyvkiadó (Kossuth Book Publishers).

Héthy, L. and Makó, Cs. (1970) *A Teljesítményelv Érvényesítése és az Üzemi Érdek-és Hatalmi Viszonyok*, Budapest, Magyar Tudományos Akadémia Szociológiai Kutató Csoport (Sociological Research Group of the Hungarian Academy of Sciences).

(1972a) *Munkásmagatartások és a Gazdasági Szervezet*, Budapest, Akadémiai Kiadó (Academy Publishers).

(1972b) 'Work performance, interests, powers and environment' in P. Halmos (ed.), *Hungarian Sociological Studies* (Sociological Review Monograph No. 17), University of Keele, pp. 123–50.

(1975) 'Labour turnover and the economic organisation', *Sociological Review*, No. 2, pp. 267–85.

(1978) *Munkások, Érdekek, Érdekegyeztetés*, Budapest, Gondolat Kiadó (Thought Publishers).

(1979) *Vezetés, Vezetőkiválasztás, Ösztönzés*, Budapest, Akadémiai Kiadó (Academy Publishers).

Hill, I. (1974) 'The private plot in Soviet agriculture', *Journal of Peasant Studies*, Vol. 2, No. 4, pp. 492–6.

(1975a) 'Some problems concerning the categorisation of the Soviet agricultural population', *Sociologia Ruralis*, Vol. 15, No. 1–2, pp. 90–106.

(1975b) 'The end of the Russian peasantry?', *Soviet Studies*, Vol. 27, pp. 109–27.

Holács, I. (1971) *A Sociological Survey of the Situation of Country Women in the South West Transdanubian Region*, Keszthely, Agricultural University of Keszthely Studies, No. 4.

(1976) 'Társadalmi változások 6 termelőszövetkezeti községben a mobilitás és as életmód összefüggésében', *Szociológia*, No. 1, pp. 86–102.

Holubenko, M. (1975) 'The Soviet working class: discontent and opposition', *Critique*, No. 4, pp. 5–25.

Horváth, J. (1976) 'A tanácsok pártirányítása', *Pártélet*, No. 6, pp. 25–8.

Horváth, L. (1980) 'Az 1980-os gazdasági szabályozók', *Közgazdasági Szemle*, No. 1, pp. 1–11.

Hough, J. F. (1969) *The Soviet Prefects: the Local Party Organs in Industrial Decision Making*, Cambridge, Mass., Harvard University Press.

Huszár, J. (1973) 'Érdekeltség és adórendszer a termelőszövetkezetekben', *Közgazdasági Szemle*, No. 5, pp. 520–37.

Illyés, Gy. (1967) *Puszták Népe*, Budapest, Szépirodalmi Könyvkiadó (Literary Publishers).

Jacobs, E. M. (1970) 'Agriculture', in G. Schöpflin (ed.), *The Soviet Union and Eastern Europe: A Handbook*, London, Anthony Blond, pp. 336–48.

Juhász, Gy. (1974) *Iparvállalatok Munkájának Pártellenőrzése*, Budapest, Kossuth Könyvkiadó (Kossuth Book Publishers).

Juhász, J. (1970) *Vezetői Döntések a Mezőgazdasági Termelőszövetkezetekben*, Budapest, Szövetkezeti Kutató Intézet Közlemények (Co-operative Research Institute Papers), No. 70.

(1973) 'Háztáji koncepciónk fejlődése', in *Szövetkezeti Kutató Intézet Evkönyv 1973*, Budapest, Közgazdasági és Jogi Könyvkiadó (Economic and Legal Book Publishers), pp. 97–127.

Juhász, P. (1973) 'A szanálás hatása a "tradicionális gazdálkodású" mezőgazdasági szövetkezetekre', in *Szövetkezeti Kutató Intézet Evkönyv 1973*, Budapest, Közgazdasági és Jogi Könyvkiadó (Economic and Legal Book Publishers), pp. 129–56.

(1975) 'A mezőgazdasági szövetkezetek dolgozóinak rétegződése munkajellegcsoportok, származás és életút szerint', in *Szövetkezeti Kutató Intézet Evkönyv 1975*, Budapest, Közgazdasági és Jogi Könyvkiadó (Economic and Legal Book Publishers), pp. 241–71.

(1976) *Megjegyzések a családi gazdálkodás elméletéhez*, Szövetkezeti Kutató Intézet Vita Anyag (Co-operative Research Institute Debate Material).

(1977) 'Megjegyzések a családi gazdálkodás elméletéhez' (a summary), in *Szövetkezeti Kutató Intézet Evkönyv 1977*, Budapest, Közgazdasági és Jogi Könyvkiadó (Economic and Legal Book Publishers), pp. 414–17.

(1979) 'Adatok és hipotézisek a mezőgazdasági szövetkezetek állandó dolgozóinak rétegződéséről', *Társadalomtudományi Közlemények*, No. 2, pp. 62–81.

Juhász, P. and Párkányi, M. (1977) 'Miért nincsenek komplexbrigádok?',

Szövetkezeti Kutató Intézet Evkönyv 1977, Budapest, Közgazdasági és Jogi Könyvkiadó (Economic and Legal Book Publishers), pp. 265–330.

Kádár, I. (1972) *A Szocialista Brigádok az Üzemi Kulturális és Politikai Nevelő Munka Bázisai*, Budapest, Szakszervezetek Elméleti Kutató Intézete (Trade Union Theoretical Research Institute).

Kádár, J. (1974) *For a Socialist Hungary*, Budapest, Corvina.

Kalocsay, F. (1970) *A Munkadíjázási Formák a Termelőszövetkezetekben*, Budapest, Agrárgazdasági Kutató Intézet Füzetei (Notebooks of the Research Institute for Agrarian Economics), No. 2.

Kaltenecker, M. and Horváth, G. (1971) 'Létszámcsökkentés – létszámhígítás hatása a vállalati érdekeltségre', *Munkaügyi Szemle*, No. 8, pp. 13–18.

Kellner, M. and Sághy, A. (1978) 'A gulyás-szigetcsoport', *Magyar Füzetek*, No. 2, pp. 94–100.

Kemény, I. (1978a) 'Hol tart a társadalmi kompromisszum Magyarországon?', *Magyar Füzetek*, No. 1, pp. 21–46.

(1978b) 'La chaîne dans une usine hongroise', *Actes de la Recherche en Sciences Sociales*, No. 24, pp. 62–77.

(1979) 'Poverty in Hungary', *Social Science Information*, Vol. 18, No. 2, pp. 247–67.

(1982) 'The unregistered economy in Hungary', *Soviet Studies*, Vol. 34, No. 3, pp. 349–66.

Keserű, J. (1966) 'A termelőszövetkezetek gazdasági irányításáról', *Társadalmi Szemle*, No. 4, pp. 3–13.

Kis, P. (1976), *Termelőszövetkezetek és Állami Gazdaságok Pénz-és Hitelgazdálkodása*, Budapest, Mezőgazdasági Kiadó (Agricultural Publishers).

Kolankiewicz, G. (1980) 'The new "awkward class": the peasant worker in Poland', *Sociologia Ruralis*, Vol. 20, No. 1–2, pp. 28–43.

Kolosi, T. (1974) *Társadalmi Struktúra és Szocializmus*, Budapest, Kossuth Könyvkiado (Kossuth Book Publishers).

Konrád, Gy. and Szelényi, I. (1974) 'Social conflicts of under-urbanisation', in A. Brown, J. A. Licari and E. Neuberger (eds), *Urban and Social Economics in Market and Planned Economies Vol. 1*, New York, Praeger, pp. 206–26.

(1979) *The Intellectuals on the Road to Class Power*, New York, Harcourt, Brace and Jovanovich.

Kornai, J. (1959) *Overcentralisation in Economic Administration*, Oxford, Clarendon Press.

Kostyál, R. and Enyedi, Z. (1977) 'A termelőszövetkezeti jövedelemszabályozás tapasztalatai, módosítások 1978–tól', *Pénzügyi Szemle*, No. 12, pp. 902–13.

Koszó K. and Molnár, Gy. (1973) *A Belkereskedelmi Vállalatok Bérpolitikája*, Budapest, Közgazdasági és Jogi Könyvkiadó (Economic and Legal Book Publishers).

Kovács, A. and Kunszabó, F. (1974) 'Nehéz talaj', *Valóság*, No. 9, pp. 38–46.

Kovács, F. (1976) *A Munkásosztály Politikai-ideológiai Műveltségéről és Aktivitásáról*, Budapest, Kossuth Könyvkiadó (Kossuth Book Publishers).

Kovács, K. (1964) 'A háztáji gazdaságok problémájához', *Közgazdasági Szemle*, No. 7–8, pp. 925–30.

Kovács, Z. (1969) *A Termelőszövetkezet-vezetők és a Termelőszövetkezetalkalmozot-*

tak *Munkadíjazása*, Budapest, Kossuth Könyvkiadó (Kossuth Book Publishers).

(1970) *Munkadíjazása a Termelőszövetkezetekben*, Budapest, A Termelőszövetkezetek Országos Tanács titkárságának kiadványa (a publication of the Secretariat of the National Producer Co-operative Council).

Kozak, Gy. and Mód, A.-né. (1974) *A Munkások Rétegződése, Munkája Ismeretei és az Üzemi Demokrácia a Duna Vasmű Két Gyarrészlegében*, Budapest, Akadémiai Kiadó (Academy Publishers).

(1975) 'Az Ózdi Kohászati Üzemek munkásai és az üzemi demokrácia', *Valóság*, No. 2, pp. 55–70.

Kulcsár, L. and Lengyel, Zs. (1979) *Szakmunkások a Mezőgazdaságban*, Budapest, Kossuth Könyvkiadó (Kossuth Book Publishers).

Kulcsár, L. and Szijjártó, A. (1980) *Iparosodás és Társadalmi Változások a Mezőgazdaságban*, Budapest, Közgazdasági és Jogi Könyvkiadó (Economic and Legal Book Publishers).

Kulcsár, R. (1975) 'A nők társadalmi mobilitása', *Statisztikai Szemle*, No. 10, pp. 968–82.

Kunszabó, F. (1970a) *A Tagok Helyzete és Csoportjai. (Szociológiai Vizsgálat Eredményei a Herédi Mátravidek Termelőszövetkezetben)*, Budapest, Agrárgazdasági Kutató Intézet Füzetei (Notebooks of the Research Institute for Agrarian Economics), No. 10.

(1970b) 'Színe és visszája', *Kortárs*, No. 8, pp. 1294–304.

(1970c) *Parázson Pirítani*, Budapest, Magvető Kiadó (Sower Publishers).

(1971) 'Rétegek és érdekek', *Valóság*, No. 8, pp. 31–8.

(1972) *Sárköz*, Budapest, Szépirodalmi Könyvkiadó (Literary Book Publishers).

(1974a) *Elnöktípusok a Termelőszövetkezetekben*, Budapest, Akadémiai Kiadó (Academy Publishers).

(1974b) 'A lakóhelyi, munkahelyi közösségek és a mezőgazdasági foglalkozások tekintélyének összefüggései', *Szociológia*, No. 1, pp. 64–86.

(1975) 'Termelő és termelés', *Valóság*, No. 7, pp. 48–56.

(1978) 'Szokatlan történet', *Elet és Irodalom*, 24 June.

(1980) *Jászföld*, Budapest, Szépirodalmi Könyvkiadó (Literary Book Publishers).

Laczó, F. (1977) 'Korszerű-e a mezőgazdasági árrendszer?', *Közgazdasági Szemle*, No. 3, pp. 320–35.

Ladányi, J. (1977) 'A községekben élő munkások', *Szociológia*, No. 1, pp. 28–40.

Laki, M. (1980) *Év Végi Hajrá az Iparban és a Külkereskedelemben*, Budapest, Magvető Kiadó (Sower Publishers).

Laky, T. (1976) 'Érdekviszonyok a fejlesztési akciók vállalati döntési eljárásában', *Gazdaság*, No. 4, pp. 40–57.

(1979) 'Enterprises in bargaining position', *Acta Oeconomica*, Vol. 22, No. 3–4, pp. 117–46.

(1980) 'A recentralizálás rejtett mechanizmusai', *Valóság*, No. 2, pp. 31–41.

Lane, D. (1971) *The End of Inequality?*, Harmondsworth, Penguin.

(1972) *Politics and Society in the USSR*, London, Weidenfeld and Nicolson.

Lane, D. and O'Dell, F. (1978) *The Soviet Industrial Worker*, Oxford, Martin Robertson.

Lantos, L. (1976) 'A gazdasági vezetők beszámoltatása', *Pártélet*, No. 5, pp. 19–22.

Lázár, I. (1976) 'The collective farm and the household plot', *New Hungarian Quarterly*, No. 63, pp. 61–77.

Lengyel, Zs. (1977a) 'A mezőgazdaság szocialista átszervezés és következményei', *Társadalomtudományi Közlemények*, No. 1, pp. 68–82.

(1977b) 'A munkásosztály és a szövetkezeti parasztság közlekedéséről', *Társadalomtudományi Közlemények*, No. 4, pp. 84–95.

(1979) *Nők a Mezőgazdaságban*, Budapest, Kossuth Könyvkiadó (Kossuth Book Publishers).

Lewin, M. (1968) *Russian Peasants and Soviet Power*, London, George Allen and Unwin.

Leys, S. (1977) *The Chairman's New Clothes*, London, Allison and Busby.

(1978) *Chinese Shadows*, Harmondsworth, Penguin.

Lökkös, J. (1978) 'A keresetszabályozás néhány problémája', *Közgazdasági Szemle*, No. 2, pp. 174–87.

Lunczer, I. (1974) 'Hogyan látják a munkások az üzemi demokráciát?' *Társadalmi Szemle*, No. 12, pp 70–8.

Macauley, M. (1969) *Labour Disputes in Soviet Russia 1957–65*, Oxford, Clarendon Press.

Mackenzie, G. (1974) 'The "affluent-worker" study: an evaluation and critique', in F. Parkin (ed.), *The Social Analysis of Class Structure*, London, Tavistock, pp. 237–56.

Macsári, K. (1974) 'A szakszervezetek szervezeti önállóságáról és pártirányításáról, a szakszervezeti jogok gyakorlásáról', *Társadalmi Szemle*, No. 4, pp. 45–53.

Magdoff, F. (1982) 'Pros and cons of agricultural mechanisation in the third world', *Monthly Review*, Vol. 34, No. 1, May, pp. 33–45.

Mandel, E. (1982) 'China: the economic crisis', in M. Eve and D. Musson (eds), *The Socialist Register 1982*, London, Merlin, pp. 185–204.

Márkus, I. (1973) 'Az utóparasztság arcképéhez', *Szociológia*, No. 1, pp. 56–67.

(1979) *Nagykőrös*, Budapest, Szépirodalmi Könyvkiadó (Literary Publishers).

Marrese, M. (1981) 'The evolution of wage regulation in Hungary', in P. G. Hare, H. K. Radice and N. Swain (eds), *Hungary: A Decade of Economic Reform*, London, Allen and Unwin, pp. 54–80.

Marx, K. (1971) *Capital Volume III*, Moscow, Progress Publishers.

Megyeri, E. (1976) *Erőforrás – Értékelés és Jövedelemszabályozás*, Budapest, Közgazdasági és Jogi Könyvkiadó (Economic and Legal Book Publishers).

Merényi, F. and Simon, F. (1979) *A Gazdaság Pártirányítása*, Budapest, Kossuth Könyvkiadó (Kossuth Book Publishers).

Meszticzky, A. (1975) 'Elnökök, szakvezetők, munkavezetők a termelőszövetkezetekben', in *Szövetkezeti Kutató Intézet Evkönyv 1975*, Budapest, Közgazdasági és Jogi Könyvkiadó (Economic and Legal Book Publishers), pp. 279–333.

Millar, J. (1970) 'Soviet rapid development and the agricultural surplus hypothesis', *Soviet Studies*, Vol. 22, pp. 77–93.
(1971) 'Financing the modernisation of kolkhozy', in J. Millar (ed.), *The Soviet Rural Community*, Urbana, Ill., University of Illinois Press.

Molnárné Venyige, J. (1979) 'Munkamegosztás és érdekviszonyok', *Közgazdasági Szemle*, No. 5, pp. 539–47.

Molyneux, M. (1979) 'Beyond the domestic labour debate', *New Left Review*, No. 116, July-August, pp. 3–27.

Nagy, Gy. (1976) 'A mezőgazdasági termelőszövetkezetek vezetésének alapkérdései', *Vezetéstudomány*, No. 4, pp. 11–17.

Nagy, L. (1976) 'Az ipari és mezőgazdasági személyi jövedelmek aránya és arányos fejlesztése', *Közgazdasági Szemle*, No. 3, pp. 279–92.

Nagy, L. V. (1973) 'A termelőszövetkezetek kiegészítő tevékenységének hatása a munkaerőgazdálkodásra', *Közgazdasági Szemle*, No. 10, pp. 1210–17.

Nemes, F. (1976) *Érdekeltség – Magatartás – Tartalékok*, Budapest, Közgazdasági és Jogi Könyvkiadó (Economic and Legal Book Publishers).

Nemes, F. and Bullányi, I. (1973) 'Ami a vállalati tartalékok mögött van', *Valóság*, No. 1, pp. 76–81.

Nolan, P. (1976) 'Collectivisation in China: some comparisons with the USSR', *Journal of Peasant Studies*, Vol. 3, No. 2, pp. 192–220.

Noumoff, S. J. (1979) 'The struggle for revolutionary authority', *Journal of Contemporary Asia*, Vol. 9, pp. 27–52.

Nove, A. (1969) *An Economic History of the USSR*, Harmondsworth, Allen Lane.
(1977) *The Soviet Economic System*, London, Allen and Unwin.
(1978) 'Agriculture', in A. Brown and M. Kaser (eds), *The Soviet Union since the Fall of Khrushchev*, London, Macmillan, 2nd edition, pp. 1–15.
(1980) *The Soviet Economic System*, London, Allen and Unwin, 2nd edition.

Nyers, R. (1971) 'Hungarian economic policy in practice', *Acta Oeconomica*, Vol. 7, No. 3–4, pp. 255–74.

Orbán, S. (1972) *Két Agrárforradalom Magyarországon*, Budapest, Akadémiai Kiadó (Academy Publishers).

Pál, J. (1977) *Az Első 558 Mezőgazdasági Termelőszövetkezeti Csoport Engedélyezését és Gazdasági Támogatását Tartalmazó Jegyzőkönyvek*, Budapest, Szövetkezeti Kutató Intézet Közlemények (Co-operative Research Institute Papers), No. 127.

Pálfalvi, N. (1975) *Jövőnk*, Szolnok, Education Department of Szolnok County Council.

Párkányi, M. (1975) 'Az üzemi szervezetre és a társadalmi helyzetre vonatkozó vélemények eltérése munkajellegcsoportok és származási rétegek szerint a mezőgazdasági szövetkezetekben', in *Szövetkezeti Kutató Intézet Évkönyv 1975*, Budapest, Mezőgazdasági és Jogi Könyvkiadó (Economic and Legal Publishers), pp. 385–441.

Pelva, A. (1960) 'A mezőgazdasági munkák gépesítése a termelőszövetkezetekben', *Statisztikai Szemle*, No. 8–9, pp. 841–9.

Portes, R. (1972) 'The strategy and tactics of economic decentralisation', *Soviet Studies*, Vol. 23, No. 4, pp. 629–58.

(1977) 'Hungary: economic performance, policy and prospects', in Joint Economic Committee (ed. John P. Hardt), *East European Economies post Helsinki*, Washington, DC, USGPO.

(1978) 'Inflation under central planning', in F. Hirsch and J. H. Goldthorpe (eds), *The Political Economy of Inflation*, Cambridge, Mass., Harvard University Press, pp. 73–87.

Pospielovsky, D. (1970) 'The "link system" in Soviet agriculture', *Soviet Studies*, Vol. 21, No. 4, pp. 411–35.

Radice, H. K. (1981) 'Industrial co-operation between Hungary and the West', in P. G. Hare, H. K. Radice and N. Swain (eds), *Hungary: A Decade of Economic Reform*, London, Allen and Unwin, pp. 109–31.

Rakovski, M. (1978a) *Towards an Eastern European Marxism*, London, Allison and Busby.

(1978b) 'La Hongrie, est-elle réellement si différente?', *Esprit*, No. 7–8.

Rawski, T. G. (1979) *Economic Growth and Employment in China*, London, Oxford University Press.

Révész, G. (1972) 'Az élőmunkát helyesítő gépesítés korlátairól', *Közgazdasági Szemle*, No. 2, pp. 142–58.

(1974) 'Stimulation, distribution according to work, income regulation', *Acta Oeconomica*, Vol. 12, No. 1, pp. 55–73.

(1978) 'Keresetszabályozásunkról', *Közgazdasági Szemle*, No. 7–8, pp. 917–34.

Richet, X. (1981) 'Is there a Hungarian model of planning?', in P. G. Hare, H. K. Radice and N. Swain (eds), *Hungary: A Decade of Economic Reform*, London, Allen and Unwin, pp. 23–37.

Robinson, J. (1977) 'The labour theory of value', *Monthly Review*, Vol. 29, No. 7, December, pp. 50–9.

Robinson, W. F. (1973) *The Pattern of Reform in Hungary*, New York, Praeger.

Rosenfeld, C. H. (1979) *Hungarian Agriculture: a Symbiosis of Collective and Individual Enterprises*, Ashford, Kent, Wye College Miscellaneous Study No. 6.

Rubery, J. (1978) 'Structured labour markets, worker organisation and low pay', *Cambridge Journal of Economics*, No. 2, pp. 17–36.

Sánta, F. (1964) *Húsz Óra*, Budapest, Magvető Zsebkönyvtár (Sower Pocket Library).

Sas, J. H. (1972) 'Expectations and demands made upon children in a rural community', in P. Halmos (eds), *Hungarian Sociological Studies* (Sociological Review Monograph No. 17), University of Keele, pp. 247–68.

(1976) *Életmód és Család. Az Emberi Viszonyok Alakulása a Családban*, Budapest, Akadémiai Kiadó (Academy Publishers).

Schapiro, L. (1965) *The Government and Politics of the Soviet Union*, New York, Vintage.

Schöpflin, G. (1977) 'Hungary: an uneasy stability', in A. Brown and J. Gray (eds), *Political Culture and Political Change in Communist States*, London, Macmillan, pp. 131–58.

(1979) 'Opposition and para-opposition: critical currents in Hungary, 1968–78', in R. Tőkés (ed.), *Opposition in Eastern Europe*, London, Macmillan, pp. 142–86.

Seccombe, W. (1974) 'The housewife and her labour under capitalism', *New Left Review*, No. 83, pp. 3–24.

Selden, M. (ed.) (1979) *The People's Republic of China*, New York and London, Monthly Review Press.

Selivanov, V. I. (1969) 'Primary rural collectives and their social functions', in G. V. Osipov (ed.), *Town, Country and People*, London, Tavistock, pp. 140–50.

Shanin, T. (1973) 'The nature and logic of the peasant economy', *Journal of Peasant Studies*, Vol. 1, Nos. 1 and 2, pp. 63–80 and 186–207.

Shubkin, V. N. (1969) 'A comparative sociological survey of a Moldavian village', in G. V. Osipov (ed.), *Town, Country and People*, London, Tavistock, pp. 151–68.

Simó, T. (1975) *A Termelőszövetkezeti Elnökök Társadalmi Mobilitása*, Budapest, Szövetkezeti Kutató Intézet Közlemények (Co-operative Research Institute Papers), No. 107.

   (1977) 'Adalékok a termelőszövetkezeti tagok és alkalmazottak tagozódásához', *Szövetkezeti Kutató Intézet Évkönyv 1977*, Budapest, Közgazdásagi és Jogi Könyvkiadó (Economic and Legal Book Publishers), pp. 451–91.

Simonyi, A. (1976) 'Az üzemi demokrácia a munkások oldaláról nézve', *Társadalmi Szemle*, No. 7, pp. 56–65.

   (1977) 'Munkásrészvétel üzemi bérezési döntésekben', *Társadalmi Szemle*, No. 10, pp. 99–101.

   (1978) 'A központból a perifériára', *Valóság*, No. 1, pp. 89–98.

Soós, A. K. (1979) 'Beruházási rendszerünk néhány általános problémája', *Közgazdasági Szemle*, No. 8–9, pp. 795–811.

Soós, G. (1969) 'A földtörvény végrehajtásárol', *Társadalmi Szemle*, No. 3, pp. 75–9.

Stuart, R. C. (1971) 'Structural change and the quality of Soviet farm management 1952–68', in J. Millar (ed.) *The Soviet Rural Community*, Urbana, Ill., University of Illinois Press, pp. 121–38.

   (1972) *The Collective Farm in Soviet Agriculture*, Lexington, Mass., D. C. Heath.

Swain, N. (1981) 'The evolution of Hungary's agricultural system since 1967', in P. G. Hare, H. K. Radice and N. Swain (eds), *Hungary: A Decade of Economic Reform*, London, Allen and Unwin, pp. 225–51.

Szabady, E. (1971) 'A magyar családok demográfiai sajátosságai', in P. Lőcsei (ed.), *Család és Házasság a Mai Magyar Társadalomban*, Budapest, Közgazdasági és Jogi Könyvikiadó (Economic and Legal Book Publishers), pp. 54–69.

Szabó, B. (1974) 'Vezetés – gazdálkodás – érdekeltség. Tények és adatok egy mezőgazdasági termelőszövetkezetből', *Valóság*, No. 6, pp. 35–44.

Szabó, F. (1964) 'A háztáji gazdaságok helyzete és megítélése', *Társadalmi Szemle*, No. 1, pp. 20–3.

Szabó, I. (1976) 'A párt gazdaságpolitikájának érvényesítése', *Pártélet*, No. 4, pp. 66–70.

Szabóné Medgyesi, É. (1976) 'A szabályozó rendszer sajátosságai a mezőgazdaságban', *Statisztikai Szemle*, No. 12, pp. 1216–28.

Szakács, S. (1964) *Földosztás és Agrárfejlődés a Magyar Népi Demokráciában*,

Budapest, Közgazdasági és Jogi Könyvkiadó (Economic and Legal Book Publishers).

Szakál, P. (1973) 'A vezetéshez szükséges információkkal kapcsolatos problémák a mezőgazdasági termelőszövetkezetekben', *Szövetkezeti Kutató Intézet Evkönyv 1973*, Budapest, Közgazdasági és Jogi Könyvkiadó (Economic and Legal Book Publishers), pp. 285–325.

Szalkai, I. (1976) 'Az ipari minisztériumok pártszervezetei', *Pártélet*, No. 8, pp. 41–3.

Székffy, K. (1978) 'A bérek és a termelékenység kapcsolata az iparban 1950–74 között', *Közgazdasági Szemle*, No. 7–8, pp. 831–47.

Szelényi, I. (1972) 'Housing system and social structure', in P. Halmos (ed.), *Hungarian Sociological Studies* (Sociological Review Monograph No. 17), University of Keele, pp. 269–97.

Szerdahelyi, P., Juhász, Gy. and Juhász, J.-né. (1976) 'A termelőszövetkezeti egyesülések tapasztalatai és eredményei', *Gazdálkodás*, No. 5, pp. 9–22.

Szijjártó, A. (1972) *Nemzedékváltás a Homokhátsági Termelőszövetkezetekben*, Budapest, Agrárgazdasági Kutató Intézet Füzetei (Notebooks of the Institute for Agrarian Economics), No. 5.

Szilágyi, J. (1969) 'A gépesítés hatása a foglalkoztatottságra a termelőszövetkezetekben', *Statisztikai Szemle*, No. 12, pp. 1201–13.

Szilárd, Cs. (1977) 'Az új bér-és jövedelemszabályozók első tapasztalatairól', *Közgazdasági Szemle*, No. 3, pp. 311–19.

Szomolányiné Szabó, J. and Kis, Z. (1970) *A Szántóföldi Gépesített Komplexbrigád Gépesítésszervezési és Szociálpszichológiai Vizsgálata*, Budapest, Agrárgazdasági Kutató Intézet Füzetei (Notebooks of the Research Institute for Agrarian Economics), No. 4.

Szymanski, A. (1979) *Is the Red Flag Flying?*, London, Zed Press.

Tardos, M. (1972) 'A gazdasági verseny problémai hazánkban', *Közgazdasági Szemle*, No. 7–8, pp. 911–27.

Tepicht, J. (1973) *Le Paysan Polonais*, Paris, Armand Colin.

Tiboldi, A. (1976) 'A pártszervezet szerepe a gazdasági döntésekben', *Pártélet*, No. 4, pp. 75–8.

Timár, A. (1978) 'A bérszabályozás rendszer 1978 január 1-i változásai', *Munkaügyi Szemle*, No. 1–2, pp. 5–8.

Timár, J. (1977) 'Foglalkoztatáspolitikánkról és a munkaerőgazdálkodásunkról', *Közgazdasági Szemle*, No. 2, pp. 129–50.

Tiszáné Gerai, V. (1975) 'A mezőgazdasági szakmunkások fluktuációjának néhány problémája', in *Szövetkezeti Kutató Intézet Evköny 1975*, Budapest, Közgazdasági és Jogi Könyvkiadó (Economic and Legal Book Publishers), pp. 545–85.

Tiszáné Gerai, V. and Meszticzky, A. (1977) 'A szántóföldi termelési rendszerek terjedésének néhany társadalom-politikai és ökonomikai hatása az üzemi viszonyokra', in *Szövetkezeti Kutató Intézet Evkönyv 1977*, Budapest, Közgazdasági és Jogi Könyvkiadó (Economic and Legal Publishers), pp. 603–54.

Trotsky, L. D. (1967) *The Revolution Betrayed*, London, New Park.

Vági, F. (1969) 'A paraszti jövedelmek és a közös gazdaság', *Társadalmi Szemle*, No. 5, pp. 26–33.

230   *References and bibliography*

Vajda, A. (1976) 'A nők beilleszkedése a foglalkozási struktúrába, 1949–70', *Statisztikai Szemle*, No. 7, pp. 672–87.
Vali, F. (1961) *Rift and Revolt in Hungary*, Cambridge, Mass., Harvard University Press.
Varga, Gy. (1982) 'A piacra termelő mezőgazdaság', *Közgazdasági Szemle*, No. 6, pp. 689–703.
Végh, A. (1972) *Erdőháton, Nyíren*, Budapest, Szépirodalmi Könyvkiadó (Literary Publishers).
Vendégh, F. and Enyedi, Z. (1976) 'A termelőszövetkezetek új jövedelemszabályozási rendszerének sajátos vonása', *Pénzügyi Szemle*, No. 9, pp. 655–65.
Villányi, L. (1977) 'A területfejlesztés és az áfészek', in *Szövetkezeti Kutató Intézet Evkönyv 1977*, Budapest, Közgazdasági és Jogi Könyvkiadó (Economic and Legal Book Publishers), pp. 679–723.
Wädekin, K. E. (1971a) 'The non-agricultural rural sector', in J. Millar (ed.), *The Soviet Rural Community*, Urbana, Ill., University of Illinois Press, pp. 159–79.
(1971b) 'Soviet rural society', *Soviet Studies*, Vol. 22, pp. 513–38.
(1973) *The Private Sector in Soviet Agriculture*, Berkeley, University of California Press.
(1975) 'Income distribution in Soviet agriculture', *Soviet Studies*, No. 1, pp. 3–26.
Wajcman, J. (1981) 'Work and the family: who gets the "best of both worlds"?' in Cambridge Women's Studies Group (ed.), *Women in Society*, London, Virago Press, pp. 9–24.
Wheelwright, E. L. and McFarlane, B. (1970) *The Chinese Road to Socialism*, New York and London, Monthly Review Press.
Wiles, P. J. D. (1974a) 'The control of inflation in Hungary', *Economie Appliquée*, Vol. 27, No. 1, pp. 119–47.
(1974b) 'Comments on chapter 10', in A. Brown, J. A. Licari and E. Neuberger (eds), *Urban and Social Economics in Planned and Market Economies Vol. 1*, New York, Praeger, pp. 258–63.
Wright, E. O. (1978) *Class, Crisis and the State*, London, New Left Books..
Wronski, H. (1971) 'Consumer co-operatives in rural areas in the USSR', in W. A. D. Jackson (ed.), *Agrarian Policies and Problems in Communist and Non-Communist Countries*, Seattle and London, University of Washington Press, pp. 159–73.
Zám, T. (1973) *Bács-Kiskunból Jövök*, Budapest, Szépirodalmi Könyvkiadó (Literary Book Publishers).
(1977) 'Javasoljuk a kongresszusnak ...', *Valóság*, No. 6, pp. 52–63.
Závondi, L. (1976) 'A pártszervezetek cselekvési prográmjának végrehajtásáért', *Pártélet*, No. 9, pp. 29–33.
Zétényi, Z. (1972) 'Mekkora a tét az építőiparban?', *Valóság*, No. 10, pp. 89–91.
Zotova, O. I. and Novikov, V. V. (1969) 'The development of collectivist attitudes among agricultural workers' in G. V. Osipov (ed.), *Town, Country and People*, London, Tavistock, pp. 202–17.

Index

accumulation fund: in China 56; in Soviet Union 55

Agrarian Theses 3, 26, 33, 34, 36, 40, 52, 67, 116

agribusiness 115

agricultural estates (pre-war) 3, 50, 204

agricultural-industrial producer co-operatives 208

agricultural machinery 37, 39, 61, 69, 77, 145, 165

agricultural producer co-operative groups 35, 201

agricultural producer co-operatives 51, 58–9, 83, 87, 90, 136, 140–2, 146–7, 161, 170–1, 179, 181, 190, 196, 201, 205; administrative workers on 87, 95, 97, 102–5, 119, 125, 158, 187; age of membership 84–5, 88, 91–4, 100, 103, 113, 122, 124, 126, 128, 158; aid to: see aid; amalgamations of 37, 48, 59, 85, 137; bankruptcies of 135, 144, 210; cancellation of debts of 54; cost of joining 31; democratic structure of: see co-operative democracy; election of presidents on 116, 120, 123, 125, 138, 147, 158–9, 207; employees on: see employees; Founding Statute of 148–9, 157; 'immobile' members of 90–1, 97, 100–1, 113, 124, 205; industrial-type jobs on 86, 89, 100, 105–6, 108, 112, 142–3, 145, 165, 167, 171, 180, 198, 208; investment control on: see investment; lawyer of 118, 209; level of members' incomes 43, 46, 49, 56, 164, 167, 176, 178, 202, 205, 211; management of: see management; managerial bonuses: see bonuses; managerial links with local government and party agencies 134, 136–8, 144; mechanisation of 28, 38–9, 66, 78, 85–6, 96, 101, 105, 117, 119; members' ultimate sanction 138, 158–60; membership's attitudes to changes in norms 154, 202; membership's knowledge of 155–6; 'mobile members' of 90–1, 97, 100–1, 112–13, 124, 126; new occupations on 83, 86, 88–90, 97, 100, 126, 143; non-industrial production on: see ancillary enterprises; organisational model of 35, 45, 117–18; Party's role in: see Hungarian Socialist Workers' Party; pensioners on 39–41, 92–3, 95–6, 99–100, 112, 141, 159, 204, 206; personnel work on 117–18, 129, 136–40, 182; right to make independent contracts 53, 135; right to own land 32, 34, 41, 63, 65, 72, 91, 205; right to own machinery 32, 36–7, 53; size of 35, 37, 42, 59–60, 115, 117, 147, 150, 156, 196; social divisions within membership 114, 116–17, 128, 186–7, 202, 205; trade unions on: see trade unions; type I 32, 35, 201; type II 32, 35, 201; type III 31–2, 35–6, 39–40, 200–2; see also agriculture

agricultural proletarians 20, 106, 108–13

agricultural specialised groups 11, 59–60, 62, 68–9, 148, 204, 209

agriculture: aid to: see aid; exports from 64; large-scale 26, 54; ministerial control of 133–5; revaluation of capital goods in 202; share of national budget 27–8, 36, 181, 185, 200; small scale, 63,

231